BUSINESS COMMUNICATION

Writing, Interviewing, and Speaking at Work

RANDALL E. MAJORS

California State University, Hayward

HARPER & ROW, PUBLISHERS, New York
Grand Rapids, Philadelphia, St. Louis,
San Francisco, London, Singapore,
Sydney, Tokyo

1817

Sponsoring Editor: Debra Riegert
Project Coordination, Text Art: R. David Newcomer Associates
Text Design: Suzanne Dyer Company
Cover Design: CIRCA 86, INC.
Production Manager: Jeanie Berke
Production Assistant: Paula Roppolo
Compositor: York Graphic Services, Inc.
Printer and Binder: Malloy Lithographing, Inc.

Business Communication: Writing, Interviewing, and Speaking at Work

Library of Congress Cataloging-in-Publication Data

Majors, Randall E.
  Business and communication.

  Includes index.
  1. Business communication. I. Title.
HF5718.M35 1989   658.4'5   88-32843
ISBN 0-06-044183-6

89 90 91 92   9 8 7 6 5 4 3 2 1

CONTENTS

The Characteristics of Effective Communication 28

The Communication Plan 44

Psychological Strategies of Communication 58

The Principles of Business Writing 77

Business Memos 97

Informative Letters 115

EMPLOYMENT AND INTERVIEWING SKILLS: JOB SEARCH, APPLICATIONS, RÉSUMÉS, AND INTERVIEWING

Unit IV   367
BUSINESS SPEAKING

20
The Principles of Business Speaking   369

DETERMINE YOUR PURPOSE AND TOPIC   370
RESEARCH YOUR TOPIC AND SELECT MATERIALS   371
ESTABLISH YOUR CREDIBILITY   371
ORGANIZE AND OUTLINE YOUR SPEECH   373
PREPARE THE DELIVERY OF THE SPEECH   374
ANTICIPATE STAGE FRIGHT   375

21
Informative Speeches   389

PRELIMINARY CONSIDERATIONS   389
**ORGANIZE AND OUTLINE THE BODY OF YOUR
  SPEECH**   390
PREPARE THE CONCLUSION   391
PREPARE THE INTRODUCTION   393
DEVELOP TRANSITIONS IN THE SPEECH   394

Speeches to Motivate 473

PREFACE

The ability to communicate clearly and accurately is one of the most valued skills in the business environment. Business people who have good communication skills have a distinct advantage in accomplishing the tasks required by their jobs: writing reports, letters, and memos; interviewing, hiring, and counseling; decision making and problem solving; and giving instructions, persuading, selling, and listening. In addition, effective communication skills are among the most attractive abilities a potential employee can offer a prospective employer. Employers want applicants who can write, interview, and speak effectively because good communication skills are strong indicators of a successful employee.

This book is a set of short lessons in four aspects of communication skills that any manager or employee needs on the job. Each lesson is followed by a set of exercises designed to reinforce and integrate these lessons. The book covers four broad areas of communication:

1. Basic principles of written and oral communication;
2. Business writing skills in letters, memos, and reports;
3. Employment and interviewing skills in the job search, applications, résumés, and job interviewing;
4. Business speaking skills for informing, instructing, selling, persuading, and motivating.

The purpose of this book is to develop practical business communication skills in each of the four communication areas. You already have skills in each area. Some people are stronger in certain areas than in others, but by reading the lessons and applying the information in the exercises, you can reinforce your areas of strength and develop your skills in the areas needing improvement. You are encouraged to deepen your knowledge by referring to the additional sources cited at the end of each chapter for more information or examples of the topics of each lesson.

Most people in the business world receive very little training in communications. It is assumed that anyone with a high school or college degree already possesses the skills in writing, interviewing, and public speaking needed on the job. Unfortunately, many employees and managers actually have a woeful lack of effective communication skills. The lessons and exercises in this text provide you with the information and practice you need to develop these valuable skills.

I wish to thank the many students who have helped me determine what is useful in developing business communication skills. The lessons and exercises in the text have been designed, tested, and refined with the participation of students at California State University at Hayward, Northeastern Illinois University at Chicago, and Iowa State University at Ames. Without their willing assistance, the book would not be as valuable. I wish to express particular thanks to the following students, whose letters are included as samples: Robert V. Arthur, Grant Bruneau, Steve Faria, Timothy S. Fullmer, Marilyn Ghiorso, Katherine Martinis, Mark H. Morris, John I. Reilly, and Mary E. Whiteley.

Equally helpful have been the colleagues who have provided suggestions, corrective feedback, and encouragement. Of particular help were Christopher DeSantis, career consultant in Chicago; Dr. Elizabeth Mechling, Chair of the Marketing Department at CSU Hayward; Dr. Ce Ce Iandoli; and Dale Kobler, all of whom spent many hours editing the manuscript and offering suggestions that have improved the text greatly.

No text is ever perfect or complete. I would like to hear from you if you have comments, suggestions, reactions, or criticisms that would make the text more practical or useful for developing skills in business communications. Please write to me at the Department of Marketing, California State University at Hayward, Hayward, CA 94543.

Randall E. Majors

BUSINESS COMMUNICATION

PRINCIPLES OF COMMUNICATION

1

The Importance of Business Communication

How well can you communicate? The skill of effective communication, more than any other business skill, will determine your career success in the coming years. That is a bold statement for an author to make. Is communication really so important? A bit of thought about your future career will show that it is.

This chapter investigates the value of effective communication skills in the workplace. It also shows you how effective communication skills can help you get the job you want and advance in your chosen career.

The Value of Effective Communication in Business

Communication is the major activity of business. Executives have estimated that they spend approximately 90 percent of their time communicating in some form: reading, writing, speaking, or listening.[1] That figure may be surprising, but if you think about it for a moment, you will realize that communication is at the heart of any business activity. Managing co-workers, talking to customers, analyzing business opportunities, or looking for a job—all these activities require direct communication between people.

Business communication is also expensive. A recent Postmaster General's study found that of 96 billion pieces of mail sent annually, 77 billion pieces were business correspondence.[2] This staggering number reflects a huge expense. Studies have estimated that the cost of producing the average business letter ranges from $4.75 to $20.00 when you compute the costs of dictation, transcription, revision, typing time, materials, and postage.[3] Business meetings, speeches, and interviews also reflect a huge expense when you calculate the value of the time that is being spent—or, sometimes, wasted—when business people attend these activities.

The high costs of business communication make clear the need for efficient and effective communication skills. If business writing and speaking are done efficiently, then money as well as time can be saved. Other benefits of effective communication are also obvious. Internally, effective communication reduces both errors and the amount of time that must be spent correcting them. Good communication in the workplace decreases absenteeism and worker turnover and increases job satisfaction and worker productivity. All these factors increase the profitability of a business. Externally, effective communication creates a positive public image for a business, increases the number of satisfied customers, and maximizes profit potential.

The Value of Effective Communication to You

Effective communication is not only a valuable skill in business but also a vital asset to your career. How important is communication in your chosen profession? Think about the want ads or job descriptions you have seen for positions you will want in the future. How many of them include one of the following requirements?

Applicants need to be able to communicate effectively.
Heavy client contact.
Good presentation and interpersonal skills a must.
Candidate must be able to talk to people comfortably.
Report- and letter-writing ability a definite plus.
Please enclose a writing sample

Almost every job demands that you write clearly, speak comfortably, and deal with people effectively. Good communication skills are required if you are going to perform well in your future job or improve your performance in your current position.

Much research has been done on the skills necessary for success on the job. Repeatedly, business people cite communication skills as the most important requirement for success. When asked about the communication skills most important for success in their jobs, executives cited the following:

advising	persuading
instructing	interviewing
exchanging information	public speaking
giving orders	problem solving
listening	working in small groups.[4]

Think for a moment about the job you will want in the future. Will it entail any of these communication skills? Will you have to talk to customers or clients? give co-workers instructions? provide explanations of projects or ideas? write letters and reports? give public presentations? If the answer to any of these questions is yes, than you are probably like most other business people. A survey of recently promoted business executives asked them to recall the college course that was most valuable in preparing them for their jobs. A course in oral and written communication was cited as most influential in helping them succeed at their current positions.[5] A similar study also found that the most important criterion for promotion was proven communication skills, which were rated as more valuable than ambition, education, confidence, appearance, or the capacity for hard work.[6]

Communication skills are also vital in helping you get the job you want. A researcher polling on-campus business recruiters asked about critical factors in their decisions to hire a candidate. Heading their list of requirements for employability was effective communication, both written and oral, which was ranked ahead of scholastic qualifications, specialized coursework, previous employment, or extracurricular activities.[7] Getting hired for a position you want is a real test of your ability to describe your accomplishments in a job interview and to persuade the interviewer that you are the right person for the job. Thus, the skills of interviewing and writing effective résumés and applications determine whether you get started in the position you want. Once you have your job, the ability to write, speak, and deal with people will determine advancement and success in your career.

Naturally, developing effective communication skills demands time and effort. It is not easy to eliminate bad habits you may have developed or to learn new ways of planning and performing communication tasks. But investing time and energy now will reap rewards in your future. For these reasons, learning effective techniques of writing, interviewing, and speaking will be worth every ounce of effort you put in.

Every job consists of a different set of communication tasks. Some jobs emphasize writing, others require interviewing, and still others entail public speaking. Thus, you should become familiar with the communication tasks you will need in the future so that you can begin to develop those skills now. You may already have some of the skills you need, but you may need to develop or strengthen others. A clear assessment of your present skills and your future communication needs will help you determine your goals for using this book.

At the end of this chapter, Exercise 1.1 asks you to conduct an assessment of your current career expectations and communication skills. By completing this exercise, you will get a clearer picture of which skills you need to improve. Exercise 1.2 provides you with the opportunity to set goals for yourself in developing communication skills. By knowing your needs in advance, you can create a plan to develop your skills so that you will have them at your command when you need them. This book will help you anticipate and develop those valuable skills early in your career. This preparation will make you the best applicant and a valuable employee.

NOTES

1. Phillip V. Lewis, *Organizational Communication: The Essence of Effective Management*, 2d ed. (Columbus, Ohio: Grid Publishing, 1980), p. 10.

2. Herta A. Murphy and Charles E. Peck, *Effective Business Communications*, 3rd ed. (New York: McGraw-Hill, 1980), p. 9.

3. Joel P. Bowman and Bernadine P. Branchaw, *Effective Business Correspondence* (New York: Harper & Row, 1979), p. 7.

4. Vincent DiSalvo, David C. Larsen, and William J. Seiler, "Communication Skills Needed by Persons in Business Organizations," *Communication Education*, Vol. 25, No. 4 (November 1975), 273.

5. H. W. Hildebrand, F. A. Bond, E. L. Miller, and A. W. Swinyard, "An Executive Appraisal of Courses Which Best Prepare One for General Management," *The Journal of Business Communication*, Vol. 19, No. 1 (Winter 1982), 8.

6. John Fielden, "What Do You Mean I Can't Write?" *Harvard Business Review* (May–June 1964), 144–145.

7. Frank S. Endicott, "Trends in Employment of College and University Graduates in Business and Industry," *Thirteenth Annual Report: A Survey of 225 Well-Known Business and Industry Concerns*, Northwestern University, 1976.

EXERCISE 1.1
Communication and Your Career

Jo Spreal graduated from college and accepted a job as an assistant manager in a large retail store. After the first week on her new job, Jo sat down and analyzed the tasks that her position required of her. To her surprise, communication skills were at the head of the list. She itemized her responsibilities and found that she spent a great deal of time writing and talking to other people—far more than she had expected. Fortunately, Jo's communication skills were good, but she found herself wishing she had taken more communication training when she was in school. Now she would have to develop those skills on the job.

Directions: Think for a moment about the career area you aspire to or the "dream job" you would like to have. What communication skills will be required on that job? Imagine what a typical day on that job would be like and identify the communication tasks you would probably have to perform. List as many of these tasks as you can under the categories below. To the right of each one, make a preliminary assessment of your current skill level in each:

1 = very little skill   3 = average skill   5 = excellent skill

Your "dream job": _____

COMMUNICATION SKILLS REQUIRED ON THE JOB

CURRENT ABILITY RATING

Writing Tasks

	Low				High
_____	1	2	3	4	5
_____	1	2	3	4	5
_____	1	2	3	4	5
_____	1	2	3	4	5
_____	1	2	3	4	5
_____	1	2	3	4	5

Interviewing Tasks	**Low**				**High**
_____	1	2	3	4	5
_____	1	2	3	4	5
_____	1	2	3	4	5
_____	1	2	3	4	5
_____	1	2	3	4	5
_____	1	2	3	4	5

Public Speaking Tasks

_____	1	2	3	4	5
_____	1	2	3	4	5
_____	1	2	3	4	5
_____	1	2	3	4	5
_____	1	2	3	4	5
_____	1	2	3	4	5

Other Communication Tasks

_____	1	2	3	4	5
_____	1	2	3	4	5
_____	1	2	3	4	5
_____	1	2	3	4	5
_____	1	2	3	4	5
_____	1	2	3	4	5

EXERCISE 1.2
Goals for This Course

Directions: Read closely the Table of Contents for this book. In the following four areas taken from that table, list the goals you want to accomplish for this course. Think about your skills and abilities in each of the four areas. Write a statement describing what you will try to learn, improve, practice, or develop in the areas of business communication.

I. Basic Writing Skills: Grammar, Punctuation, Mechanics, and Style

_____

_____

_____

_____

_____

_____

II. Business Writing: Letters, Memos, and Reports

_____

_____

_____

_____

_____

_____

_____

III. Employment and Interviewing Skills: Job Search, Applications, Résumés, and Interviewing

_____

_____

_____

_____

_____

_____

_____

IV. Business Speaking

_____

_____

_____

_____

_____

_____

_____

EXERCISE 1.3
Diagnostic Memo

Directions: Write a brief memo to your instructor providing a personal assessment of the strengths and weaknesses of your present writing abilities, and explaining the writing requirements of your present job if you are employed or a former job you have held.

Memorandum

To: _____ Date: _____

From: _____

Subject: _____

_____

_____

_____

_____

_____

_____

_____

_____

_____

_____

_____

_____

_____

_____

_____

_____

_____

_____

EXERCISE 1.4
Introductory Interview: Meeting a Stranger

Directions: To familiarize you with the process of interviewing, select a member of your class and conduct a five-minute interview in which you get to know that person. You may want to explore areas such as educational background, employment experience, career goals, hobbies, and favorite social activities. You can take notes in the spaces provided below.

Interviewer: _____

Person Interviewed: _____

Educational Background:

_____

_____

_____

_____

Employment Experience:

_____

_____

_____

_____

Career Goals:

_____

_____

_____

_____

Hobbies/Interests:

_____

_____

_____

_____

EXERCISE 1.5
Introductory Speech: Introduce Yourself

Directions: Give a one-minute speech in which you introduce yourself to the rest of your class. You may outline your remarks in the spaces provided below.

As you listen to other students introduce themselves, notice which speakers are effective in holding the audience's attention and interest. Be prepared to discuss the elements of speaking that make speakers interesting.

My Educational Background:

_____

_____

_____

_____

My Career Plans:

_____

_____

_____

_____

My Hobbies/Interests:

_____

_____

_____

_____

Most Interesting Thing About Me:

_____

_____

_____

_____

2

The Elements of Effective Communication

Whichever type of communication skill is required in your job, all communication events have certain elements in common. By understanding the similarity of communication events, you will develop a general insight into how communication works effectively. This insight is the key to being adaptable as a communicator. You cannot prepare for every possible communication event, but you can develop a general sense of how to be an effective communicator in just about any situation. This adaptability is the most valuable "transferable skill" you can take from job to job. Whatever the demands of your job, if you know how the communication process operates, you can plan effective communication, anticipate possible breakdowns, and use feedback effectively.

All human communication consists of one person trying to convey meaning to another person. When you want to communicate, you have thoughts you want another person to understand. A key problem in communication is that the meaning you intend to send is never received in exactly the same way you send it. The other person's unique experiences, values, or perceptions always slightly change the meaning you intend. Thus, *pure* communication—the exact transmission of meaning from one person to another—is an unattainable ideal. But *effective* communication is possible—the transmission of meaning as accurately as possible within the constraints of the situation and given the skills of the people involved.

The Communication Process

Every communication event—a letter, an interview, or a speech—has the same basic elements. The same types of problems can arise in each of these situations, and you can use the same techniques to ensure effectiveness and success as a communicator. Figure 2.1 depicts the basic process that underlies every communication event. As each element of the communication process is discussed below, follow the flow of meaning through the diagram.

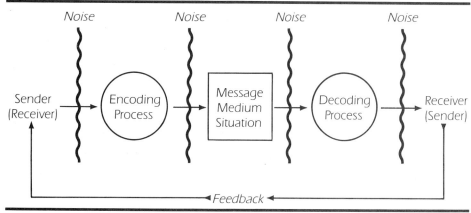

FIGURE 2.1 Basic Communication Process

SENDER

The *sender* is the person who initiates a piece of communication with the intention of transmitting an idea or a thought to another person (the receiver).

ENCODING PROCESS

The sender must put the communication into some form of signal—for example, written signs, nonverbal gestures, or spoken words. The *encoding process* is the selection of the signal in which the message will be transmitted.

MESSAGE

Once the sender's idea is encoded, it is called the *message*. Messages can be either intentional or unintentional. Senders can intentionally transmit ideas to receivers, but they often transmit unintended messages as well. Messages are often complex, with many ideas being transmitted at once.

MEDIUM

The *medium* is the means, or apparatus, by which a message is transmitted. Oral language consists of words, and written language employs symbols. Nonverbal signals must be seen, and words must be heard. The medium dramatically affects the message by adding additional layers of meaning to it. Thus, the choice of medium is as important as the choice of signal in transmitting.

SITUATION

The *situation* consists of the environmental conditions in which the transmission of the message takes place. The place in which the transmission occurs, the timing, the physical setting, and distractions can affect how clearly the message is transmitted.

DECODING PROCESS

When a message is transmitted, the receiver interprets the sender's signals in order to understand the sender's intended message. The selection and interpretation of signals is called the *decoding process*.

RECEIVER

The *receiver* is the person to whom a message is directed or who attributes meaning to unintentional signals.

FEEDBACK

Communication is a two-way activity. As a sender transmits a message, the receiver is also transmitting a return message—eye contact, nonverbal signals, or simultaneous verbal messages. These return messages are called *feedback* because they send back information about how the transmitted message is being received. If feedback from the receiver indicates that he or she is uninterested in the message, upset by it, or unclear about it, the sender can respond by adjusting the message to solve the problem in transmission.

NOISE

Unfortunately, barriers and breakdowns can occur at any stage of the communication process; these are depicted as wavy lines in each phase of the model. *Noise* is the general term for anything that creates such a blockage or distortion of communication. There are four basic types of noise: physical, semantic, psychological, and situational. Figure 2.2 defines and provides examples of these types of noise.

Physical noise: problems in the physical transmission of the message signals. Examples: sound distractions, poor lighting, illegible handwriting, computer breakdown.

Semantic noise: a barrier to effective communication caused by a speaker's choice of language. Examples: offensive terms, unclear pronunciation, garbled organization of words.

Psychological noise: mental factors that distort the sender's encoding or the receiver's decoding. Examples: attitudes, prejudices, personality factors.

Situational noise: environmental conditions that hamper good communications. Examples: fatigue that prevents the receiver from paying attention, the time delay caused by a lost letter, having to rush through an interview because not enough time was planned for it.

FIGURE 2.2   Four Types of Communication Noise

Common Problems in Communication

No matter how carefully a sender transmits a message, noise—barriers to and breakdowns in communication—is bound to occur. Therefore, good communication must build in safeguards against breakdowns and barriers. The safest approach to noise-free communication is careful planning and attention to detail when analyzing the situation and encoding the message. The more you understand the complexity of communication and the many ways it might break down, the better you can plan to avoid these problems. Study the following discussion of common communication problems, and evaluate the solutions that are proposed to prevent or correct them.

MULTIPLE MESSAGES

Rarely do you send one message at a time. Usually a sender transmits many different messages at once—emotions, nonverbal signals, and situational messages that surround the words of a verbal message. Multiple messages cause problems when they are inconsistent with the verbal content of the intended message. For example, if an applicant writes a letter saying that he is a careful and detail-oriented worker but the letter is full of typographical errors, then the receiver gets an inconsistent message. People believe the unintended message—in this example the sloppiness of the typing—far more often than the intended verbal content.

Multiple messages can arise in any of the elements of the communication process. The verbal message itself may have contradictory ideas. The choice of medium may be inappropriate to the message. The message may not be appropriate to the situation. A speaker's nonverbal messages may be inconsistent with the verbal content. A speaker's clothing and grooming may be inconsistent with the intended personal image. Whatever the communication event, multiple messages will always be present.

The phenomenon of multiple messages is both a blessing and a curse for a sender. In some ways, multiple messages can work to a sender's advantage. If all the messages are consistent, the intended verbal message is strengthened. If, however, the messages are inconsistent, people will believe the nonverbal and unintentional message far more readily than the verbal one. For this reason, effective communicators should make their multiple messages as consistent as possible.

POOR ENCODING CHOICES

Communication breakdown often occurs because the sender does not consider the receiver's ability to interpret the message accurately. A sender should encode in a way that will increase the likelihood of being understood. For example, if a speaker uses an unusual word, the receiver may not know what the word means. Thus, the sender should either select a simpler, more common word to express the idea or define the word in order to ensure the receiver's accurate decoding of the message.

The solution of the problem of poor encoding is for the sender to be sensitive to the receiver's abilities. Senders create noise when they do not anticipate the difficulty that receivers may have in decoding. The more carefully the sender considers encoding choices, the more likely it is that the intended meaning will be accurately understood by the receiver.

POOR SELECTION OF A MEDIUM

A sender must select an appropriate medium with the same care as the words of a message. There are dramatic differences between delivering a message in person and delivering it over the telephone or in writing. The writing medium is affected by such small elements as the paper used, the color of the ink, and various graphic effects. In public speaking, the message is affected by the size of the hall, the number of people in the audience, and other physical factors.

The choice of medium has a powerful nonverbal message, which often speaks louder than the sender's words. A sender should choose a medium that is consistent with the intended message and that avoids potential noise.

POOR ADAPTATION TO THE SITUATION

The communication situation consists of all the conditions that affect both the sender and the receiver. Since people are easily affected by environmental conditions, an effective communicator must consider the situation in which a message is transmitted. Without this awareness, poor choices can be made. The situation can be affected by the timing of a message, the presence of other messages, the needs of the receiver, or the attitudes of the receiver. The sender must be sensitive to these conditions and encode the message accordingly.

As an example of poor adaptation to the situation, John, an assistant manager at a drugstore, wanted to ask his boss, Eric, for a raise. John carefully considered the reasons he deserved a raise and planned a clear, logical message. Unfortunately, he approached Eric about a raise on the day the health inspector was coming to the store. Eric was distracted by his concern about whether the store would pass the inspection. Furthermore, John was not aware of the fact that Eric had received instructions from company headquarters to keep costs—especially staff salaries—within budgeted limits for the next six months. Once John learned this fact, he realized that his arguments were not going to work. John's choice of the day to present his case for a raise coincided with Eric's being distracted by other concerns. John's case was further weakened by the timing of the message. He was not aware of the budget constraint until it was too late. The most effective communication analyzes the situation thoroughly and adapts the message to suit the unique conditions of the situation.

POOR DECODING

Many communication problems occur when the receiver does not listen to the message, is distracted by noise, or misinterprets the message. Just as the sender has responsibilities to encode clearly, the receiver should be aware of decoding errors that can be avoided by using effective listening skills. Effective listening techniques are reviewed in Figure 2.3.

Have a reason for listening: know what you can gain by paying close attention.

Create a good listening situation: prepare yourself for good listening by eliminating or avoiding sources of noise that will impair your ability to pay close attention.

Avoid distractions: do not let yourself be distracted by physical, psychological, or semantic noise.

Take notes only if absolutely necessary: note taking is often distracting, so use it judiciously.

Listen for overall meaning, not just for details: try to get a sense of the general meaning of the sender and do not quibble over petty details.

Try to understand the organization of the sender: if the message is well organized, discovering the structure will help you understand and remember the details.

Do not argue with the sender mentally while listening: if you disagree with the message, wait until the sender has finished. Mentally preparing your rebuttal prevents you from hearing the complete message.

FIGURE 2.3 Techniques for Effective Listening

LACK OF FEEDBACK

A final common problem in communication is the lack of feedback. Senders are often so busy sending their messages that they overlook whatever feedback signals are coming their way. In order to adjust their message to the situation, senders need feedback, so they should watch closely for signs of their effectiveness and make necessary corrections. Likewise, receivers often do not give feedback because of time or physical constraints. If communication is to be effective, both senders and receivers have a responsibility to use feedback to send and interpret more accurate messages. Thus, the communication process in every work situation should include feedback systems. Both senders and receivers should remain sensitive to the importance of feedback and use this valuable tool to maximize their communication effectiveness.

RESOURCES

DeVito, Joseph. *Communicology: An Introduction to the Study of Communication*. New York: Harper & Row, 1981.

This book provides an interesting overview and analysis of the communication process and the types of breakdowns that can occur when people communicate.

Littlejohn, Stephen W. *Theories of Human Communication*. New York: Macmillan, 1983.

This book is a thorough review of various theories of communication processes. The complexity of communication problems is analyzed in detail.

Rogers, Carl R., and Richard E. Larsen. "Active Listening." In Richard Houseman et al., eds. *Readings in Interpersonal and Organizational Communication*, 3rd ed. Boston: Holbrook, 1977.

This classic article introduced the term "active listening" and reviews techniques for more effective listening.

Steil, Lyman, Joan Summerfield, and George de Mare. *Listening: It Can Change Your Life*. New York: Wiley, 1983.

This is an interesting and practical handbook on improving listening skills in personal and work situations.

EXERCISE 2.1
Recognizing Elements in the Communication Process

Directions: Jan, a salesperson, wants to sell office supplies to Meg, an office manager in a court-reporting firm. In the following phrases that describe the telephone conversation between Jan and Meg, identify the elements of the communication process. An item may represent more than one element.

sender	medium	receiver
encoding process	situation	feedback
message	decoding process	noise

Aspects of Telephone Call	**Communication Element**
1. Jan, who calls Meg	_____
2. The telephone	_____
3. The greeting Jan uses	_____
4. Meg's response	_____
5. Jan's sales pitch	_____
6. The time of day Jan calls	_____
7. Jan's angry tone of voice	_____
8. Meg's pause before answering	_____
9. Static on the telephone line	_____
10. Meg's need for supplies	_____
11. Meg's headache	_____
12. Meg's agreement to purchase	_____

EXERCISE 2.2
Solving Problems in the Communication Process

Directions: In each of the following situations, identify the cause of the communication breakdown or barrier, and suggest a technique for overcoming or avoiding the problem.

1. Tom asks his secretary to type a letter "as soon as you can." The secretary interprets his request to mean "as soon as is convenient" and does not plan to type the letter until the end of the day. An hour later, Tom returns and is upset because the letter has not been typed.

Problem: _____

_____

_____

Solution: _____

_____

_____

2. Tom wants to take a client, Bill, to lunch to get to know him better, but he does not know which would be a more appropriate place—an inexpensive diner to demonstrate his frugality or an expensive French restaurant to demonstrate his fine taste.

Problem: _____

_____

_____

Solution: _____

_____

_____

3. On a job interview, Sarah becomes upset when the interviewer says that the "girls in the office are expected to bring in cakes for the managers' birthdays."

Problem: _____

_____

_____

Solution: _____

_____

_____

4. Fred, a store owner, orders ten brooms for his janitorial staff. He is upset when ten *dozen* brooms are delivered and he is expected to pay for them. He calls Mark, the salesperson who took the order, and Mark says he "swears he can remember Fred said ten dozen."

Problem: _____

_____

_____

Solution: _____

_____

5. While listening to her boss give instructions on how to operate the photocopy machine, Helen suddenly remembers that she left the oven on at home and starts worrying about it.

Problem: _____

_____

_____

Solution: _____

_____

_____

6. Irene applies for a job and becomes discouraged when she does not receive any word—positive or negative—about her application. She assumes that the company must not have wanted her for the position, when in fact her application has been accidentally misplaced in the office.

Problem: _____

_____

_____

Solution: _____

_____

_____

The Elements of Effective Communication

1. Describe a communication situation that you recently experienced. For example, describe a letter you wrote, a newspaper article you read, an interview you participated in, a speech you listened to, or a conversation you had. Using this situation as your example, identify and describe the parts of the communication process as they occurred in that situation—sender, encoding process, message, medium, decoding process, receiver, feedback, noise.

2. For each of the following common communication problems, describe a hypothetical situation that would serve as an example of the problem. In addition, identify a strategy for each situation that would have prevented or solved the problem.

    Multiple messages
    Poor encoding choices
    Poor medium selection
    Poor adaptation to the situation
    Poor decoding
    Lack of feedback

3. Describe how feedback is given in the following communication situations. What kinds of feedback might the receiver of the message give the sender? What areas might the feedback cover?

    Writing a letter
    Conducting an interview
    Giving a public speech

3

The Characteristics of Effective Communication

Everyone knows how to communicate. You have studied and practiced communication every day of your life. Since you talk with or write to people every day and write occasionally, you probably assume that you have effective communication skills. Most people take their communication abilities for granted, however, and do not realize that there is a tremendous difference between average performance and truly effective strategy and technique in communicating. This chapter explores the qualities that create effective communication and introduces strategies that will help you use language more effectively when you communicate.

The Qualities of Effective Communication

There are clear differences between effective and ineffective communication, whether in writing, interviewing, or speaking. Most people recognize some differences intuitively. Exhibit 3.A presents three excerpts from letters written by people requesting a refund from a company for a recently purchased electric toaster that is defective. Which letter do you believe will be the most effective in accomplishing its purpose?

Letter #1
You dumb clucks! I can't believe that a company with your so-called reputation for customer service could sell a piece of garbage like the Moonbeam toaster I bought last week. Not only will the timer not work, but the poor design of the thing caused it to shock me seriously when I stuck a knife down inside of it! So what are you going to do about my toaster? I want a refund.

Letter #2
Pursuant to our telephone conversation of July 28, I am writing to request the possible consideration of monetary reimbursement for one Moonbeam toaster which I purchased from your downtown sales outlet at 3:40 p.m. on the afternoon of July 21 with my Rolo-Credit card (number 296-59-189), granted to me by the President of Newark Bank, Mr. Don Q. Trusty. In your estimable opinion, am I or am I not entitled to special consideration of my need? I wish to return your toaster.

Letter #3
I have enjoyed shopping at your store for many years. Unfortunately, a recent purchase disappointed me. A Moonbeam toaster (model 64K) seems to have a defective timing mechanism. I returned it to your service desk. The manager there said that it was indeed defective and that I should write you a letter requesting a refund. Please credit my charge account in the amount shown on the enclosed copy of the receipt. Thank you for this service.

EXHIBIT 3.A   Three Excerpts from Letters of Complaint

What is the difference in these three letters? The first is rude and demanding. It is incomplete in details and not likely to prompt an enthusiastic response. The second one is vague, pretentious in tone, and not likely to motivate the reader to respond. The third letter is far more effective because it creates a positive tone, provides sufficient details, and requests specific actions. The last letter is most likely to get the response desired by the writer. The characteristics displayed in Letter #3 reflect several of the basic qualities of good communication. By keeping these qualities in mind, you can begin the process of adapting your writing and speaking to make it more effective.

There are five basic qualities to develop in your communication style: accuracy, clarity, completeness, appropriateness, and dynamism. Specific uses of these qualities are discussed in greater detail in later chapters, but this preview of effective communication characteristics will give you a general idea of how messages should be planned.

ACCURACY

You need to be as accurate as possible with every aspect of communication under your control. A minor inaccuracy, such as a misspelled word or an incorrect reference, can undermine your credibility. Some readers are very demanding, and you must carefully watch the small details of your writing to ensure accuracy. When writing, you must carefully control accuracy in grammar, punctuation, mechanics, and spelling.

In speaking as well as writing, you must also use accurate facts. Double-check your facts, proofread for errors, and do thorough research on a topic before communicating about it.

CLARITY

Have you ever tried to look through a dirty window? Some communication is like that: you can see shapes and movements, but you cannot be certain about the specific details of what you are seeing. Good communication needs to have a clear purpose and clear language in order to avoid confusion or misunderstanding.

Clarity of purpose is created by analyzing your goal in advance of communicating. A writer or speaker needs to communicate the purpose clearly to the audience. A clear organizational pattern also helps the receiver to understand the logic and structure of the message. These techniques ensure that the reader or listener will understand what is being said and what action is desired as a result.

You create clarity of language by selecting precise and specific terms to convey your thoughts. For example, in the letters in Exhibit 3.A, which is clearer—to ask for a "monetary reimbursement" or a "refund"? The simpler word is usually the better word if it conveys the exact sense of the writer. Vague or abstract words should be avoided unless they are more accurate than simpler, smaller words. Another problem in clarity arises in letter #2 when the writer asks to "return" the toaster. Does "return" mean the writer wants to exchange it for another or to get a refund? Precise and specific terms help avoid such confusion.

COMPLETENESS

As a communicator, you need to determine how much you should say. It is often difficult to decide how much information is enough without saying too much or saying too little. In general, good business communication is concise and to the point. Extraneous details should be avoided. The writer or speaker has to analyze how much information is necessary to conduct the business at hand and limit the message to just what is necessary. Of course, you can be so concise as to be blunt or you can be so complete as to rattle on and on, so some balance has to be found between the two extremes.

One good technique to ensure completeness is to put yourself in the shoes of the reader or listener. What questions is the reader likely to ask about the topic? Likewise, how much information does the reader need to do what you want? Anticipate the responses of the reader and supply the information that will be needed at that next step. Look for any hidden implications in your writing and speaking that you need to address directly. Do not force the reader to have to ask you for the information that you should have included in the first place. For example, when requesting a refund on the toaster, the writer of letter #3 anticipated that the receipt would be necessary and attached it to the letter. Irrelevant details such as the time of day and the name of the credit card provider were deliberately omitted.

APPROPRIATENESS

Many values are transmitted simultaneously by the verbal and nonverbal elements of a piece of business communication. For example, a résumé hand-written on the back of a paper towel might contain all the necessary information, but a prospective employer will find the medium to be inappropriate. A writer needs to consider the reader's values and adapt to them as much as possible. Likewise, a speaker needs to understand the viewpoint of the audience and plan remarks accordingly.

Above all, you need to create a positive relationship with the receiver. You need to send messages of respect, sensitivity, and positive regard in the language and format you select for your communicating. In writing, such elements as the paper, the typing, the layout of the information on the page, and the neat appearance of the writing communicate important messages of sensitivity to the reader's values. Analyze the reader's values and adapt the nonverbal messages to them. Likewise, the language you employ when writing or speaking must be suitable to the values of the receiver. The second section of this chapter, on using language effectively, has several suggestions for adapting your language to suit the values and frame of reference of the receiver.

An effective technique for creating a positive relationship in communication is to include the common courtesies that often become "uncommon" in a hectic workplace. Include thanks, praise, and positive regard when it is appropriate to so do. Of course, you do not want to go overboard and sound insincere when communicating, but good manners are never insincere, so be careful to include the social rituals of opening pleasantries and concluding good wishes in order to make your messages more positive. When speaking, take the time for introductory and concluding pleasantries that add grace and personality to your style.

DYNAMISM

Good communication grabs the receiver's attention and makes him or her want to hear more of what you have to say. Dynamism is the expression of your personality as you write or speak. This message becomes most important when you are trying to influence the receiver to do something—to give you a job, to agree with your findings, to buy a product you have for sale, or to find you interesting as a speaker.

Dynamism is largely a matter of word choice, and several techniques for creating dynamic language are suggested in the following section. Use active and vivid verbs to convey a sense of action in your writing. Use colorful descriptions and interesting details where appropriate to your purpose. Use the pronoun "I" when talking about yourself. Avoid awkward circumlocutions such as "the author" or "the speaker" except in very formal circumstances. Finally, include "action steps" in your writing and speaking when you want the listener to do something. Always leave the receiver knowing exactly what steps or behaviors should occur next in order to satisfy you. If readers or audience members have to guess what you want them to do, chances are they will do nothing.

Using Language Effectively

Now that you know the qualities of effective communication, you may be wondering how these are achieved. Word choice is the means by which you incorporate the qualities of effective communication into the way you write and speak. The following suggestions will help you create accuracy, clarity, completeness, appropriateness, and dynamism in your language. These techniques will also help you avoid the common problems of vagueness, abstractness, redundancy, loaded language, triteness, and dullness, which suck the life and energy out of your writing and speaking.

USE SPECIFIC AND PRECISE LANGUAGE

To be specific, you must use language that precisely captures and transmits your meaning. There are two major dimensions of precision in language. The first is the degree of specific detail versus generality. You need to select the most specific words possible to describe or explain the content of your message. There may be times when you *want* to be vague, but in general it is better to be specific and precise. The two passages from letters of application in Exhibit 3.B illustrate how vague language creeps into writing. Notice how the more specific wording in the second example has greater impact and interest.

A second quality of precision is the degree of abstraction versus concreteness in language. Abstraction is the use of general language that makes no reference to specific things, while concreteness refers to the use of specific concepts and examples. Concrete words usually have stronger emotional impact than abstract words, so you must use them carefully. Skillful use of concrete language, however, will make your meaning clearer and improve the dynamism of your messages.

Figure 3.1 contains a list of common abstractions and generalities that are often used in business communication, along with their more concrete equivalents. Strive to avoid these in your own language and to substitute more concrete and specific usages.

Application #1

I have had a great deal of experience in managing people. I have held several jobs, all of which demanded that I use management skills effectively. I have never had any problems with employees, and I have always gotten high ratings on my management evaluations.

Application #2

I have held the position of Manager and Assistant Manager in five different stores in the last ten years. In each position, I was responsible for scheduling, budgeting, staff evaluations, and employee training. My supervisors have rated my performance above average and superior, and in my last position I was rated "Most Effective Manager" by store employees. I feel confident in saying that I am an effective manager.

EXHIBIT 3.B   Two Excerpts from Job Application Letters

Abstract Usages	Concrete Usages
please advise me	please tell me
at an early date	soon
at such time as	when
due in large measure to	due to (because)
I am desirous of	I want
acquaint me with	inform me
of the opinion that	think (believe)
enclosed herewith	enclosed
hold in abeyance	postpone (delay)
if you so desire	if you wish (want)
not in a position to	cannot
the thought occurred to me	I thought
pursuant to your request	as you requested
take the liberty to	may
afford an opportunity to	allow
in an active manner	actively
come into contact with	meet
render assistance to	help (aid, assist)
ascertain	learn
this constitutes	this is
we deem it	we think
we shall endeavor	we will try
personnel	people (employees, staff)
terminate	end (fire)
ameliorate	lessen (improve)
peruse	read
utilize	use
salience	importance

FIGURE 3.1 Common Abstractions and Preferable Usages

KEEP YOUR LANGUAGE CONCISE

Conciseness consists of the economical use of time and space when writing and speaking. Most business situations require you to work quickly and efficiently. Wasted time is wasted money, and you can improve your worth as an employee or manager if you know how to use your time effectively. You should always analyze a message to ensure that you include only essential and important ideas and omit trivial, tangential, or irrelevant ones. Conversely, you do not want to be so concise that your style becomes abrupt or brusque. Likewise, you should not omit important details or considerations in a piece of communication merely to make it shorter.

You should practice economy in messages whenever possible by means of your word choice. Most of the abstract usages in Figure 3.1 are less concise than their concrete counterparts. Another common but inefficient conven-

the month of August	the city of Denver
10:00 a.m. in the morning	advance warning
assemble together	alternative choice
close proximity	and also (but however)
combined together	depreciate in value
end result	completely eliminate
exactly the same	few in number
general consensus of opinion	final outcome
full and complete	important essentials
past history	personal opinion
real reason	true fact
refer back again	small size
selective in nature	the field of accounting
the subject of music	a figure of $10.00
a later date	a total of 5000

FIGURE 3.2 Common Redundancies to Avoid

tion in business language is the use of redundant words or phrases to "puff up" the importance of the idea expressed. Figure 3.2 lists some of these redundancies. Notice how in many cases one of the words could be omitted without any loss of meaning.

USE JARGON AND SLANG JUDICIOUSLY

Every profession has its own specialized vocabulary, or *jargon*. It usually consists of technical words and phrases that only a member of the profession is trained in using. Most professions also develop a slang consisting of words and phrases that facilitate communication among insiders, as when a riveter calls a superheated steel rivet a "hot one" or computer professionals refer to IBM as "Big Blue."

Jargon and professional slang are useful because they can be precise and economical. But jargon and slang may be misunderstood by someone not familiar with the special meanings of the words or phrases. As you prepare a message, be aware of the receiver's frame of reference. You may know exactly what you mean, but some words or phrases may be new to the hearer. Know the difference between the slang and jargon of your profession and common English descriptions of the same information. When you are uncertain about the audience's knowledge, clarify your terms before you use them or select more common usages so that everyone will understand.

When in a new professional setting, try to adapt quickly to the new language. Watch for new terms and try to learn them rapidly. Do not be intimidated by your lack of the language—see it as a challenge, not a threat. After all, every newcomer has to learn the language. Use the new vocabulary appropriately as a way of demonstrating your knowledge of the profession.

conceptual	time frame
input/output	compatible
interface	access
network	user-friendly
optimize	minimize/maximize
prioritize	systematize
impact	viable
feedback	parameter
contingency	overshot
cost-effective	paradigm

FIGURE 3.3   Common Business Jargon and Slang Terms

Figure 3.3 lists common business jargon and slang terms which, when used outside the business context, are often meaningless to listeners. Most of the words have precise meanings that can be suitably used in a message. They are often misused, however, when taken out of their appropriate context. For example, one computer may "interface" with another, but two people do not. Be careful with the use of these words.

AVOID LOADED LANGUAGE

All language is emotionally "loaded" to some degree. Few communications are completely neutral. The way in which you use language creates emotional responses in your receivers. Avoid unintentionally loaded language and carefully consider your word choice in situations that require tact.

The most obviously loaded words are those which imply a judgment: "stupid," "dumb," "irrational," "illogical," "immoral," "indecent," "useless," "worthless," "inferior," "incompetent," and many others. In some instances, you cannot avoid loaded words. You can soften the impact of loaded language, however, by including the criteria or reasons for your judgment. For example, if returning a piece of merchandise, merely saying that "This thing is useless to me" may not be as diplomatic as saying "I cannot use this item at the moment." By considering how the receiver will interpret the emotional loading in your words, you can avoid unintentionally offending or irritating.

Everyone has individual preferences and dislikes for certain words, based on their past experiences. These differences are called "red flag words" or hidden antagonizers if they trigger unpleasant associations in the listener. You need to understand the emotional terrain of the communication situation and avoid pitfalls of offending people with loaded language. Watch closely how people respond to certain language. Vulgarity, inappropriate formality or informality, and highly emotional words are often perceived as offensive. As you increase your understanding of the reactions of other people to language, you can tailor your language choice to be more effective in motivating or persuading them. When dealing with strangers, maintain a non-judgmental and open-minded cordiality.

allow me to express	at a loss to understand
do not hesitate to	without further delay
it has come to my attention	enclosed please find
in reply to your request	pursuant to your request
with utmost urgency	please be advised that
let me take this opportunity	in response to same
as a matter of fact	be that as it may
it goes without saying	as you already know
obviously	in case you did not know
this is to inform you	I am writing to tell you
permit me to say that	thanking you in advance
thank you for your time	anxiously awaiting your reply
hoping to hear from you	very truly yours

FIGURE 3.4 Common Trite Expressions to Avoid

AVOID TRITE EXPRESSIONS

Another area of language to consider is the use of trite and tired expressions. These are words and phrases that are so commonly used that they become empty and almost meaningless platitudes. The most common trite expressions are overused similes and metaphors such as "poor as a churchmouse" or "an angel of mercy." Avoid these expressions "like the plague"!

Senders often use trite expressions when they are not aware of their overuse. As you develop more experience in business communication, notice how other speakers and writers avoid triteness by being direct and creative. The list in Figure 3.4 contains commonly used expressions which should be avoided because of their triteness. Think of more original ways of conveying the same idea.

RESOURCES

Henze, Geraldine. *From Murk to Masterpiece: Style for Business Writing.* Homewood, Ill.: Richard D. Irwin, 1984.

> This book is an interesting and entertaining set of guidelines for improving business language. It emphasizes the most common errors and ways of avoiding them.

Strunk, William, and E. B. White. *The Elements of Style.* New York: Macmillan, 1984.

> This is a classic book on proper and not-so-proper language uses. It is full of witty examples and helpful advice.

Zinsser, William. *On Writing Well.* New York: Harper & Row, 1976.

> This book provides much useful information on planning, drafting, and revising writing.

EXERCISE 3.1
Recognizing Poor Writing

Directions: The following samples of writing reflect violations of the characteristics of good writing introduced in this chapter. Analyze each one briefly and identify the errors in the space below each sample.

1. From a letter requesting information:

   Dear Travel Agent: I am going on a trip to Europe sometime next year. Please send me some information about how to get there and what to do for the two weeks of my vacation.

   Errors: _____

   _____

   _____

   _____

2. From a response to a help-wanted ad:

   Dear Sir or Madame: I deserve the job you offer because I am the best possible person for it. I have a degree in Management Science, or I will have in June if I pass all my courses, and I have a great deal of experience managing people. I can accomplish anything I set my mind to—and I want the job you have. So I will stop by your office next Tuesday to discuss any details of the enclosed résumé or to answer any questions you might have about my qualifications.

   Errors: _____

   _____

   _____

   _____

3. From a sales letter:

   Dear Customer: CommData software is like an abacus. The Chinese revolutionized the early accounting world with their simple, easy-to-operate calculating system. On the basis of one simple piece of hardware, Genghis Khan and his hordes of would-be accountants just about conquered the world. You can be the king of the hill if you use CommData accounting software to revolutionize your office accounting system.

   Errors: _____

   _____

   _____

_____

_____

_____

_____

_____

4. From a letter of complaint to a landlord:

Dear Joe: You've got a problem—I am real upset with the lack of water pressure in this apartment. I mean, I came home from my aerobics class, like I was all hot and sweaty and yucky (you know?) and I wanted to take a cool refreshing shower and what did I get? No water pressure! The water just kind of trickled out of the nozzle like Jell-O trying to roll off a table. I mean really, it was just totally upsetting to not be able to take a shower in that condition. So what are you going to do about my shower?

Errors: _____

_____

_____

_____

_____

_____

5. From the introduction to a monthly sales report:

Statement of Purpose: The Sales Manager will contend in the following brief review of sales performance that while sales have for the most part been up slightly in all categories, nonetheless performance is not reaching an optimal level of inroads to the new market sectors which the firm has identified as its most prioritized, nor have all sales personnel achieved at anywhere near exemplary standards. Furthermore, even though profit level has showed propitious signs of increase, in view of the voluminous public response to our latest direct-mail campaign, goals that might have been acceptable two months ago must be reconsidered and recalibrated in this dynamically new market environment.

Errors: _____

_____

_____

_____

_____

EXERCISE 3.2
Language Correction Drill

Directions: The following sentences contain poor language usages. Identify each kind of error the sender has made from the concepts covered in this chapter. Rewrite each sentence, using more effective wording.

1. The meeting of the Public Airlines Board of Directors will convene and come to order at 11:30 a.m. on the morning of June 5, 1987, at the Delphi Hotel in the city of San Francisco.

   Error(s): _____

   Correction: _____

   _____

   _____

2. The airline company is losing money. It may have to go out of business soon. The company president, Joe Jones, said so.

   Error(s): _____

   Correction: _____

   _____

   _____

3. Importunate as it may at first glance appear, the dissolution of the airline would not be greeted with any great disfavor by the general public at large.

   Error(s): _____

   Correction: _____

   _____

   _____

4. Joe called the shots as he saw them and laid the blame for the failure of the airline on the shoulders of the workers.

   Error(s): _____

   Correction: _____

   _____

   _____

5. Most workers were reported as being rude to the public.

   Error(s): _____

   Correction: _____

   _____

   _____

6. Jones said that the workers are just being crybabies about the whole matter and that they should just grow up.

   Error(s): _____

   Correction: _____

   _____

   _____

7. The workers closed up shop and partied down in the parking lot.

   Error(s): _____

   Correction: _____

   _____

   _____

8. The strike was ultimately curtailed, Jones was aggrieved to report, by the intercessional efforts of the FAA.

   Error(s): _____

   Correction: _____

   _____

   _____

9. As per your recent request, a summary of the strikers' demands is being sent under separate cover.

   Error(s): _____

   Correction: _____

   _____

   _____

10. The strikers may find it advisable to articulate their demands more carefully future-wise if they wish to actualize their desires.

Error(s): _____

Correction: _____

_____

_____

11. The workers were barking up the wrong tree if they thought Joe Jones
would roll over and play dead.

Error(s): _____

Correction: _____

_____

_____

12. Those strikers were robbed—the FAA cheated them of their rights.

Error(s): _____

Correction: _____

_____

_____

The Characteristics of Effective Communication

1. Find an example of what you consider to be especially ineffective writing. For example, select a business letter, an inter-office memo, a letter to the editor from the newspaper, a magazine article, or an advertisement. Highlight the elements of the writing that make it ineffective—inaccuracy, lack of clarity, incompleteness, inappropriateness, or lack of dynamism. Be prepared to discuss your evaluations.

2. Observe a conversation or a public discussion. For example, attend a speech or a lecture, overhear two people arguing or discussing a topic, or listen to two friends having a conversation. Identify instances in the communication when language was used ineffectively—vagueness, imprecise language, wordiness, jargon or slang, loaded language, or trite expressions. You may wish to take notes unobtrusively as you listen to the exchange. Be prepared to discuss your observations.

3. How bad can your writing be? Imagine a situation at work or at school in which you might be required to write a letter or a memo. Write a letter or memo that is intentionally vague, wordy, slangy, inappropriate, full of loaded language, and trite. Be prepared to read your letter or memo aloud.

4

The Communication Plan

When you must write an important letter, do you often find yourself staring at a blank page for a long time, wondering where to begin? When you have to give a speech to a group, do you find yourself dreading it because you do not know what to say or how to organize your thoughts? When you anticipate an interview, are you seized by fear because you do not really know how to prepare for the interaction?

These misgivings about communicating are common. Many people suffer in this way because they do not understand the basic techniques of planning for effective communication. This chapter investigates seven steps you can use in creating effective communication:

Determine your purpose
Analyze your audience
Organize your thoughts
Research your subject
Construct the first draft
Edit the first draft
Reconstruct the final draft

These seven techniques are equally useful in writing, speaking, and interviewing. Using them will prepare you to tackle any communication situation. These techniques are closely related to the characteristics of effective communication discussed in the last chapter. As we discuss these seven steps in planning, notice how accuracy, clarity, completeness, appropriateness, and dynamism can be incorporated into your communications as you plan them.

Determine Your Purpose

The first thing to ask yourself when you must communicate is, "What is my purpose?" Several other questions may help you answer that initial question: What are you trying to accomplish? Do you have a single goal or several goals? Are your goals clear? If your purpose is unclear, how can you clarify it? You must answer these questions if you are to construct an effective message and present it in an appropriate form.

Most situations have an obvious purpose: to inform, to persuade, to impress, to convince, or to entertain. However, communicators often fail to see that their purpose can be complex. In most situations, the sender tries to do several things at once. In job interviews, for example, you might think that the applicant has only one task: to persuade the interviewer to offer the job. If you analyze the situation closely, however, an interview has several purposes that an applicant should address. Applicants inform the interviewer about their skills and abilities, convince the interviewer that they can do the required tasks, create a favorable nonverbal impression, and create a pleasant and confident atmosphere for the interview. By understanding the complexity of the situation and its several purposes, the sender develops strategies that can satisfy these multiple goals.

In essence, the key to determining and understanding your purpose in a communication situation is to break it into several smaller goals. Each subgoal may contribute to a large overall purpose. By seeing your purpose in its full complexity, however, you will find it easier to begin making choices about your communication techniques. Thus, when you are stumped by "not knowing where to start," you can begin by identifying your overall purpose and listing the subgoals that will help you accomplish that purpose. Once you make your list, return to each item and determine the strategies or techniques that will help you accomplish each subgoal. This analysis provides you with the elements you need to construct your message.

Analyze Your Audience

One of the best techniques for clarifying your purpose is to see the situation from the audience's point of view. What does the reader or listener want? The answer to this question may help you clarify your own purpose, because the two purposes are often interconnected. In most situations, you are required to write or speak because the receiver wants information from you. Analyze the audience; anticipate what they need to hear. This technique helps you focus on what you need to say. Knowing your audience also helps you determine what *not* to say. You can avoid the errors of irrelevance or redundancy by anticipating what the audience already knows. There is no need to inform the audience of things they already understand. You may find it appropriate to review information briefly, but new information must be interesting and relevant.

Another important aspect of audience analysis is anticipating the audience's values and attitudes. Knowing the general attitudes of the audience aids you in choosing a general approach for a topic, the format for your presentation, and the language you will use. Appropriateness is determined by matching the audience's or the reader's expectations. You can shock or surprise an audience to some degree in order to be novel and exciting, but if your approach is too inappropriate for an audience, you risk losing their goodwill. Your credibility will also suffer.

Organize Your Thoughts

Once you have determined your purpose and analyzed your audience, you are ready to begin actual construction of the message. The best way to begin construction is with a blueprint—a skeletal plan that will generally direct your building of the message. In communication terms, this plan is called an *outline*.

Many people are gripped by dread when they hear the word "outline." Did that just happen to you when you read the last sentence? People usually have this reaction because they think there is only one type of outline—the long, formal outline, complete with roman numerals and sub-sub-subpoints. In fact, there are many easy and useful ways to employ outlining that will dramatically improve your planning and construction of letters, speeches, or interviews.

The most useful organizing technique is what some people call "thinking on paper"—getting your ideas down on paper in any form so that you can start arranging them logically. Some people think in logical, sequential order. Other people think in bursts of unrelated, tangential ideas. It is this second group of people who have the hardest time using outlines, because most of them think that outlines have to be linear. On the contrary, initial attempts at outlines can take any form.

Figure 4.1 illustrates two different forms of initial outlines: the jot list (for sequential thinkers) and the idea bubble (for tangential thinkers). The jot list is for people who think easily in linear, logical order. Their ideas seem to emerge in the planning stage already organized. The idea-bubble type of outline is for people who think in creative, tangential bursts of ideas. Their thoughts often come in random, loosely connected order. Note how the two forms of outlines reflect these two ways of creating ideas.

These two types of initial outlines are extremely useful for the first stage of planning a message. Merely jot down ideas as they occur to you. Do not attempt to organize them—just get anything you might use down on paper. If you need to, you can organize the ideas later into a more complete outline.

Jot List (Sequential)	Idea Bubble (Tangential)

Thoughts for a letter

Purpose: invitation to a party
Occasion: end of school year
Time: 6:30 Saturday, May 2
Place: my house, address
What to wear: casual
Activity: dancing afterward
Who will be there: soccer team
    and guests
What to bring: dessert
Special note: Jim will be there

FIGURE 4.1 Two Forms of Preliminary Outlines

    Once you have an initial idea of what you want your message to include, you should organize it into a preliminary outline—a logical arrangement of the ideas. As you create the preliminary outline, you may want to delete some ideas because they are irrelevant or add ideas that will improve the balance of the message. The preliminary outline is just a planning document; it should grow and change as the message is developed. If you have to do research in order to compose your message, the preliminary outline will guide your search for information so that you do not waste time looking in areas that are useless to you.

    Figure 4.2 illustrates a preliminary outline created from the earlier jot lists. Notice how the ideas are grouped under headings and subordinated.

    Some situations require a formal outline of the entire message. The full outline should be constructed once all research and rewriting has been done. Figure 4.3 illustrates the format for formal outlines. Note how numerals and letters are used to organize the main sections, main points, and subpoints of the outline. Every outline will be different because of varying numbers of sections and points of information different messages include, but the sample outline shows you the general format.

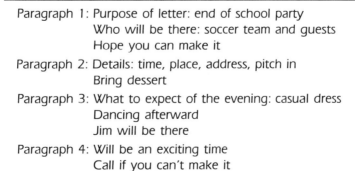

Paragraph 1: Purpose of letter: end of school party
        Who will be there: soccer team and guests
        Hope you can make it
Paragraph 2: Details: time, place, address, pitch in
        Bring dessert
Paragraph 3: What to expect of the evening: casual dress
        Dancing afterward
        Jim will be there
Paragraph 4: Will be an exciting time
        Call if you can't make it

FIGURE 4.2 A Sample Preliminary Outline for a Letter

```
I. First Section
   A. First Main Point
      1. Subpoint
         a. Supporting point
         b. Supporting point
      2. Subpoint
         a. Supporting point
         b. Supporting point
   B. Second Main Point
      1. Subpoint
         a. Supporting point
         b. Supporting point
      2. Subpoint
         a. Supporting point
         b. Supporting point
II. Second Section
   A. First Main Point
      1. Subpoint
         a. Supporting point
         b. Supporting point
      2. Subpoint
         a. Supporting point
         b. Supporting point
   B. Second Main Point
      1. Subpoint
         a. Supporting point
         b. Supporting point
      2. Subpoint
      3. Subpoint
         a. Supporting point
         b. Supporting point
   C. Third Main Point
   D. Fourth Main Point
III. Third Section
   A. First Main Point
      1. Subpoint
      2. Subpoint
   B. Second Main Point
```

FIGURE 4.3 Format for Formal Outlines

Research Your Subject

In some cases, your own knowledge and experience will supply you with the information you need to construct a message. In other situations, you may need to do research. In either case, you need to consider carefully the information you have assembled in your preliminary outline and evaluate its relevance, sufficiency, and authority.

Information is *relevant* when it applies directly to the issues at hand in the message. Determine which information is most relevant to suit the purposes of the audience and yourself as you focus the message. Relevant information attracts the receiver's interest and attention because it is useful and practical.

Sufficiency of information means that enough material is offered to explain the crucial issues thoroughly. Senders can err in either direction. If too little information is offered, the issues will remain unclear; if too much information is presented, the receivers will be overwhelmed or bored by the amount of detail. You need to find the proper balance in the amount of information you provide.

Authority in information is determined by the credibility of the source. The opinions and beliefs of experts carry more authority than your personal opinion in some matters. You need to determine how authoritative the situation demands you to be in your message. How detailed, how exact, how specific do you need to be? Reporting what authoritative sources have to say about your subject will help you create stronger support for your ideas.

You can conduct effective research in numerous places. Library holdings, current periodicals, interviews with experts, popular media, business records, and your personal experiences provide a wealth of relevant and authoritative data that can make your messages more interesting and more believable.

Construct the First Draft

Once you have assembled the information you need, you are ready to construct the message. An effective technique is to plan to write several drafts before you complete the final effort. If you anticipate revisions, you will be aware that the first draft does not have to be perfect, so you will feel freer to experiment with different formats or approaches. Using the multiple-draft technique also helps planners who suffer from "writer's block"—the inability to get started. By writing a first draft that is purposely unorganized, rambling, or illogical, the sender can overcome inhibitions about being "perfect." The logic problems can be easily solved by composing an outline from the first rough draft and then composing a second, more suitable effort.

Preparing a first draft works for letters, speeches, and interviews. Letters obviously can be rewritten before they are mailed. Speech outlines can be written in advance. Speeches can be rehearsed, evaluated, and revised before being given to the actual audience. Likewise, interviews can be planned and rehearsed. Many writers and speakers attest to the usefulness of the first-draft technique. The only way to write well, they say, is to rewrite, rewrite, and rewrite.

Edit the First Draft

A major factor in the drafting process is editing the initial drafts. The standards for editing include the characteristics of effective communication discussed earlier. Review your writing, outlines, and presentations for clarity and accuracy. Is your purpose clear? Are your points clearly stated? Are your facts accurate? Are the grammar, punctuation, and spelling correct? Likewise consider the completeness factor. Have you covered your topic thoroughly but without belaboring it or cluttering it with irrelevant detail? Finally, review your work for appropriateness and dynamism. Is your choice of medium suited to the situation? Is your language appropriate to the occasion? Have you communicated a sense of personality and energy in your message?

An objective scrutiny of your first version of a letter, speech, or interview will help you identify any weaknesses that need correction. This careful attention to detail ensures you of the chance to make necessary corrections before you communicate with the receiver.

Reconstruct the Final Draft

The last step in the planning process takes advantage of all that has gone before. By determining your purpose, analyzing your audience, organizing your material, and researching facts adequately, your first effort should be an effective message. By adding the extra dimension of careful editing and revision of your first draft, however, you have the chance to strengthen the final product. This attention to reconstruction takes time and effort, but if you are concerned about the quality and effectiveness of your message, the effort will reap great rewards.

Good communication ultimately boils down to two principles: careful planning and attention to detail. The seven steps we have reviewed in this chapter provide the tools to create effective and interesting messages. The more you work with these tools, the more comfortable they will become to you. At first, some of the tools may seem awkward or unfamiliar, but practice with them will make you an adept communicator. And the messages you create will be both attractive and powerful.

RESOURCES

Dumaine, Deborah. *Write to the Top: Writing for Corporate Success.* New York: Random House, 1983.

This book contains useful information on the outlining and first-draft techniques reviewed in this chapter.

Einstein, Charles. *How to Communicate.* New York: McGraw-Hill, 1985.

This book contains a witty review of rules of grammar and a practical philosophy about communicating for the writer and speaker.

Munter, Mary. *Guide to Managerial Communication.* Englewood Cliffs, N.J.: Prentice-Hall, 1987.

This book is an excellent summary of the planning process for all three communication modes. It contains several useful checklists for the revision process.

EXERCISE 4.1
Analyzing Communication Situations

Directions: In each of the following situations, determine the errors the sender has committed in the message sent. Which step of the planning process would have prevented the communicator from committing the error?

1. Tom has been planning a dinner party for several weeks for important business clients. He invited several business associates several weeks in advance and asked that they write to accept or refuse the invitation. The day of his dinner party, he received the following message from Joe, one of his guests:

> Tom,
>
> Sorry I can't make it tonight. Something came up. I'll call later.
>
> Joe

Error committed by Joe: _____

_____

Planning step violated: _____

_____

2. Matty, a manager in a lumberyard, has been asked to speak to a meeting of all the secretaries in her company. The occasion is the annual awards banquet for the staff. Since no one told her what to speak about, Matty thinks that she will show slides of her recent lumber-buying trip to Malaysia.

Error committed by Matty: _____

_____

Planning step violated: _____

_____

3. Phil is preparing for a job interview. He assumes that the company offering the new job, General Communications, is very similar to his current employer, Communications Limited. At the interview, the first question his interviewer asks is, "What do you know about General Communications?" Phil answers, "Well, I think it's kind of like Communications Limited, isn't it?"

Error committed by Phil: _____

_____

Planning step violated: _____

_____

4. Ellen is a customer service manager for a retail store. A customer has complained that the store does not have child care service. Ellen composes the following letter:

> Dear Madame:
>
> What makes you think we should provide child care service? Do any other stores in town provide it? No! Stop and think the next time before you offer your free opinions. We try to do a good job in providing customer service, but you don't seem to appreciate our efforts. But thanks for shopping with us. We value your patronage.
>
> Sincere appreciation,
Ellen Glump

Error committed by Ellen: _____

_____

Planning step violated: _____

_____

EXERCISE 4.2
Writing Preliminary Outlines

Directions: In order to give you practice using the jot-list and the idea-bubble forms of organizing, create the following documents:

1. A jot list of what you would include in a speech on "How to Organize Your Desk."
2. An idea-bubble list of what you would include in a speech on "How to Use a Dictionary."
3. A preliminary outline of either the desk or the dictionary speech based on the jot list or the idea-bubble list.

1. *Jot List:* "How to Organize Your Desk"

_____

_____

_____

_____

_____

_____

_____

_____

_____

_____

_____

_____

_____

_____

_____

_____

_____

2. *Idea-Bubble List:* "How to Use a Dictionary"

3. *Preliminary Outline*

    Topic: _____

EXERCISE 4.3
Editing Drill

Directions: The following is a letter of recommendation which is in need of editing. Revise each paragraph of the letter in the space provided. Be prepared to explain the revisions that you make in terms of the seven planning steps discussed in this chapter.

---

84 Bucolic Way
San Simeon, CA 93827
April 24, 19XX

Carole Masterwrighter
Sinclair Publishers
8095 Fragrant Street
San Clemente, CA 92718

To the Dearest Reader:

As you peruse this letter, hark back to the halcyon days of your own youth and recall the splendor of youthful juvenile enthusiasm. Were you anxiously awaiting your first tenure of employ? Were you champing at the bit to set foot on the road to great adventure? Sarah Stevens shares that enthusiasm with you—she is ready for the great adventure into employment

_____

_____

_____

_____

_____

_____

Notwithstanding the fact that Sarah was constantly employed during the entirety of her academic training, she managed, despite various learning difficulties, to attain a 4.0 grade average. She matriculated and sustained her college career at Okogobee University and graduated with an M.S. degree in Management Science. Moreover, she distinguished herself with the attainment of the Outstanding Scholarship Award of the Business School during her senior year.

_____

_____

_____

_____

_____

_____

Sarah is a great worker. She can get things done. She is willing to help out. She goes the extra step to anticipate problems. She thinks through problems, and she always comes up with good solutions.

_____

_____

_____

_____

_____

Wow! What else can I say? Sarah is just a super kid—a great personality—a dynamite worker—and super with the public.

_____

_____

_____

_____

_____

That just about wraps it up. Thanks for your consideration of Sarah for the job. I hope and pray you will give her your serious consideration. If there is anything else I can do, please do not hesitate to give me a call. Anxiously awaiting your decision, I remain

Most warmly cordial,
Eleanor Primrose

_____

_____

_____

_____

_____

ACTION ASSIGNMENT

4
The Communication Plan

1. Assume that you are going to join a club. One of the requirements of joining the club is that all new members must give a ten-minute speech to introduce themselves at their first meeting to the other members. Create the situation—the type of club it would be, the other members, the activities of the club, and the location of the first meeting. Plan your speech by listing what you would do to accomplish each of the steps of the following communication plan:

   Determine your purpose
   Analyze your audience
   Organize your thoughts
   Research your subject
   Construct your first draft
   Edit the first draft
   Reconstruct the final draft

2. If you were going to write a résumé to apply for a job, what type of research would you do? Where would you do the research?

3. Search through your files for a term paper, report, or business letter that you wrote some time ago. Read the document and evaluate its effectiveness now that you have some perspective on it. If you had the chance, would you revise it? Would the document be improved by a revision? In what ways?

5
Psychological Strategies of Communication

Have you ever noticed that some speakers seem to grab your attention while others are boring and lifeless? Do some pieces of direct-mail advertising capture your interest while others are bland and dull? When you meet strangers for the first time, have you ever found some of them to be fascinating and easy to listen to while others seem self-centered and uninteresting? Effective communicators in these three situations use psychological strategies to create attention, interest, and persuasiveness and to build a positive relationship with the audience. This chapter looks at a set of strategies that can help you capture attention, make you interesting as a speaker or writer, and ultimately make you more effective in accomplishing your communication purpose.

Use the "You" Orientation

Basic human nature makes people self-centered. Most people think in terms of how they can benefit from what is being discussed—that is, they operate by the WIIFM principle, "What's In It For Me?" Effective communicators use this fundamental human concern to their advantage when they construct messages from the viewpoint of the receiver rather than the sender. The listener is more likely to pay attention and be affected by the message when the sender acknowledges the WIIFM principle.

The "you" orientation can be used in two ways—in an unspoken form and in the actual language you use. The unspoken "you" orientation occurs when you plan your message with the needs, interests, and values of the audience or reader in mind. You determine what to say, how much to include, and how to phrase the content of your message in a way that you know will interest and be easily understood by the receiver.

Another application of the "you" strategy is to actually use the pronoun "you" more often then the pronoun "I" or "we." When the writer starts a sentence with the word "you," the receiver becomes personally involved in

"I"-Oriented Sentences	"You"-Oriented Sentences
I wish to apply for the position as an apprentice with your firm which you advertised.	You say in your ad that you are looking for a hard-working apprentice. I wish to apply.
We wish to point out that the monthly rent is overdue.	You may have overlooked the monthly rent.
We are pleased to announce the opening of our new store.	You will be glad to know about the opening of our new store.
I am sending your order today.	Your order is being sent today.

FIGURE 5.1 "I" Orientation Versus "You" Orientation

the message. By discussing the receiver's experience or needs, the sender captures attention and gets a better hearing. Notice in Figure 5.1 how the "I" and the "you" orientations influence the effectiveness of the sentences.

Create Needs in the Receiver

In some communication situations, the receiver will have a strong desire to hear what you have to say. In such cases, the sender has to pay less attention to creating interest, because the situation has already provided it. In many instances, however, the receiver may not automatically be interested in what you have to say. You may have to work harder to create interest and attention for your message. An effective device for building attention is "need creation"—pointing out the positive benefits that your message can have for the receiver.

As with the "you" orientation, "need creation" focuses on the needs and interests of the receiver instead of the sender. To create needs, the sender must answer the following questions:

Why is the receiver listening?
What does the receiver hope to gain?
What else can the receiver gain?
How is this information relevant and applicable to the receiver?

To attract the receiver, incorporate the answers to these questions in the opening lines of your message. By promising benefits and solutions to problems at the beginning, you will capture the interest of the listener more easily. Analyze the content of your message thoroughly for the benefits you are offering the receiver. Include as many realistic statements as possible to stress how the reader or listener will gain from accepting and attending to your message.

Create a Positive Tone

Tone is the overall emotional reaction you create in a message. It can be either demanding, critical, complaining, hostile, and defensive or friendly, pleasant, relaxed, and confident. In general, you should strive always to create a positive emotional climate for your messages. Even when negative information must be communicated, you can do so in a diplomatic, tactful way that will not affront the receiver. Take care not to be insincere or condescending when communicating bad news, but do stress any possible positive aspects more than negative ones. Figure 5.2 illustrates differences in negative and positive tone.

Another technique to create positive tone is to avoid, or at least carefully control, any negative sentiments you express to the receiver. Only in very rare circumstances should you express anger, try to intimidate with threats, or accuse the receiver of wrongdoing. It is far better to argue with rational appeals than to resort to name calling, loaded language, or threats. In general, negative tone in a message creates a negative response, not a positive one. The more you try to appeal to the receiver in a rational and positive tone, the greater the chances are of a reasonable, positive response.

Establish Your Credibility

Another important question that you should consider when planning messages is "Why should the audience listen to me—personally?" The answer to this question determines your *credibility*, or your authority and believability as a sender. If you create an image of professionalism in business communications, you will increase your chances of getting an open reception from the receiver. You can accomplish these goals by consciously using devices that enhance your credibility.

Research shows that your professional associations, your rank and title in a business, and the use of expert opinions and data in your messages improve your credibility dramatically. Building trust with the listener also

Negative Tone	Positive Tone
Do not expect an answer before May 30.	You can expect an answer after May 30.
We guarantee you will never need a replacement.	This product will last indefinitely.
None of our products have ever malfunctioned.	All of our products have functioned perfectly.
I do not have experience in word processing, but I can type 50 words per minute.	I have excellent typing skills at 50 words per minute.

FIGURE 5.2 Negative Versus Positive Tone

improves your credibility. Demonstrating good intentions toward the receiver, which are suggested by the "you" orientation and "need creation," increase trust. Appearing to be fair and open-minded also heightens the sense of trust. The quality of dynamism also increases credibility, because it makes you appear personally involved and committed to your message. Most people find dynamism an attractive characteristic, so it enhances your appeal.

When planning messages, give attention to your credibility and include as many enhancing devices as are appropriate in the situation. Even if you have low initial credibility, you can improve it by what you say about yourself, either verbally or nonverbally, in your message.

Use a Clear Organizational Structure

People attach strong positive value to messages that are logically organized, and they place lower value on messages that are rambling and disorganized. Research also shows that people more easily remember messages that are highly organized. For these reasons, you should construct messages in a logical, orderly fashion.

Chapter 4 discussed the importance of outlines as a planning tool for effective messages. When you construct a letter, plan a speech, or prepare for an interview, use an outline as a means for organizing your thoughts and controlling your presentation of those ideas. The best approach to outlining is to use a three-part structure for any message, planning the beginning, middle, and end of your message.

Any message must have a beginning, or an *introduction*, in which you establish a positive relationship with the receiver and make your purpose clear. Introductions are also good places in which to establish some credibility and point out the relevance of your message for the receiver. If your message is fairly lengthy, you may also wish to offer a preview of the ideas you will be presenting, so that the receiver will understand the overall structure of your message.

The middle, or *body*, of a message consists of the actual business to be conducted. It should be logically divided into main points. Letters are customarily divided into paragraphs, each devoted to a separate idea. Speeches are divided into main points. Interviews cover main areas of questioning. Each main point should be supported with facts, statistics, examples, demonstrations, or whatever else is necessary to accomplish your purpose.

The ending, or *conclusion*, of a message should accomplish your purpose. You can summarize all your main points, emphasize one key point, make a strong appeal for action, or reestablish a positive relationship with the receiver.

An old formula for business writing is the "Relationship—Business—Relationship" technique. This formula neatly summarizes the functions of the three parts and is particularly useful for persuasive messages. An old Army adage for public speakers is "Tell them what you are going to tell them, tell them, and then tell them what you told them." This advice summarizes the functions of the three parts of a communication, particularly in informative settings.

To preview something: *I will cover, I wish to do three things . . .*

To add something: *furthermore, besides, in addition, moreover, even greater, next, finally . . .*

To compare something: *likewise, similarly, at the same time, the same thing is true for . . .*

To contrast something: *in contrast, although, however, on the other hand, still, yet . . .*

To show the result of something: *thus, therefore, as a result, as a consequence . . .*

To give an example of something: *for example, for instance, to demonstrate, to illustrate, as a case in point . . .*

To show greater or lesser rank: *moreover, first, last, even greater, worse yet, more importantly . . .*

To show time and place: *first, second, then, after, during, while, finally, soon, here, next to, above . . .*

To summarize and conclude: *in summary, finally, in closing, thus, one final thought . . .*

FIGURE 5.3 Common Transitional Devices

Use Transitions to Increase Clarity

Once you have developed an outline, you can insert transitions to make the logical pattern of your thought clear to the receiver. *Transitions* are words or phrases that link the parts of a message together. They act as signposts to tell the reader or listener where you are and where you are going with your train of thought. Without transitions, messages can wander into unrelated diversions or in uncertain directions, and the receiver will become lost.

Listed in Figure 5.3 are examples of transitional words and phrases. Use these devices to explain your structure in advance, to explain where you are in the structure, and to review where you have been.

Use Emphasis for Effect

Invariably, some elements of a message are more important than others. To draw attention to the important parts of a message or to reduce attention to insignificant elements, you can use several emphasis techniques: location, amount, and repetition.

The most important and memorable *locations* are the beginnings and endings of messages. Thus, you should place key ideas in those locations to heighten attention and memory. First lines in letters and speeches should be powerful and interesting. The first sentence in a paragraph should clearly explain the key idea of that paragraph. The last line of a letter or speech should produce the desired response you want from the receiver. The post-script in a letter is a technique for emphasizing one last idea.

The *amount* of time and space you spend on an idea in proportion to the rest of the message also communicates its importance. Thus, you should commit your time and space proportional to the value of the ideas in your message. Spend most of your time on the important issues and less time on trivial or tangential matters.

Repetition is another powerful device for improving memory. The more you repeat a message or an idea, the more a receiver will tend to remember it. Of course, you can overuse repetition and become redundant, so this technique should be used judiciously. If certain facts or ideas are extremely important, however, appropriate repetition will ensure that the receiver's attention is drawn to them.

Use Verbs to Increase Dynamism

The single most important writing element that can electrify your readers and capture their interest is the use of the verb. Verbs are like the motors that propel your language, just as an engine pulls a train along the tracks. By selecting and using verbs wisely, you can create a sense of energy and forcefulness which will capture attention and interest.

In general, you should prefer the active voice to the passive voice in verbs. Voice refers to the way in which the action of a sentence is constructed. In the *active voice*, the subject of the sentence does something to an object. In the *passive voice*, something is done to the subject by someone (the indirect object). Note these examples:

> Tony hit the ball. (active voice)
> The committee passed the bill. (active voice)
> The ball was hit by Tony. (passive voice)
> The bill was passed. (note: the indirect object is not stated)

If you want a sense of force and vigor in your language, use the active voice as often as you can.

There are times when the passive voice can be useful. Most commonly writers use the passive voice to diffuse the blame or responsibility for an action or to emphasize the result rather than the actor:

> An error was made in counting the inventory. (note: the sentence does not name who committed the error)

In most instances, however, you want a sense of force and liveliness, so do not let the "creeping passive" habit drain the life out of your sentences. Control the passive voice closely, and use the active voice whenever possible.

As you select language for your message, choose lively and specific verbs. Speakers often play it safe by using weak and dull verbs. By employing more lively synonyms, you can make your language brighter and more vigorous. Note the differences among the following verbs:

to talk: telephone, chat, discuss, argue, murmur
to try: attempt, struggle, grapple
to do: accomplish, achieve, attain
to end: terminate, finish, complete
to think: assume, consider, ponder, debate

Of course, your language should be appropriate to the situation, so do not select verbs that are overly dramatic; but when a vivid synonym states the action more precisely, utilize it.

You can improve your writing by avoiding several "weak verb" constructions. In many cases, you can avoid the verb "to be" in all its forms—"am," "is," "was," "are," "were," "will be"—when used as a linking verb. Wherever possible, use a more interesting verb instead of the linking verb:

Sam *is* a happy fellow. (weak linking verb)
Sam *radiates* happiness. (vivid action verb)

To strengthen your language, you can also avoid those verbs which are synonymous with the verb "to be": "occur," "take place," "exist," "entail," "constitute." Use a more vivid action verb to replace one of these.

Verbs that qualify the sender's ideas also dilute the energy of communication. Words such as "think," "seem," "tend," "feel," "believe," and "appear" convey a sense of indecision and weakness in the sender. Do not qualify your opinions and statements except when it is necessary to do so or when you intend to communicate indecision or tentativeness.

The "preposition verb" is a particularly common weak construction that combines a dull verb with a preposition to create a second weak verb. Notice in the following list how the weak preposition verbs can be replaced by more vivid, interesting ones:

get up = arise	think about = consider
look over = analyze	walk out on = leave
work out = exercise	go over = read, review
talk out = discuss	put together = assemble

One final technique will help you attain a vigorous communication style: avoiding the "smothered verb," one that is hidden as a noun within a sentence. Notice how the second sentence in each of the following pairs reads with greater force and energy because the smothered verb is set free:

The committee *held a meeting* last week. (smothered)
The committee *met* last week. (vivid)
A *decision was reached* regarding the hiring of more janitors. (smothered)
They *decided* to hire new janitors. (vivid)
Finding a good janitor *is something* nobody wants to do. (smothered)
Nobody *wants to find* a new janitor. (vivid)
The group *made alterations* in the process of hiring janitors. (smothered)
The group *altered* the way they will hire janitors. (vivid)

Use Action Steps

When you want the receiver to take some action, you need to specify exactly what you want done, when it should be done, and how the receiver should do it. Including specific action steps in your message will increase the chances of getting the response you seek.

Action steps should be specific suggestions or instructions on how to accomplish the desired result. The more specific they are, the better the receiver will understand what to do. It is a good tactic to make the first step in a series an easy one, since that increases the chance of a response. You can also volunteer to be actively involved in the first steps of the plan if the receiver wants your participation.

Anticipate the receiver's probable objections to your ideas or desires. Plan action steps that will overcome or deal with these objections reasonably. By analyzing the way in which the receiver will respond to your message, you can plan more effectively and overcome the objections as you construct your message. Look at your message with a critical, objective eye. Spot the weaknesses in your message that may inhibit the response you seek. Then edit your message to provide greater relevance, more motivation, or data that refute any objection the receiver might have. These techniques will ensure a more positive response.

RESOURCES

Glorfield, Louis, David A. Lauerman, and Norman C. Stageberg. *A Concise Guide for Writers*. New York: Holt, Rinehart and Winston, 1984.

This book provides useful advice on improving your language style, with special emphasis on problems to avoid.

Treece, Malra. *Communication for Business and the Professions*. Boston: Allyn and Bacon, 1983.

This book contains an interesting discussion of psychological strategies for the business writer.

EXERCISE 5.1
Psychological Strategy Drill

Directions: In the following sentences, identify the reason a positive relationship is not formed: lack of the "you" orientation, no "need creation," poor tone, or lack of credibility. Rewrite the sentences so as to create a more positive relationship with the reader.

1. I am going to graduate in June, and I would like to work for a company like yours.

   Error: _____

   Correction: _____

   _____

2. To avoid breakdowns in operating, do not exceed suggested load capacity.

   Error: _____

   Correction: _____

   _____

3. I want you to give money to the Red Cross.

   Error: _____

   Correction: _____

   _____

4. I am quite upset with the inferior service I received yesterday.

   Error: _____

   Correction: _____

   _____

5. Nobody seems at all interested in this company's doing a better job.

   Error: _____

   _____

   Correction: _____

   _____

6. I have a B.S. degree in business administration.

    Error: _____

    _____

    Correction: _____

    _____

7. Please pay your rent promptly, or we will start eviction proceedings.

    Error: _____

    _____

    Correction: _____

    _____

8. Everybody ought to consider a degree in business administration—it is the right thing for you.

    Error: _____

    _____

    Correction: _____

    _____

9. I suppose you think that I do not have any relevant experience—in fact, I have quite a bit.

    Error: _____

    _____

    Correction: _____

    _____

EXERCISE 5.2
Improving Verb Choice

Directions: The following sales letter has several poor verb usages. Read the letter and identify the verb problems by circling any passive constructions, underlining any smothered verbs, and drawing an "X" through any weak verbs (forms of "to be" and preposition verbs). Rewrite the letter in the lines provided, improving the verb choices.

```
                    PHOTO-STORAGE SYSTEMS
                       1849 Polaroid Way
                     Huntsville, AL 29584


                                        January 30. 19XX

Brownie I. Matic
13 Silver Nitrate Lane
Boron, NV  89473

Dear Sir:

    You are being contacted in regards to a new product that is

being manufactured by us.  This product is photo-file, a plastic

storage system designed for photographs, that we think could

easily be a replacement to the shoebox storage system that most

people may use now.

    The photo-file system is constructed of high-impact plastic.

It is to be offered in red, blue, or yellow, and offerings will

be made in various model sizes.  Several unique features

constitute the photofiles's best selling points:  see-through

top, compartment dividers, and easy carrying handle.  A money-

back guarantee will be honored on each unit sold.  Replacements

will be made for any defective units.

    We feel that the photo-file would fit in with the products

offered in your catalogue, and we wish you would try it out.  One

of our sales representatives will show up in your area the first

part of next month, and we would like to set up an appointment at

your convenience.

    High hopes are held by us for a long and profitable

relationship.

                                    Sincerely,

                                    I. C. Starrs
```

```
                          PHOTO-STORAGE SYSTEMS
                            1849 Polaroid Way
                          Huntsville, AL  29584


                                                      January 30. 19XX

      Brownie I. Matic
      13 Silver Nitrate Lane
      Boron, NV  89473

      Dear Sir:


      _____

      _____

      _____

      _____

      _____

      _____

      _____

      _____

      _____

      _____

      _____

      _____

      _____

      _____

      _____

      _____

      _____

      _____

      _____

      _____

      _____

      _____
```

EXERCISE 5.3
Verb Replacement Drill

Directions: The following list of twenty verbs could be replaced with more specific and vivid synonyms. Identify each of the words as a "weak" verb, a "smothered" verb, or a "preposition" verb. Write its replacement in the line at the right.

POOR VERB	TYPE OF PROBLEM	REPLACEMENT
1. I take pleasure in		
2. it is recommended		
3. come up with		
4. work together		
5. the job entails		
6. I am of the opinion		
7. I will endeavor		
8. she perused		
9. come into contact		
10. a condition exists		
11. please forbear		
12. make an amendment		
13. come to an end		
14. it is to be wished		
15. utilize a tool		
16. I have a concern		
17. my wish is that		
18. to provide service		
19. to think over		
20. to give advice		

ACTION ASSIGNMENT

5
Psychological Strategies of Communication

1. Each of these sentences is from a sales speech for a product. Each attempts to create a sense of need in the receiver regarding the message that follows. Rewrite each sentence to create more of a sense of need.
   a. I do not know much about this product, but it is supposed to be good.
   b. I have never used this product before, but many people have.
   c. Do you think you might be able to use this product?
   d. Many people say that this product saves them time.
   e. Why would anybody want to buy this product? Would you?

2. Add transitional sentences or words in the spaces indicated to make these sentences flow more smoothly and logically:

   In the middle of the night, I was awakened by a calamitous noise.

   _____ I arose from my bed. _____

   _____ I looked out the window. _____

   I went downstairs. _____ I looked out the back

   door. _____ A wild raccoon had overturned the trash

   can and was making a racket. _____ I picked up a
   shoe and threw it at the raccoon, and it scampered off into the night.

   _____ I climbed the stairs and went back to my
   peaceful sleep.

3. Write a paragraph describing your most recent vacation. Describe where you went, what you did, who accompanied you, and what you liked (or disliked) about the vacation. Once you have completed this paragraph, revise it by changing all the active-voice verbs into passive-voice verbs. Read the revised paragraph aloud. Does it sound strange? Rewrite the paragraph using more vivid verbs than you originally used. Does it sound more interesting?

BUSINESS WRITING: LETTERS, MEMOS, AND REPORTS

6

The Principles of Business Writing

Writing is a requirement of all formalized education and most business careers. You have probably written term papers, book reviews, research reports, and essays in your school career. If you have been employed, you have probably had to write business letters, memos, reports, and recommendations.

Unfortunately, despite all this practice and experience in writing, most people hate it. If at all possible, most people avoid writing. The consequence of this aversion is that most people cannot write very well. Thus, their dislike of writing creates a vicious cycle: by avoiding writing, people never develop the skills necessary to do it well or the sense of accomplishment that comes from being a good writer.

This chapter helps you to conquer the problem of hating and avoiding the writing process. Unless you confront and defeat your negative attitude toward writing, you can never develop your skills and acquire this important business skill. You already know how to write. This chapter prepares you to write more effectively by applying the principles of effective communication that you learned in the first unit of this book.

Develop a Positive Attitude Toward Writing

The reasons for your hatred of and aversion to writing are understandable. What were your early writing experiences like? Most people complain that they were forced to write about things they thought were irrelevant, forced to write arbitrary numbers of words or pages, criticized for not doing it well, and bored by merciless grammar and punctuation drills.[1] Negative reinforcement of this sort is bound to squelch any enthusiasm a person might have in an activity. Thus, many people avoid writing altogether.

The reality of the workplace, however, demands that you know how to write easily and effectively. Success in your business career depends on your ability to present your ideas and opinions in writing. Without the skill to write effectively, you will be at a severe disadvantage in a competitive job marketplace, and you will not be able to achieve work goals at the rate you desire.

So what can be done about this vicious cycle of avoidance? If you dislike writing, you must first try to create a more positive attitude toward writing. Several good reasons for changing your attitude were discussed in Chapter 1. Writing is a large part of most jobs, and your career success depends on your ability to write. If you are ambitious about your career, you should become convinced of the value that writing can have in your future. If you are not convinced of this fact yet, interview several people who hold positions to which you aspire. Ask them about their experiences with and attitudes toward writing. Do they think it is valuable to their jobs? Do they find it easy or difficult—and why? Do they have any recommendations for you about developing your writing skills? A few candid interviews with professional people will prove the value of writing in most business settings.

Beyond the value of writing in the workplace, writing can also be enjoyable—if you develop a solid set of basic skills. It can even be easy—if you learn some simple, fundamental techniques. As you develop the ability to write clearly and gracefully, you will become more comfortable with putting your thoughts on paper. The guidelines for effective communication discussed in the first unit of this book should help you increase the clarity and accuracy of your writing. As these basic skills improve, then you can become more strategically persuasive in the way you write. Issues of completeness and appropriateness become more important as your skills develop. Finally, once you are comfortable with writing, your personality—or "voice," as it is sometimes called—will begin to develop in your writing. You will become as persuasive on paper as you are in person, and your writing can become a source of professional influence and personal satisfaction to you.

It is a long journey to the goal of being a good writer, and most people have gotten off to a bad start. If you commit yourself to changing your attitudes about writing, however, you can create a plan for developing the skills that will make you a success. The following chapters in this unit are designed to give you the basic planning and composition skills you need to develop as a writer. They must be supplemented by a positive attitude, however, or you will never escape from the vicious cycle of hating to write. If you do apply yourself to developing your skills, you will improve. Once you start getting a sense of accomplishment from your writing, you may even want to expand the types of writing that you do. After writing a simple business letter becomes a relatively easy task, you may discover a hidden novelist or journalist inside you. You will never know about these latent talents until you try to enjoy writing.

The First Rule of Writing: Be Adaptable

It may sound strange to you, but there is no right way to write. Trying to write "right" is one of the biggest stumbling blocks for beginning writers, especially if they are strongly motivated to achieve or if they have received serious criticism in their early writing careers. The frustration of "not knowing where to start" or "not being able to do it well" often becomes a block to writers.

The most important rule of writing is to realize that the best writer is the one who adapts to the situation at hand. A good writer has to be aware of the "rules" of writing—the commonly accepted standards of English usage. These rules may be broken, however, as long as the writer knows exactly when to break them and what effect will be created. For example, how do you spell the word that refers to the place where you see a movie—a "theater" or a "theatre"? The "right" answers depends on several things. Are you in England or the United States? Does the movie house use one of those spellings in its own name? How does your boss want it spelled? Who is the audience to whom you are writing, and what will they think of the spelling? The answers to these questions tell you how to spell the word—not the dictionary or any other "rule" of English usage.

The same need to adapt applies to every rule of writing offered in this book. You need to analyze the situation and decide how best to express the message you want to convey. Grammar, punctuation, format, salutation, word choice—indeed, every aspect of writing—is a matter of judiciously adapting to the situation in order to create the desired effect. You should know the commonly accepted rules, but then you may free yourself from worrying too much about them. Just write. Get some feedback. Then rewrite if you must.

The best way to develop adaptability as a writer is to find writing you admire. Look for role models. Analyze these writers' letters or memos for techniques that you might find useful. Collect samples of reports or résumés if you know you must write them in the future. Look at how other people write, and trust your own instincts about what is good. What formats appeal to you? What is a good opening line for a letter requesting an interview? What complimentary close should you use when writing a letter to your boss? Other people's solutions to these writing problems will help you make your own decisions. Research your company's policy or informal standards for the format of a letter or the organization of a sales report. Scrutinize your immediate superior's style of writing for clues about how to make your writing more acceptable. If you want to be "upwardly mobile" in your profession, look at the writing of the people who are already at the level to which you aspire.

You have to know the options available to you in order to adapt most effectively. Too many writers can write only one way—they get something down on paper and then they think it is cast in concrete. Poor writers consider no changes, make no revisions, and never stop to think that there might be a better way to express their thoughts. This attitude undermines any chance of improvement because it prohibits feedback, one of the most valuable tools for a writer. Look for feedback in your writing environment. Ask for feedback and use it to make your writing even more effective or acceptable.

You can become a good writer, perhaps a truly dynamic one, if you apply yourself to the task of learning the rules and then breaking them all—on purpose. The first step is to learn the rules thoroughly. The second is to develop a sense of your own style. The third is to look for role models of good writing in other people. The final step is to let your style develop as you become comfortable with the rules, your own preferences, and the practices of others you admire. The result of this process is your own unique writing style, one that gives you a sense of accomplishment and is effective in communicating to others.

Remember the Qualities of Effective Writing

Chapter 3 discussed the five qualities of effective communication: accuracy, clarity, completeness, appropriateness, and dynamism. As you begin writing, keep these criteria in mind. Use them as guidelines for selecting what you will write. As an example, let us say that you have to write a letter to a client asking to extend a deadline for delivery of a shipment. What would you say in your letter? Figure 6.1 illustrates how the qualities of effective communication create competent writing in this example.

You can also use this figure as a checklist to review your writing once the first draft is completed. Make sure that all facts are accurate and specifically stated. Be certain that you include everything necessary, and delete any trivial details. Check your language for tone and liveliness. Use the psychological strategies discussed in Chapter 5 wherever appropriate to enhance the effectiveness of your writing.

Develop Your Writing Plan

Chapter 4 introduced the idea of the communication plan—an outline to assist you in planning any communication activity. You may wish to develop a more specific writing plan for letters, memos, and reports. Since writing can be entirely planned and rewritten before it is ever communicated to the reader, a good writing plan can be especially effective. The following sections expand upon the communication plan introduced in Chapter 4. They provide you with a writing plan that will ensure clear, readable, and accurate pieces of writing.

Accuracy:	What are the precise facts about the shipment?
	When was the shipment due?
	What is the new arrival date?
Clarity:	What are the reasons for the delay?
	Does the client have any alternative courses of action?
Completeness:	Have you said everything that needs to be said?
	Will the client have any questions?
Appropriateness:	What tone do you want the letter to have?
	How can you maintain a positive relationship?
Dynamism:	What kind of image do you want to project?
	How personal do you want to be with the client?

FIGURE 6.1   An Example of Effective Communication Criteria in Use

ESTABLISH YOUR PURPOSE

Before writing, think for a moment about whom you are writing to and what your exact purpose is. Establish your point of view and plan exact and specific things to say about it. When you begin to write, stick to your purpose. Do not wander from your goal or clutter your writing with unnecessary details.

CONSIDER YOUR TONE

Decide in advance the exact emotional atmosphere you want to communicate in your writing. Do you want to sound stern, pleasant, angry, humble, or informal? As you select opening and closing lines, choose words and thoughts that clearly communicate the tone you want.

PLAN AND OUTLINE YOUR THOUGHTS

Any piece of writing benefits from planning. Either jot down your main points quickly or, if you have time, develop a more complete outline. Once your ideas are planned, review the outline carefully to ensure that it is complete. Once you start to write, stick to your outline. If new ideas come to you while writing, rework your outline to make sure that the entire composition does not lose its focus or balance.

CONSTRUCT GOOD PARAGRAPHS

Organize your thoughts into paragraphs. Each paragraph should have a clear *thesis statement*—a sentence that explains what will be considered in the paragraph. As you move from idea to idea in your composition, each main idea should have its own paragraph. Coordinate the main points in your outline with the paragraphs in your writing.

SUPPORT YOUR IDEAS WITH EVIDENCE
AND EXAMPLES

Once you announce a new paragraph with a thesis statement, support that idea with facts, opinions, statistics, examples, or other forms of evidence. Make sure that descriptions, anecdotes, or examples are relevant. Use expert and well-documented evidence when possible. If you rely on your own opinions and observations, make sure they are accurate and thorough.

CONSIDER THE STYLE YOU ARE USING

Style consists of word choices. Use words that are exact and specific and that create a professional image. Avoid jargon, unnecessary wordiness, and stuffy, pretentious language. In general, use active and vivid verbs that energize your writing.

CREATE A STRONG ENDING

End a composition with a firm, resounding statement. You may want to reiterate a key idea or refer to an opening device you used in starting the message. Establish a good relationship with the reader, and anticipate an ongoing relationship.

READ THE COMPOSITION, EDIT, AND REDRAFT

The key to effective writing is in editing. Once you have completed the first draft, reread it for balance, clarity, tone, and the other qualities of effective writing. If possible, let some time pass between writing the initial draft and editing it. You can be more objective if you revise your draft after you have set it aside for a time.

PROOFREAD YOUR FINAL PRODUCT

Always, always reread your final draft and correct any misspellings, punctuation errors, and grammatical errors. Look closely for sentence fragments or poorly constructed paragraphs that may need last-minute revision. Check your outline to make sure you have thoroughly covered each aspect of your initial purpose.

Figure 6.2 summarizes these steps in the writing process. Use it as a checklist for preparing your compositions.

Establish your purpose.

Consider your tone.

Plan and outline your thoughts.

Construct good paragraphs.

Support your ideas with evidence and examples.

Consider the style you are using.

Create a strong ending.

Read the composition, edit, and redraft.

Proofread the final draft.

FIGURE 6.2 The Writing Plan

1. **Don't sit and stare at an empty page.** If you don't know where to start, just start anywhere. You can always go back and rearrange or reorganize your writing later.

2. **Don't try to write perfectly.** Just get your thoughts down on paper. You can always return to them and improve them later.

3. **Be bold.** Be innovative in the way you write and in what you say. Write first drafts that you would never send (because they might be inappropriate) but that are fun to write anyway. Stretch your horizons as a writer—you may surprise yourself.

4. **Be humorous.** Try to use your sense of humor where appropriate. You will have more fun writing, and the reader will enjoy it more, too.

5. **Be creative.** Try writing in a way that you have never done before. Experiment with formats, type styles, stationery, artwork, layout, and other writing devices to give "pizzazz" to your writing.

6. **Express yourself.** Try kinds of writing projects that you have never tackled before. Write a small book of recipes or stories. Create a coloring book for a child you know. Write a play or create a training videotape. Start with easy projects and work up to more difficult ones. By trying new formats, you may discover hidden writing talents.

7. **Have fun.** Most important, do not let yourself get bored when you write, because if you are bored, the reader will probably be bored too. If writing becomes drudgery, do something quickly to make it more interesting. Keep the task of writing lively and creative, and you will learn to enjoy it more.

FIGURE 6.3 Suggestions for Becoming a Better Writer

Getting Started

While much advice is available about becoming a better writer, students have found the suggestions listed in Figure 6.3 to be helpful in making their writing more enjoyable and getting started on a writing project. Try to incorporate these suggestions into your attitudes about writing.

While writing requires hard work, it establishes your competency. Writing, unlike speaking, lasts and verifies your abilities over time. Most of us are scared to write or hate to write, but the payoffs of learning this valuable skill are well worth the effort required. Good luck, and happy writing.

NOTE

1. See John Holt, *How Children Fail* (New York: Delacorte, 1982).

EXERCISE 6.1
Writing Attitude Self-Assessment

Directions: Complete the following attitude survey of your opinions about writing. For each item, circle the appropriate number on the scale from 1 to 10. Be prepared to discuss your answers.

1. My general attitude about writing is that:

   I hate it   I enjoy it
   1   2   3   4   5   6   7   8   9   10

2. When I have to do a writing project:

   I avoid it   I look forward to it
   1   2   3   4   5   6   7   8   9   10

3. I feel I can communicate my thoughts on paper:

   Not very well   Very well
   1   2   3   4   5   6   7   8   9   10

4. For me, writing is:

   A difficult task   An easy task
   1   2   3   4   5   6   7   8   9   10

5. When it comes to creativity in my writing, I am:

   A boring writer   An interesting writer
   1   2   3   4   5   6   7   8   9   10

6. For me, writing is:

   Sheer drudgery   Great fun
   1   2   3   4   5   6   7   8   9   10

EXERCISE 6.2
Action Plan for Writing Improvement

Directions: The following questionnaire is designed to help you create an action plan that you can follow in improving your writing skills. Answer the questions as truthfully and as completely as you can. Give careful consideration to the ways in which you might improve as a writer. Discuss possible solutions with an instructor, or look for suggestions from someone whose writing you respect.

1. Writing could be of value to me and my career in the following ways:

_____

_____

_____

_____

_____

_____

2. As a writer, my strong points include:

_____

_____

_____

_____

_____

_____

3. The areas in which I need to improve as a writer include:

_____

_____

_____

_____

_____

_____

4. For each of the areas that need improvement, these are the specific things I can do to improve:

Improvement area #1: _____

_____

_____

_____

_____

Improvement area #2: _____

_____

_____

_____

_____

Improvement area #3: _____

_____

_____

_____

_____

Improvement area #4: _____

_____

_____

_____

_____

EXERCISE 6.3
Having Fun with Writing

Directions: This exercise is designed to give free rein to your imagination and sense of fun. There are no right answers; merely follow your sense of enjoyment in writing a letter that responds to the following situation:

Imagine that you work in a small room (10 feet square) with another person, who is a smoker. You have been placed together only two weeks, and your co-worker smokes at least a pack of cigarettes a day in your small room. You have hinted subtly that the smoking bothers you, but your partner does not take the hint. Now you are forced to write an official letter asking your partner not to smoke during working hours. There is no official company policy—your boss has said that you two have to work it out together. There can be no room assignment changes unless one of you quits the job.

1. Write down the first thing that comes to your mind. Don't think—just write one sentence.

   _____

   _____

   _____

2. Look at what you just wrote—and get bolder. Pull out all the stops and let the person know exactly what you are thinking.

   _____

   _____

   _____

3. Now look at both sentences and consider which elements you would actually want to send to your partner. Put together a new sentence that is a bit more tactful but still bold.

   _____

   _____

   _____

4. Rewrite the following sentence to make it bolder:
   "If you would just smoke a little bit less during work hours, I would certainly appreciate it."

   _____

   _____

   _____

5. Rewrite the following sentence using humor:
"From what I understand of the Surgeon General's report, smoking increases the likelihood of lung cancer or sudden heart attack. That disturbs me—as it should you."

_____

_____

_____

6. Let your mind run free for a moment. How could you communicate these same messages without speaking them or putting them into a letter? Be as creative as you can.

_____

_____

_____

_____

7. Now compose a short letter to your imaginary roommate that is direct, bold, creative, humorous, and communicates your message effectively. As you craft each sentence, consider its tone, its boldness, its appropriateness, and other ways in which you might say the same thing. Write the first draft quickly. Once it is done, read it to yourself. Are you satisfied? What would you say differently?

_____

_____

_____

_____

_____

_____

_____

_____

_____

EXERCISE 6.4
Expanding Horizons as a Writer

Directions: Compose a short essay on the following topic:

Imagine that you were given a magic pen that would allow you to write beautiful prose with absolutely no effort.

What types of projects would you write?
For whom would you write them?
What would be your motive for writing them?
What prevents you from writing them now?
Would you be willing to try and write them without the magic pen?

Title: _____

Author: _____

_____

_____

_____

_____

_____

_____

_____

_____

_____

_____

_____

_____

_____

_____

_____

_____

EXERCISE 6.5
Having Fun with First Drafts

Directions: Select one of the following situations and write a letter in response to it. Create any necessary facts you need to write a clever, entertaining letter. Since you will never mail this letter, let your imagination run free. Have fun. Create a personality such as "Dear Abby" or "Miss Manners" or "G.I. Joe" to be the voice in your letter.

Situation #1: You are an old hand at your job. You have been there for two years and have seen many people come and go. A new person has just been hired and has written you a letter asking for advice on how to succeed at the new job. The new employee asks such questions as: What should I wear? How should I talk to the boss? How should I act in the office cafeteria? Write to the person and give your sincere advice on how to succeed.

Situation #2: Your nephew or niece has written to you asking for your advice on going to college. He or she asks the following questions: Should I go to college? What is the best major for me? Which is more important—borrowing money or working through school? Should I go to a residential school or live at home and commute? Write to your nephew or niece and give your sincere advice on going to college.

6

The Principles of Business Writing

1. Identify three types of writing that you will be required to do in your future career. Obtain one sample of each type from someone you know in that industry or from library books. For example, you may wish to include reports, magazine articles, news stories, business letters, or proposals. For each of your samples, list the qualities that make it especially effective or ineffective. Be prepared to discuss your answers.

2. Write a short essay (500 words, 2 to 3 typed and double-spaced pages) on the following topic: "The Qualities of an Effective Educator." You will be asked to share this essay with your fellow students. Before you begin your essay, jot notes about the following steps of your writing plan:

   Your purpose
   The relevant attitudes of your reader
   The tone you want to create
   The main points of your essay (select three)
   The supporting material for each main point
   Lively and specific words and images to create a vigorous style
   A strong ending to summarize your purpose

3. Make copies of the essay you composed in Action Assignment 2 and distribute them to the other members of your class. Read each essay and discuss how effectively it performs the steps of the writing process discussed in this chapter.

7
Business Memos

The *memo* (short for "memorandum") is the most widely used form of writing in many businesses. The memo is used extensively to share information, make requests, influence decisions, and document actions. Since memos are widely used, any aspiring business writer must learn to write them effectively and quickly. Memos, unlike business letters, are written for readers within an organization—people who usually know the company and each other already. Thus, memos use a direct style, a more informal structure, and more informal language than letters.

This chapter looks at the formats you can use in writing memos, suggests techniques for making your memos effective, and provides examples of the three basic types of memos: informative, persuasive, and documentary. By incorporating the general suggestions for effective writing discussed in the preceding chapter with the specific memo-writing techniques presented in this chapter, you can learn to plan and compose memos that will work for you.

Formats for Memos

Memos are a distinctive form of business writing because their formats are unique. When writing memos, use the following format techniques.

USE STANDARD MEMO HEADINGS

The standard memo heading, illustrated in Figure 7.1, demonstrates the five elements used most commonly in memos: the title line, the sender line, the receiver line, the date, and the subject line. All memos should have these five elements in some form.

MEMORANDUM

TO:

FROM:

DATE:

SUBJECT:

FIGURE 7.1   Standard Memo Features

The *memo title line* is necessary to identify immediately the memo as an internal document. This line signals the reader that the memo is for in-house business and should not be shared casually with people outside the firm.

The *sender line* identifies the writer of the memo. Often the sender's job title is included if the name is not immediately recognizable. As with the receiver line, specific names add more personality to memos than just job titles or general rank categories.

The *receiver line* identifies the intended recipient of the composition. The reader may be either an individual or a group of people. When addressing memos to a group, it is advisable to include everyone's name if possible. A person is more likely to read a memo if it is addressed by name to him or her. When writing to large groups, a general receiver line, such as "To: All Employees," may be necessary.

The *date line* identifies the date of the writing of the memo. This fact is important for filing and maintaining records of actions taken. Always date your memos accurately.

The *subject line,* which may consist of the letters "Re" (for "about") instead of "Subject"), provides a brief summary of the topic and the purpose of the memo. This reference alerts readers to how valuable the memo may be for them. It also grabs attention, so it should be used carefully to focus the reader's interest on the content of the memo. The subject line should include both the general subject area and a hint about the specific purpose of the memo. Vague subject lines are useless in grabbing attention or clarifying the purpose.

VARY THE FORMAT WHEN NECESSARY

Other types of memo formats adapt this standard format. They maintain the five elements of the memo heading but add other format devices to fill particular needs. The *circular memo* includes a list of names of intended recipients, who check off their names once they have read the memo and then pass it along to the next person on the list. This technique ensures that everyone on the list has read the memo, and it reduces the number of duplications of the memo. The *quick-response memo* includes a response sheet at the bottom that requests the recipient to respond to the sender in some way. For example, a memo requesting your preference among three vendors might include a list of the three vendors at the bottom and instruct you to check the one you prefer. You would mark the memo and then return it to the sender, thus eliminating the need to write a response memo of your own. *Memo reports* are long, formal reports written as memos. They are such common business documents that they are discussed in detail in Chapter 12.

USE ITEMIZATION AND LISTS FOR CLARITY

The body of a memo often contains a number of items or points. These can be made more readable by itemizing them or listing them with numbers, bullets, or asterisks. Use itemization whenever the material in the memo includes several items that need to be considered separately. Lists are useful for organizing figures or statistical data. The sample memos in this chapter illustrate the use of itemization and lists.

USE ACTION STEPS TO GET A RESPONSE

If the purpose of the memo is to provoke some action from the readers, use specific instructions about what you want them to do. Specific action steps tell the readers what to do in order to fulfill your desires. Word the action items positively and pleasantly. Avoid commands or demands. Action steps make memos more effective because they clarify your purpose and provide specific instructions to readers. Note how action steps are used in several of the sample memos in this chapter.

Techniques for Effective Memos

Beyond the choice of appropriate format for your memo, there are several other techniques for improving the clarity and effectiveness of a memo. Consider the following suggestions as you plan and write.

MAKE SURE THE MEMO IS NECESSARY

The most common complaint about memos is that there are too many of them. Business people often feel swamped by the number of memos that cross their desks each week. For this reason, consider carefully whether you need to write a memo, before you do so. Would a phone call or a brief personal word suffice? Likewise, consider who should receive the memo. Does everyone in the office need a copy, or can you narrow your list of receivers to just a few? Each situation will result in different answers to these questions, but a preliminary thought may save considerable effort.

CLARIFY PURPOSE AND GRAB ATTENTION

Another common complaint about memos is that they are often confusing. The first thing most people ask when they get a memo is, "Do I need to read this?" You can avoid this problem by using an effective subject line and by starting the memo with a specific statement of purpose. In the first paragraph, explain what the memo is about, why it is being written, and what action will be required from the reader. If these items are relevant to the receiver of the memo, the reader will pay attention. A clear opening makes the memo easy to read. By combining a clear subject line with a clear first paragraph, you announce your purpose and grab your reader's attention easily.

ORGANIZE THE BODY FOR EASY READING

Make your main points immediately clear with itemization, enumeration, or underlining. Look at the memo from the reader's perspective. Is it easy to read at a glance? Do the main points jump off the page and demand attention? Is the information well organized? Do your paragraphs make sense and assist the reader in organizing the information? If the memo is very long, consider breaking it into sections with subheadings. You can use this technique effectively in short reports as well. In essence, try to make your memos as easy to read as possible through the way you organize, arrange, and highlight the contents.

USE INFORMAL, PROFESSIONAL LANGUAGE

Generally, memos are written in a more informal style than letters. Since writer and reader both work for the same employer, certain assumptions can be made about shared knowledge, language, and values. For these reasons, technical jargon is more widely used in memos than in letters. Likewise, writers of memos need not spend much time developing a positive relationship with the reader—the relationship is assumed to be positive. Most memos begin with a statement of purpose and then go straight to the business at hand unless the writer specifically wants to build a relationship with the reader along with the message.

KEEP YOUR TONE POSITIVE

Because many memos are written in haste, they can often become rather dry and demanding. Whenever appropriate to do so, begin and end your memos on a positive tone. Word your ideas and suggestions in terms that motivate the reader. Avoid an announcing or commanding tone.

Common Types of Memos

Memos are written for three basic purposes: to inform, to persuade, and to document actions or ideas. The following sections provide suggestions about how to accomplish these three purposes.

INFORMATIVE MEMOS

Memos are often used to announce information, disseminate ideas, and make requests. In a typical business setting, memos provide many useful means of communicating work-related information:

Give instructions
Announce a meeting
Record minutes of a meeting
Announce policy changes
Request a meeting

Explain processes
List job duties
Post company policies and rules
Provide project timetables
Offer feedback

Exhibit 7.A is an example of an informative memo. Note the techniques that make the memo effective.

PERSUASIVE MEMOS

Various persuasive purposes can be accomplished using memos, including the following:

Propose an improvement
Recommend a procedure
Ask for cooperation or support
Motivate people to attend a meeting
Sell a product or service

Recommend a purchase
Support a position
Ask for a raise
Solicit volunteers
Motivate compliance

When writing persuasive memos, the psychological techniques of effective communication become important. You must appeal to the values of your readers in ways that will encourage them to agree with you. Clear explanations of your reasons are vital, and you must use credible evidence to support your arguments. The persuasive memo should end with a clear call for action. Make your purpose specific, and ask for a specific response from your reader.

Exhibit 7.B illustrates an effective persuasive memo. Note the psychological strategies used within the memo format.

```
                              MEMO

To: All Staff Members

From: Jim Harriman, Personnel Manager

Date: June 4, 19XX

Re: Selecting Your Flexible Schedule Hours

As you know, we are considering adopting a flexible schedule for work
hours among the staff members in the Baker Street office. The flexible
schedule should make your jobs easier because it gives you the opportunity
to set your own hours to some degree.

I need to know your preferences for arrival and departure hours so that I
can begin to develop a schedule that will be satisfying to as many people as
possible. On the bottom of this memo is a response sheet, which will give
me an initial indication of your preferences. Please mark your first and
second choices for arrival, lunch break, and departure hours.

Please remember the rules:

1. You must work a total of eight hours per day, and those hours must be
   in two segments of four hours each.
2. You can arrive anytime between the hours of 6:00 a.m. and 9:00 a.m.
3. Lunch can last any number of hours, or you can work straight through
   lunch if you prefer.
4. Departure hours must be between 2:00 p.m. and 8:00 p.m., when the
   building is locked.

I appreciate your cooperation in making the transition to flexible
scheduling easy. Not all employees will be able to get exactly the schedule
they want, since the office must be covered by a certain number of
personnel at any given time. However, I will make very effort to get you as
close to your desired schedule as possible.
-------------------------------------------------------------------------------

Response Sheet (tear off and return to me by 6/10/XX)

    Your Name:

    Preferred Arrival Time:    1st _____  2nd _____

    Preferred Lunch Period:    1st _____  2nd _____

    Preferred Departure Time: 1st _____  2nd _____
```

EXHIBIT 7.A   Sample Informative Memo

```
┌─────────────────────────────────────────────────────────────┐
│                        MEMORANDUM                             │
│                                                               │
│   TO: Helen Morgan, President                                 │
│                                                               │
│   FROM: Wayne Elmiron, V.P. Planning                          │
│                                                               │
│   DATE: May 18, 19XX                                          │
│                                                               │
│   SUBJECT: Why We Should Move the Office                      │
│                                                               │
│   Helen, I appreciate your ideas, and I have analyzed the     │
│   suggestions you made when I talked to you last week         │
│   concerning our space problems. I would like to summarize    │
│   the problem as I see it and to make several recommendations │
│   for the board of directors to consider at their next        │
│   meeting.                                                    │
│                                                               │
│   The Space Problem:  There are several reasons for the       │
│   current overcrowded situation we face at present:           │
│                                                               │
│   1. We have tripled the number of orders processed weekly    │
│      since moving to the current office site five years ago.  │
│   2. We have doubled the number of employees.                 │
│   3. Size of inventory has increased 50 percent.              │
│                                                               │
│   These factors have resulted in tremendously cramped working │
│   quarters. We had to give up the employee lunch room and     │
│   convert one of the two bathrooms into inventory storage. It │
│   is my feeling that we must address this space shortage issue│
│   or we will soon begin having employee motivation problems.  │
│                                                               │
│   Recommendations:  For the above reasons, I propose the      │
│   following course of action:                                 │
│                                                               │
│   1. We investigate the costs of space expansion at the       │
│      current site.                                            │
│   2. We investigate the costs of a move to a new office site. │
│   3. We communicate the search for a solution to the employees│
│      and ask for their ideas as to space preferences.         │
│   4. The company commit itself in writing via the newsletter  │
│      to solving the problem by the end of the year.           │
│                                                               │
│   This is not an insurmountable problem. By providing the     │
│   space we need, I feel sure that the company stands to grow  │
│   even faster in the coming years. Our employees have worked  │
│   hard, and I believe they deserve some improvement in their  │
│   working conditions.                                         │
└─────────────────────────────────────────────────────────────┘
```

EXHIBIT 7.B   Sample Persuasive Memo

DOCUMENTARY MEMOS

A third use of the memo is to document actions or ideas in business situations. People often need a written record of events, so that tangible proof exists that an action took place or an idea was discussed. Documentary memos are a form of self-protection for some employees who want to ensure

```
┌─────────────────────────────────────────────────────────────┐
│                    Electron Distributing                     │
│                                                               │
│  MEMO                                                         │
│                                                               │
│                                                               │
│  To: Bill Haloman, Manager                                    │
│                                                               │
│  From: Jean Sax, Sales                                        │
│                                                               │
│  Date: August 30, 19XX                                        │
│                                                               │
│  Re: Telephone Conversation with Omni-Fax Sales               │
│                                                               │
│  Bill, I have enjoyed my first few weeks here at ED, and I    │
│  have appreciated your help in making my transition into the  │
│  company an easy one. I feel that I will be able to perform   │
│  well now that I have learned the ropes a bit.                │
│                                                               │
│  I was talking with a client yesterday, and I thought you     │
│  might be interested in the conversation. I know one of the   │
│  sales people at Omni-Fax because we belong to the same       │
│  health club. He mentioned that Omni-Fax expects to expand    │
│  production more than two-fold in the next two months         │
│  due to a facilities expansion. That means that they will be  │
│  in the market for our services even sooner than we thought.  │
│                                                               │
│  I suggest that we put together a sales presentation designed │
│  specifically for Omni-Fax and get it to them as soon as      │
│  possible. I think we would have a good chance of picking up  │
│  a large part of their expanded business if we were the       │
│  first ones on the scene with a reasonable offer.             │
│                                                               │
│  I would appreciate your reactions to this idea. I know I     │
│  would like to be involved in the presentation, if you think  │
│  that would be appropriate. I will not move without your      │
│  O.K., so please get back to me as soon as you can.           │
│                                                               │
└─────────────────────────────────────────────────────────────┘
```

EXHIBIT 7.C   Sample Documentary Memo

that verbal agreements or interpersonal situations are written down and can be verified. Examples of situations that might need documentation are the following:

> On being hired, a new employee is promised a raise in six months.
>
> A superior has required an employee to perform a certain task which the employee feels will result in "disaster"; for example, delaying the reordering of paper goods until after a heavy work period.
>
> An employee has a telephone conversation with a client that may have serious consequences; for example, the client threatens to drop the account unless a specific action is taken.
>
> A manager observes unethical behavior in an employee and wants to document it in the employee's personnel file.

Another use of the documentary memo is to demonstrate excellent performance. Memos can show that an employee has good ideas, can express them well, takes initiative to propose improvements and solutions, has good problem-solving skills, is sensitive toward other people, and is assertive and decisive. You can use documentary memos to advance your career by putting onto paper your innovative ideas, perceptions of problems, proposed solutions, and recommendations. If you document your ideas by means of memos, you are more likely to get credit for them and to be perceived as a valuable employee. You might wish to document situations such as the following:

Propose an improvement
Suggest the solution to a problem
Bring attention to a hidden problem with serious consequences
Share praise, be thoughtful, give compliments, express appreciation

You should be careful not to overuse the documentary memo, because it can be perceived as "grandstanding" if you use it inappropriately. A judiciously composed memo, however, can be used on occasion to highlight your insight and good ideas. Exhibit 7.C is an example of an effective documentary memo.

EXERCISE 7.1
Recognizing Problems in Memos

Directions: Below is a memo that you might receive one day. Identify the problems in the grammar, style, and tone of this memo in the spaces that follow.

MEMORANDUM

TO: Everbody in the Office

FROM: Randall E. Majors

DATE: October 8, 19XX

SUBJECT: Shorter Memos

I want to know what in the heck is going on around here! It has recently been bouught to my attention that the quality of memos received in this office has substantially declined (at least in my humble opinion) over the last several years. The memos I have been receiving have been neither dynamic nor effective. With run-on sentences, unnecessary and excessive verbiage, unclear purposes, and seemingly nonexistent organization. No organization should be hampered by such poor writing—it is a sign of weakness which will no doubt substantially negatively impact upon our profitbility and success. It is my opinion that memos should be clearly focused, to the point, succinct, and free of any unnecessary reduncancy whatsoever. When are people going to realize that nobody has the time to sit around and try to figure out what you mean in a memo if it rambles on and on? So, in conclusion, let's take the bull by the horns make our memos shorter and clearer.

_____

_____

_____

_____

_____

_____

_____

_____

_____

EXERCISE 7.2
Correcting Weak Memos

Directions On the basis of the suggestions in this chapter, revise the following memos so that they are more effective.

MEMO #1

To: Secretarial Pool

From: Supervisor

Date: September 14, 19XX

Re: Break-Time Rules

People seem to be taking advantage of the flexibility of coffee break hours. If we do not limit ourselves to 15-minute breaks, then a more rigidly imposed coffee break schedule will be necessary. So please take only 15-minute breaks.

MEMO #1 Revision

To: _____

From: _____

Date: _____

Re: _____

_____

_____

_____

_____

_____

_____

_____

```
                          MEMO #2

To: Jim, Ellen, Florence, Mike, and Bob

From: Gerald Hosener, Manager

Date: March 10, 19XX

Re: Work Hours

Since we hired three new people last week, things have gotten a little
confusing around here in regards to office assignments for working hours.
I know we do not have adequate office space, so you people are just going
to have to work it out between yourselves as to who gets what office when.
What I suggest you do is: Jim take room #47 upstairs in the old section of
the building, Ellen take room #3 next to my office, Florence can have room
#4 next to Ellen, and Mike and Bob will have to share Mike's current
office, room #45, until we can find a better place for Bob. Like I said, you
all work it out between yourselves and let me know what you are going to
do.
```

MEMO #2 Revision

To: _____

From: _____

Date: _____

Re: _____

_____

_____

_____

_____

_____

_____

_____

_____

_____

_____

_____

EXERCISE 7.3
Composing a Persuasive Memo

Directions: Compose a persuasive memo in which you propose an improvement for your current classroom or work situation. The issue need not be a large one. You can propose a minor change in some policy, some method of conducting business, or a response to a problem you see. Remember to include a clear statement of the problem, evidence for the problem, and a clear action plan for the solution. Maintain a positive relationship with the reader.

MEMORANDUM

To: _____

From: _____

Date: _____

Re: _____

_____

_____

_____

_____

_____

_____

_____

_____

_____

_____

_____

_____

_____

_____

_____

_____

Business Memos

1. Make copies of the persuasive memo you composed in Exercise 7.3. Form a group of five people to act as reader/critics and distribute these copies to the group members. Read each memo and critique it on the basis of the suggestions made in this chapter.

2. Find an example of a poorly written memo in your workplace or in a business writing textbook. (You may have to delete specific names or information to keep it anonymous.) List the elements that make the memo ineffective. Be prepared to discuss your analysis.

3. Compose a quick-response memo that meets the needs of the following situation. You have volunteered to be the planner for a companywide garage sale for the firm where you work. More than 50 people are interested in bringing household items for sale to the company parking lot on Saturday morning. You are responsible for providing tables and chairs from the company's supply room, so you need to know how many tables and chairs the participants will need. Carefully consider what other information should be included in the memo.

4. If you are employed, write a memo to your immediate superior asking for a raise. If you are a student, write a memo to an instructor asking him or her to reconsider a grade assigned to you for a course.

8

Informative Letters

The lifeblood of business is the flow of information between organizations. The routine exchange of business letters is the means for this communication. In order to be an accomplished business writer, you must be able to compose correspondence that both accomplishes your purpose and maintains a positive relationship with your reader. This chapter investigates five types of informative business letters—the request for information, the reply, purchase orders, acknowledgments, and informative announcements—and offers you strategies for writing these communications effectively.

The Informative Strategy: Relationship, Business, Relationship

The basic strategy of any informative letter is first to establish a positive relationship with the reader, then to conduct the business of the letter, and finally to close with a reinforcement of the relationship. This heavy reliance on relationship building in letters is difficult for some writers, because they are not accustomed to the devices of typical business writing. At first, these conventions may seem artificial. Some experience in the world of business, however, soon proves how useful it is to create positive introductions and closings to your correspondence.

You create goodwill and a more conducive environment for profitable business when you use positive and polite openings in your letters. Spend some time planning ways in which you can establish a positive relationship with the reader before you turn to the business you have to conduct in your letter.

Figure 8.1 lists several devices you can use to begin letters positively. Use these devices judiciously. Insincere praise can be interpreted as flattery and may make the reader suspicious of your motives. Likewise, straining too hard to be positive or to find commonalities may make your letter sound forced.

Express positive regard for the reader.

Refer to some prior contact you have had with the reader.

Refer to people, purposes, or events you have in common.

Use a "you" orientation in the opening paragraph.

Use "need creation" in the opening.

Include thanks and appreciation wherever appropriate.

Use praise when sincere and appropriate.

Refer to recent achievements or successes.

Use positive language throughout the letter.

FIGURE 8.1 Devices for Establishing Positive Relationship

Be as friendly and sincere as is comfortable for you, yet do not be too anxious to rush immediately into the business of the letter. Take the time to build a friendly tone.

Relationship also can be reinforced in the closing paragraph of a letter. You can use the same devices listed in Figure 8.1 in your conclusion or another common closing device—reference to the next contact you plan to have with the reader. By looking toward the future with the reader in mind, you reinforce your positive regard for him or her. Expressions of thanks are usually appropriate at the end of a letter as well.

Above all, a positive tone throughout a letter maintains a sense of respect and pleasant relations. Avoid being demanding, sarcastic, caustic, or overly critical. Use diplomatic and positive ways of phrasing your remarks. Try always to be reasonable, polite, and courteous. Avoid any "cute" expressions, and be careful when using humor. What is an attempt at humor to you might be misinterpreted by the reader. Likewise, do not be overly familiar with the reader or presume too much about the relationship you have established. Figure 8.2 lists common expressions of presumption that creep into letters. Avoid these.

By incorporating elements of positive relationship throughout a business letter, you create a favorable impression and generate a readiness in the reader to accept the business you propose. Find the devices that you are most comfortable using in the opening and closing of your letters.

Each of the five types of informative letters should begin and end by employing the relationship devices just discussed. Most commonly, the introduction to any informative letter consists of relationship building and a

"As you already know . . ."

"I am sure you are aware that . . ."

"Of course, you will want to . . ."

"I am sure that you will agree that . . ."

"No doubt you feel that . . ."

"It is obvious that . . ."

"Wouldn't you like to . . ."

"This is certainly a case in which . . ."

"I don't want to presume, but . . ."

FIGURE 8.2 Common Expressions of Presumption to Avoid

statement of the purpose of the letter. Because the purpose of each type of letter is distinctive, a different formula can be used to outline the body of each letter. The following sections discuss each type briefly and suggest an outline formula you can use when composing informative letters.

Request Letters

Informative letters often request information or some action from the reader. For example, you might write to a business and request a catalogue, a price list, a policy statement, a list of hours, or some other piece of information. The informative letter merely informs the reader of your need. Because this type of request is an expected part of business, you are not required to persuade the reader to take the action you desire. Admittedly, in some situations you might need to be more persuasive, and these are discussed in the next chapter, on persuasive letters.

Figure 8.3 outlines the formula for the letter of request. Use this formula when making requests through correspondence. Note how these techniques are used in the request letter in Exhibit 8.A.

When making a request, do not assume that the reader will comply. Phrases such as "thanking you in advance" are presumptuous. Only thank the reader for considering your request. If the reader complies with your request, you can write a follow-up note expressing your thanks.

The key elements of request letters are the clarity and completeness of the request. Include all the details about what you want. Do not expect the recipient of the letter to be able to read your mind. If the request is complex, itemize it in a list to make it easier for the reader to comply. Remove any obstacles that impede your getting what you request. As you edit your first draft of the request, look for places in which the reader might misinterpret your request, be unable to give you what you want because of incomplete information, or misunderstand your intentions. Correct these shortcomings in the second draft.

Introduction:	Establish positive relationship (see Figure 8.1).
	State the general purpose of the letter.
Body:	State the specific details of the request.
	Provide any relevant and necessary reasons for your making the request.
	If the request is an unusual or a difficult one, mention some benefit to the reader for complying.
	If you face a deadline, inform the reader of the time constraints you are under.
Conclusion:	Reinforce positive relationship.
	Thank the reader for considering your request.

FIGURE 8.3 Formula for Request Letters

```
                                            JIR Accounting Services
                                                   1382 Sunset Way
                                              Pittsburg, CA  94565




                                                December 9, 19XX

         Mr. Ted Brooks
         Laser Computer Co.
         2879 Buchanan Rd.
         Edminton, CA 98767

         Dear Mr. Brooks:

         Your firm was recommended to us by Mr. Joseph Bell on the basis
         of a purchase he made three months ago.  He said that your firm
         offered high-quality printers at reasonable prices.

         My company needs four printers to complete the stations in our
         network. We need high-speed dot matrix printers with tractor-type
         paper feeders that are capable of printing at least 160 charac-
         ters per minute.  They should handle both standard 8½" by 11"
         paper as well as 14½" by 11" paper.  Please send me information
         on printers that meet these specifications.  Also, because noise
         is a problem at the work stations, we are interested in pur-
         chasing noise-supression covers for the printers.

         Since our target for completion of the project is February 7, can
         you provide a list of printers and noise supressors that meet
         these specifications, along with a price list, no later than
         January 7?

         I am looking forward to working with you.  If you have any
         questions, please call me.  Thank you for your consideration.

                                                Sincerely,

                                                John I. Reilly
```

EXHIBIT 8.A Request Letter

Reply Letters

The response you write to a request for information or action is called a reply letter. Replies are easiest to write when the response is a positive one. Figure 8.4 illustrates the steps for writing a positive reply to a request.

The key to effective reply letters is the addition of information that was not specifically asked for in the initial letter of request but may be of interest to the reader. Of course, you should provide a response to what was requested, but it is also useful to go beyond the requester's need and offer more

Introduction:	Establish positive relationship with reader (see Figure 8.1).
	Refer to the request.
	Express appreciation for the interest.
Body:	Respond to the request.
	Itemize response items if necessary.
	Include additional comments that may be of interest.
	Include any additional promotional message.
Conclusion:	Close cordially.

FIGURE 8.4 Formula for Reply Letters

than the original request. Going this extra step makes your reply letter even more useful to the reader, and it establishes you as an insightful and helpful business associate. A sample letter of reply is given in Exhibit 8.B.

More diplomacy is required when the reply to a request must be qualified or denied. These types of replies are dealt with in Chapter 10, on diplomatic letters.

Purchase Orders

An extremely common informative business letter is the one in which an individual or a business places an order to purchase goods or services. The key to effective orders is completeness. The recipient of the letter needs to know every specific detail necessary to complete the order. If the sender omits a necessary detail, then the receiver of the order must delay the fulfillment of the order and engage in an exchange of letters to clarify the missing details. Figure 8.5 outlines a simple order-letter format. Note that relationship building in the opening of the letter is optional. Since the sender is placing an order, it can be assumed that a positive relationship already exists between the writer and receiver of the letter. If there are specific relationship comments that would be helpful to the exchange, however, it is acceptable to include them in the introduction.

When writing orders, examine the specific details of the order closely to ensure that all necessary facts have been included. The order should include any necessary details such as color, quantity, model number, unit price, or total price. Special concerns might include shipping arrangements, delivery timetables, credit arrangements, or other features of the transaction. Each of these should be addressed separately and clearly in the letter so that the order can be fulfilled on the basis of the single piece of correspondence. A sample order letter is provided in Exhibit 8.C.

Introduction:	Establish positive relationship (optional).
	State the general purpose of the letter.
Body:	Provide specific details of the order.
	Explain any special concerns about the order.
Conclusion:	Close briefly but cordially.

FIGURE 8.5 Formula for Purchase-Order Letters

```
                        SAMPSON'S GYM
              212 Stanton Drive, Hayward, CA 92675 (415) 298-0914


                                               December 2. 19XX



    Lisa Martin
    235 Nugilla Avenue
    Hayward, CA 92675

    Dear Ms. Martin:

    Thank you for your interest in Sampson's Gym.  You stated in your
    letter that you were interested in joining our gym, but that you
    wanted more information about our memberships and services.

    Our business has been in operation since 1975.  In our 13 years
    of service, we have established a large clientele and have built
    an excellent reputation.

    Our facilities are very pleasant.  We offer the following
    conveniences:
         · Aerobic dance floor (2500 square feet)
         · 24 Nautilus machines
         · Complete free weights
         · Olympic-size lap pool
         · Sauna
         · Jacuzzi
         · Separate locker rooms and showers for men and women

    Some items may be of special interest to you.  The pool, sauna,
    and Jacuzzi are all located indoors, and they are all coed.  Our
    hours are 6:00 a.m. to 11:00 p.m. seven days a week.  We have
    trained personnel on duty at all times to assist you in your
    training program.

    Our one-time initiation fee is $80, and our monthly dues are $39.
    You will receive two free months for each person you get to join
    our gym.  Feel free to come in any time next week for a guided
    tour and a sample workout.  We look forward to serving you.

    Cordially,

    Robert V. Arthur,
    Membership Counselor
```

EXHIBIT 8.B Letter of Reply

Letters of Acknowledgment

Letters of acknowledgment are the normal responses to orders. In the acknowledgment, the writer verifies that the order has been received, assumes that it is in the process of being fulfilled, and states when the buyer can expect it to arrive. Acknowledgments may also contain mentions of special concerns: requests for clarification, explanations about changes in availabil-

```
                                          Vintage Videos
                                          821-B 29th Ave.
                                          Union City, CA




          Mr. Roland Stark
          AAA Office Equipment
          3232 Broadway
          Oakland, CA  92031

          December 20, 19XX

          Dear Mr. Stark:

              Thank you for sending us your catalogue.  We would like to
          place an order for a number of items.
              Please ship one each of the following:

              1.  BD-9110 Copier System priced at $3524.95.  We understand
                  that this model comes with a free case of toner and five
                  reams of bond paper.

              2.  Model 30100 Fascimile machine priced at $539.00.

              3.  Luxsteel Executive Chair, item #437, priced at $324.50.
                  Our choice of upholstery fabric is the tan leatherette.

              Our offices will be closed until January 4, so we cannot
          take delivery until after that date.  However, we do need
          everything prior to January 10.  Will this be a problem?  Also,
          please note that all deliveries are taken at our Starr Street
          entrance.
              We are happy to have this opportunity to do business with
          you.  We look forward to a mutually satisfying future.

              Yours,

              Katherine Martinis

              Katherine Martinis
              Office Manager
```

EXHIBIT 8.C Order Letter

ity or price, warnings about delay in delivery, or other situations that may affect the satisfactory completion of the order. The key to writing an effective letter of acknowledgment is to be direct about any special concerns that will affect the order. By asking for clarification or by providing explanation immediately, the writer advises the buyer of the status of the order. With this complete information, the business can be conducted in the most efficient manner possible. The buyer can adjust to potential problems with the completion of the order and will be more satisfied with the service received. Figure 8.6 outlines the normal steps in a letter of acknowledgment. A sample acknowledgment letter is given in Exhibit 8.D.

Introduction:	Refer to the order.
	Thank the customer for the order.
Body:	Respond to the details of the order.
	Mention any special concerns about completion of the order.
	Provide any additional business or promotional issues.
Conclusion:	Repeat thanks.
	Anticipate doing business again.

FIGURE 8.6 Formula for Letters of Acknowledgment

ROB'S FISHING EMPORIUM
71693 West First Street, Hayward, CA 94548 (415) 782-2200

December 2, 19XX

Dennis A. Ruhtra
1692 Birch Street
San Lorenzo, CA 94577

Dear Mr. Ruhtra:

We have received your order, and we thank you for your patronage.
Your interest in fishing has led you to the right tackle supply
company, Rob's Fishing Emporium. We are here to provide you with
all the essential tackle for a successful fishing trip.

The following items will be shipped to you immediately:
 ·500 yards of 8 lb. test Strength monofilament line
 ·3 Deep Diver Bass Boppers
 ·2 Lisa Lures

We are temporarily out of stock of the Garz 320 spinning reel.
We have therefore back-ordered your request--reference number
32069C. We expect delivery on December 13. As soon as we
receive the shipment, your order will be filled. We will only
bill your account $13.79 for the items being shipped. This
amount includes the shipping charge of $2.00. We will not charge
additional shipping fees for your back order. The cost of your
spinning reel, $32.52, will be billed to your account when the
reel is shipped.

Remember, your order is important to us. When it comes to price,
Rob's will not be beat. If you find a lower advertised price for
any item that we sell, we will beat that price by 5 percent
because we want your business. Thanks for shopping with us!

Cordially,

Robert V. Arthur

Robert V. Arthur,
President

EXHIBIT 8.D Letter of Acknowledgment

Once the business of the initial order is completed, the acknowledgment letter can add other business or promotional concerns. The provider of the order may have other goods or services that would interest the buyer, or there may be other business details that are worth including. Additional business should be included only if the initial order will be completed with few adjustments. If there are significant problems in completing an order, comments about additional business should be postponed until a more favorable occasion arises.

Informative Announcements

Informative letters announce important business events, such as an imminent sale, a change of policy, an expansion of services, or a change of personnel. When the purpose of an informative letter is to announce some event, the piece of news should be emphasized by being mentioned first in the letter. Positive relationship building can be included, but it should be subordinated to the announcement.

Specific techniques for emphasis of items in letters include using a subject line immediately after the salutation, beginning the letter with the announcement item, or underlining the item for visual emphasis. All these devices focus attention on the importance of the event and fulfill the purpose of the letter more effectively. Figure 8.7 outlines the steps in writing an informative announcement. Exhibit 8.E presents a sample informative announcement.

The key to writing an effective announcement is to put the business of the letter first and relationship building second. In situations when you wish to motivate the reader toward some action, the body may include more persuasive material. Persuasive announcements are dealt with in greater detail in the next chapter.

Business letters do not consist of just business. Underneath all correspondence lies a relationship between two people. Good business letters should establish and maintain a positive relationship between the writer and the reader. Once you establish a positive working relationship, then the business of the letter can be accomplished. Clarity and completeness are the fundamental ingredients of the business sections of a letter. By combining relationship and business factors in your letters, you ensure a positive reception by the reader and you reduce the chance of misreading, misunderstanding, and ineffectiveness.

Introduction: Focus attention on the announcement item.
Body: Provide necessary details about the announcement.
Conclusion: Establish positive relationship.
                 Close cordially.

FIGURE 8.7   Formula for Informative Announcements

```
                                        McLains Auto Supply
                                        1802 Vicksburg Dr.
                                        Scenic, CA 92064
                                        (402) 853-7643


                                        December 8, 19XX


Mr. David Ferguson
Manager
Valley Auto Parts
862 Ocean St.
Antioch, CA 94509

Dear Mr. Ferguson:

McLains is changing its credit policy from 2/10, n 30 to 3/10, n
30.  All accounts not paid within 30 days will be subject to a
service charge of 2 percent a month.  The new policy will go into
effect next January 2.  In order to receive the discount, payment
must be received within ten days after delivery of the
merchandise.

We are changing our policy in order to lower the finance costs of
our receivables.  We hope to encourage you, our valued customer,
to take advantage of the larger purchase discounts--discounts
that will provide a signigicant savings for your company.

As you may recall, when you inquired about the larger discounts
last August, we were unable to honor your request because of an
agreement with our suppliers.  Fortunately, our suppliers now
support this new policy.  We hope you will see these new changes
as financially advantageous for your firm.  If you have any
questions, please call me.

                                        Sincerely,

                                        John I. Reilly
                                        Credit Manager
```

EXHIBIT 8.E   Informative Announcement

EXERCISE 8.1
Writing a Letter of Request

Directions: Write a letter of request based on one of the following situations.

1. You wish to take a family member on a vacation to visit Epcot Center at Walt Disney World in Orlando, Florida. You need information about overnight lodging, admission costs to Epcot Center, and general tourist information about the surrounding area. The address of the Orlando Chamber of Tourism is 248 Orange Grove Boulevard, Orlando, FL 32419.

2. You wish to purchase a personal computer from Apple. You need information regarding the models available, their capacities, prices, and availability. You may have additional concerns to include in your letter as well. The address of Apple Information Center is 400 Apple Road, San Jose, CA 93123.

3. You have just moved to a new town and you want to find a new dentist. A friend has recommended Dr. Elizabeth Brown. Write and ask for information regarding office hours, prices, and distinctive features of the services provided. Dr. Brown's office is at 49 Powell Street, Lima, OH 48758.

EXERCISE 8.2
Writing a Letter of Reply

Directions: Assume that you are the recipient of one of the letters from Exercise 8.1. Compose a letter of reply. You may have to invent specific details to make your letter sound convincing.

_____

_____

_____

_____

_____

_____

_____

_____

_____

_____

_____

_____

_____

_____

_____

_____

_____

_____

_____

_____

_____

_____

EXERCISE 8.3
Writing an Informative Announcement

Directions: Compose a letter announcing one of the following events. Address the letter to a relevant person or group of people. You may need to invent more details than are provided below.

1. You are president of the Friends of Animals, a nonprofit organization devoted to supporting the local Humane Shelter. Your group is planning a fund-raising dog fashion show in the student union to take place on Wednesday from 12:00 noon until 1:00. You plan to hold the show in the cafeteria and will pass a collection plate during the show to raise money for the Humane Shelter.

2. You are secretary of the Business Majors Club. You have been asked to announce the annual bake sale fund-raiser, which will take place on the sidewalk outside the Business Building on Friday from 9:00 a.m. until 4:00 p.m. All students are welcome.

3. You work at a local clothing boutique. Your boss plans to have a special sale with 50 percent off all merchandise for any college student with a valid student ID. You are asked to write an announcement letter that will be mailed to every student in the dorms.

_____

_____

_____

_____

_____

_____

_____

_____

_____

_____

_____

_____

_____

_____

_____

_____

_____

_____

_____

_____

_____

_____

_____

_____

Informative Letters

1. Make copies of the informative announcement you composed for Exercise 8.3 and distribute them to your classmates. Read and critique each announcement on the basis of the guidelines suggested in this chapter.

2. Write a letter ordering some item from a mail-order catalogue. (Do not use the order form provided in the catalogue.) Share the letter with a friend and ask him or her to serve as a devil's advocate. Can your friend spot *any possible way* in which your order could be garbled or misunderstood? Is the information *complete?*

3. Pretend that you are the recipient of the order in Action Assignment 2. You must communicate to the buyer that you are permanently out of stock of the item which was ordered, but you have several similar items that you would like to suggest as replacements.

9 Persuasive Letters

In addition to informative letters, business people use persuasive letters widely—to sell, to convince, to motivate action, and to build interest in their products and services. In a highly competitive market, persuasive letters keep consumers informed, support sales efforts, and cope with problems that may emerge. The ability to write convincing and dynamic persuasive letters increases your value as an employee because these letters enhance your ability to influence others. Many people can argue effectively face-to-face, but if you can become an effective persuader through letters, then you will save time and money for your employer. Likewise, you can use persuasive letters to conduct your own affairs more efficiently and effectively.

This chapter investigates four types of persuasive letters: claim letters, collection letters, sales letters, and persuasive announcements. Each type of letter is based on common persuasive principles. By mastering the basic principles, you can adapt them to specific situations to accomplish your particular purpose.

The Persuasive Strategy: Interest, Convince, Motivate Action

All persuasive letters share three goals: to attract the interest of the reader, to convince, and to motivate action. Most letters use these elements in that order. The first paragraph grabs attention and states the purpose of the letter. The body of the letter consists of evidence presented to convince the reader about your purpose. The conclusion of the letter outlines specific steps for the reader to take and makes a final appeal for action.

There are many techniques for attracting interest. You are already familiar with several means for grabbing the attention of a reader: using a subject line, underlining and other visual emphasis, and beginning with a bold statement of your purpose. Figure 9.1 lists additional persuasive techniques for attention getting.

Refer to some need the reader may feel.

Emphasize a problem the reader may have.

Mention the benefits that other people have gained.

Offer a promise of benefits to the reader.

Excite the reader's curiosity.

Reveal startling statistics about problems or benefits.

Make a bold claim and challenge the reader to explore it.

FIGURE 9.1 Methods for Grabbing Interest in Persuasive Letters

Throughout the opening, you can use techniques for establishing a positive relationship with the reader, but your main purpose should be to compel the reader to continue reading the letter. Many people immediately "turn off" when they encounter an obvious persuasive appeal in a letter. Your purpose in the introduction should be to convince them to continue reading in order to receive the entire message.

The body of the persuasive letter contains the evidence that is intended to convince readers about your purpose. Evidence consists of facts, statistics, testimony, or other elements that convince the reader that your claims are true, applicable, or relevant. For example, if you were trying to persuade a reader to support your favorite charity, the Mountain View Animal Shelter (MVAS), evidence can be stated in many ways. Figure 9.2 illustrates the use of evidence in such a case.

Fill a persuasive letter with enough evidence to convince the reader, but not so much as to overwhelm. Likewise, select evidence that is most relevant and credible for the reader. Try to understand the reader's point of view, and relate your appeals to the reader's needs and values. The more your evidence satisfies some need of the reader, the more likely it is that your persuasive purpose will be accepted.

The conclusion of a persuasive letter provides the reader with action steps—the things he or she must do to receive the benefits you have described in the introduction and body of your letter. Depending on the situation, you may wish to chart a course of action with specific steps, give details such as time and place, or provide several alternative methods for satisfying your purpose. The key to an effective persuasive conclusion is to ask yourself,

Fact: "Hundreds of animals are abandoned in our city each year."

Statistic: "The MVAS saves 500 animals' lives every year."

Testimony: "The mayor of Mountain View endorses it enthusiastically."

Explanation: "This is what the MVAS does . . ."

Personal Endorsement: "I belong to MVAS."

Relevance: "MVAS serves you directly by . . ."

Credibility: "I am president of the Friends of MVAS."

Comparison/Contrast: "MVAS is more effective than any other animal-welfare organization in the states."

FIGURE 9.2 Uses of Evidence in Persuasive Letters

"Does the reader have all the information necessary to do what I want him or her to do?" If there are any missing or confusing details, clarify these in the conclusion of your letter.

As with informative letters, take care not to be presumptuous with the reader. Maintain positive relationship at the close of the letter. Allow the reader room to refuse your offer at present, because he or she may be interested at a later date. Being overly presumptuous will only offend the reader and ruin your chances for later persuasion.

Each of the four types of persuasion letters analyzed in this chapter uses the basic pattern of interest, convince, and motivate action. Since each type of situation is unique, however, the formula for each letter differs. In the following sections, note the ways in which basic techniques are combined with specific methods for each situation to produce effective persuasive letters.

Claim Letters

When you feel that the reader owes you something but you do not have any legal recourse for getting satisfaction, you write a claim letter. For example, you may want a service station to correct a faulty car repair at no cost, you may want a company to extend a warranty coverage beyond the contract period, you may want a favor from someone, or you may want the reader to "bend the rules" slightly in your favor. Claim letters are also used to argue for a refund, a reimbursement, an additional service at no cost, a reconsideration of a decision, or another chance to do something. In each case, you might argue that the reader should do something for you—and you will provide the reasons—but the reader is not required to give you what you want. If the reader is required by law to fulfill your wishes, then a collection letter should be used; such letters are discussed in the next section.

The keys to effective claim letters are to maintain a positive tone and to specify the action you want taken. Too often, writers fall into the error of just complaining about a problem. A letter of complaint merely vents the writer's emotions and tries to make the reader feel bad enough to do something about the problem. This use of negative reinforcement may work occasionally, but it will not work as effectively as positive reinforcement. Figure 9.3 illustrates

DON'T	DO
Start negatively	Start positively
Get angry	Express concern
Call the reader names	Express respect
Be sarcastic or scornful	Be direct and sincere
Use emotional language	Be objective and reasonable
Blame the reader	Focus on the problem
Write in generalities	Specify the problem
Threaten	Request specific action

FIGURE 9.3 Tactics to Avoid and to Use in Claim Letters

Introduction:	Establish positive relationship.
	State that a problem exists.
Body:	Describe the problem situation in detail.
	Detail the negative effects of the problem.
	Explain why the reader should act.
Conclusion:	Outline specific action steps for the reader.
	Reiterate positive relationship.
	End on a confident, positive tone.

FIGURE 9.4 Formula for Claim Letters

poor persuasive techniques that you should avoid and provides suggestions for better tactics that you should use in a claim letter.

The claim letter outlines a specific course of action you want taken and convinces the reader to provide the satisfaction you desire. It avoids the pitfalls of the complaint letter and maintains a positive, cooperative tone. In effect, the claim letter maintains positive relationship while being persuasive. Figure 9.4 lists the steps in a claim letter.

The most difficult aspect of the claim letter is convincing the reader to solve your problem. The strongest arguments are that such an action is standard policy for other people, that it is morally right (fair, honest, reasonable), or that the reader has done it in the past. Weaker arguments are expressions of appreciation, bids for pity or sympathy, and pleading. You should use the strongest arguments you have in the situation. You can also offer to negotiate if you feel that doing so will strengthen your case. Offer to trade some benefit to the reader for the solution you desire.

A common weakness in claim letters is the lack of a specific plan of action. Spell out exactly what you want, when and how you want it, and under what circumstances. The more specific you can be, the clearer the response you will get from the reader. Do not end the letter with "Please, do something." State exactly what you want done. Do not demand, but be firm in your request while maintaining a positive, cooperative attitude. If you intend to discuss the problem in more detail, take the initiative and say that you will call. Do not put yourself in the position to wait for the reader to call you.

The two sample claim letters in Exhibits 9.A and 9.B illustrate these techniques. Note how the letters use the formula outlined in Figure 9.4 while maintaining a positive tone.

Collection Letters

In some situations the reader is legally obligated to give the writer satisfaction. Collection letters request payment, reimbursement, delivery of goods, or adherence to other contractual obligations. Most collection letters are written in a sequence of increasingly intense and demanding tactics. Initial collection letters often are only reminders that payment is due. As a final resort, the sender may threaten to sue or take other legal action against the sender. The strategy behind this escalation is to maintain positive relation-

```
Jane Galloway
64 Markham Street
Des Moines, IA  54321




December 14, 19XX

Mr. Donald Thompson
Thompson's Repair Shop
467 Main Street
West Des Moines, IA  54324

Dear Mr. Thompson:

I appreciate the prompt, courteous service I receive from your
shop.  In the six years I have been using your services, I have
never encountered a problem.  Unfortunately, a recent repair has
concerned me, and I wish to see if we can resolve the difficulty.

On November 13, your shop replaced the power steering valve (part
number 1894A) on my Ford Ranger.  The work order was numbered
45L987.  At first, the leak in the valve seemed to be fixed, but
it has begun leaking again.  I have monitored the leakage onto
the floor of my garage, and I am certain that the power steering
valve is still leaking.

I am planning a trip for the end of this month, and I need my car
to be in working order.  Under the circumstances, I think that it
is reasonable for you to repair the leaking valve again at no
cost to me.  Your company has a reputation for excellent,
thorough service, and I know you stand behind your work.  The 90
day warranty on repairs is also in effect.

I would like to schedule an inspection and repair appointment for
my car during the next week.  I will call you on Friday, December
18, to arrange a convenient time for you to look at the problem.
If the valve is faulty, then it should be replaced, but if the
leak is not related to the original repair, I want you to do any
necessary additional work to complete the repair.

I have enjoyed our association in the past.  There is no shop I
would rather work with in the future.  Thompson's is still number
one in my mind.

Yours truly,


Jane Galloway
```

EXHIBIT 9.A Claim Letter

ship with the reader as long as possible. Some companies use a collection sequence of 12 to 15 letters. Others have only 3 to 6 steps. Figure 9.5 illustrates common tactics in the typical sequence of collection letters.

The obvious escalation of tactics in the collection sequence illustrates the breakdown of any positive relationship between sender and receiver. The key to effective collection letters is to maintain positive relationship as long as possible so that your business association with the reader can continue. These letters are often produced by a computerized collection department in a large organization, but in smaller companies you may need to write such letters individually. Figure 9.6 outlines a formula that you might use in writing an early-stage collection letter.

```
                    PACIFIC PRESS PRODUCTIONS
             4700 Industrial Blvd., Pleasanton, CA 94566
                          (415) 462-7500




                                                November 25, 19XX

      Mr. Lee Knight
      Bay Printing Supply
      34500 Easton Road
      Oakland, CA 94546

      Dear Mr. Knight:

      Thank you for the prompt delivery of order #13537.  The estab-
      lishment of my new printing firm has been simplified by your
      company's assistance.

      The order was delivered to my warehouse on November 17, via your
      delivery truck.  All of the items arrived in excellent condition.
      Unfortunately, an exchange of one of the items is necessary.

      Apparantly, a mistake was made in filling the ink order.  I
      received 20 pounds of OS872, which is a metallic gold ink.  This
      ink is the wrong color and costs $3.85 more per pound than OS427,
      which I ordered.  I was, however, invoiced and billed for OS427.

      Since I cannot use the ink and it represents a $77.00 loss to
      your company, I suggest an exchange.  I will return the ink I
      received if you will kindly send me 20 pounds of OS427.

      I appreciate your prompt attention in this matter, and I look
      forward to doing more business with your company in the future.

                                      Sincerely,



                                      Timothy S. Fullmer
                                      President
```

EXHIBIT 9.B Claim Letter

Early Stage:	Remind reader of payment due.
	Remind that payment is overdue.
	Provide possible excuse for overdue payment.
Middle Stage:	Repeat firmly that payment is overdue.
	Give first warning of impending legal action.
	Spell out steps in impending legal action.
Late Stage:	Make final courteous attempt to solicit payment.
	Give final warning of impending legal action.
	Provide notification of legal action.

FIGURE 9.5 Tactics in Escalating Stages of the Collection Sequence

```
                                        Appliances Unlimited
                                        7690 Meridian Blvd.
                                        San Mateo, CA  97857
                                        (415) 874-3430




          Mr. Daniel Burnett
          325 Hartcourt Dr.
          San Lorenzo, CA 98733

          February 6, 19XX

          Dear Mr. Burnett:

          We hope your family has been enjoying the new stove you purchased
          from us on December 7.  This letter is to let you know that we
          appreciate your patronage and to remind you that your January
          payment is overdue.

          Perhaps the holidays have kept you so busy you have forgotton to
          send in your payment, which is now 30 days past due.  Please
          remit your January 5, 19XX payment of $75 as soon as possible.

          We are sure that this has been an oversight on your part and that
          it can be quickly remedied.  Please disregard this request if you
          have already mailed your payment.

          Sincerely,

          M. E. Whiteley

          M. E. Whiteley
          Appliances Unlimited
```

EXHIBIT 9.C   Early-Stage Collection Letter

Sample collection letters are provided in Exhibits 9.C, 9.D, and 9.E. Note how three different levels of appeal are made that affect the tone of the letters.

Introduction:	Establish positive relationship.
Body:	State purpose—to collect payment.
	Clarify present status to correct any errors.
	Provide steps for immediate action.
Conclusion:	Reaffirm positive relationship.

FIGURE 9.6   Formula for Early-Stage Collection Letters

```
                                    Appliances Unlimited
                                    7690 Meridian Blvd.
                                    San Mateo, CA 97857
                                    (415) 874-3430




Mr. Daniel Burnett
325 Hartcourt Dr.
San Lorenzo, CA 98733

March 5, 19XX

Dear Mr. Burnett:

Your account with us is now two months overdue.  Undoubtedly you
have a reason for this delay in sending us payment for January
and February.  Your account is now $150 past due.

Your patronage is appreciated, but your credit could suffer with
any further delays.  Help us avoid having to turn your account
over to a collection agency.

Please send in your payment or, if you are currently unable to do
so, call us.  We want to help you maintain your good credit.

Sincerely,

M. E. Whiteley
M. E. Whiteley
Appliances Unlimited
```

EXHIBIT 9.D   Middle-Stage Collection Letter

Sales Letters

Prospective buyers are often mailed letters or flyers that explain the features and benefits of products or services. No doubt you have received these types of letters yourself. The most effective sales letters are those which capture the attention of the reader, convince the reader of the benefits of the product, and prompt the reader to take action.

You can gain attention and interest in a sales letter with the format you use. Sales letters often break all the rules of formal business letter writing. The stationery is often modified to look more like a flyer or handbill. Color

```
                                        Appliances Unlimited
                                        7690 Meridian Blvd.
                                        San Mateo, CA 97857
                                        (415) 874-3430




    Mr. Daniel Burnett
    325 Hartcourt Dr.
    San Lorenzo, CA 98733

    April 17, 19XX

    Dear Mr. Burnett:

    We have sent you several letters requesting payment on your
    delinquent account.  Your overdue balance is now $225, which
    represents your January, February, and March payments.  We are
    now forced to turn your account over to a collection agency.
    This is not something we wish to do.  We would much rather
    have worked out terms with you.

    Your account will be forwarded to Retail Dealers Collections,
    Inc., on May 1, 19XX.  This allows you two weeks to make some
    form of remittance to us before such action is taken.  Receipt
    of your check for $225 or a substantial portion of that amount
    received before May 1 will allow us to cancel collection
    proceedings.

    Sincerely,

    M. E. Whiteley
    M. E. Whiteley
    Appliances Unlimited
```

EXHIBIT 9.E   Late-Stage Collection Letter

and dramatic visual effects such as photographs or artwork are used extensively. The language is also more dramatic and colorful to elicit excitement and interest in the product. In some cases, a formal format can be used, but the opening paragraphs tend to attract interest by emphasizing the reader's needs and potential benefits.

The major elements of sales letters are the coverage of the features and benefits of the product that is for sale. Features are both tangible and intangible elements of the product. Tangible features include size, shape, color, and price. Intangible features include such considerations as ways in which the product can be used, where it can be obtained, and conditions for purchase. Each feature offers a potential benefit for the buyer. For example, a low price (a feature) may have a benefit (saves you money). If the price is high, the benefit could be better quality (it is a common assumption that better quality creates higher price) or longevity.

When writing a sales letter, you should analyze your product carefully for relevant features and benefits to the reader. Not all features will be relevant, and not all benefits will be applicable to a specific reader. You should also analyze your reader's values and select the features and benefits that most nearly match the reader's needs. Use evidence to support your arguments about how the product will satisfy the reader's needs. Anticipate any objections the reader might have, and develop counterarguments to overcome these objections.

```
OMNI                              P.O. Box 64, Milton, CA 94573
MARKETING                                    309 (456-6790)



                          INCREASE SALES

                         RAISE VISIBILITY

                 PROMOTE SERVICE TO YOUR COMMUNITY


OMNI MARKETING is introducing the Rainbow Passbook of Savings as
a sales promotion marketing tool designed to increase foot
traffic for businesses in our community while raising money for
charity.  The booklet offers customers the oppurtunity to receive
"free" goods and services or discounts on merchandise at Milton
stores.  Working with store owners, OMNI MARKETING will assess
the individual needs of each business and design a plan to
increase the business's customer base.

The ultimate goals of the Rainbow Passbook are threefold:

          1)  To increase awareness of Milton businesses.

          2)  To keep more consumer dollars within the community.

          3)  To raise money for the Community Chest.

The Passbook will be sold to the public through a direct-response
ad in newspapers and at prime locations throughout the city.
This distribution method ensures that the book will be targeted
to a receptive audience.  Expected distribution exceeds 10,000
books with 10% of all net sales going to the Community Chest.

If you wish to participate, the cost for a one-page display ad in
the passbook is $250.00. (Discount coupons in the ads should be
good for a full year.)  Your business will also be listed in a
directory in the Passbook.  In addition to the increased foot
traffic in your store and the contribution to the Community
Chest, each participating business will receive ten free
Passbooks.

We are eager to talk with you about the Rainbow Passbook of
Savings, and we look forward to working with you.

If you have any questions, give either of us a call at the above
number.

          Phil Siegel                      Larry Campbell
```

EXHIBIT 9.F Sales Letter to Businesses

End the sales letter with specific action steps that explain how the reader can obtain the benefits you offer. Provide any necessary details about point of purchase, terms of agreement, or other business aspects that may affect the reader's ability to buy your product.

Figure 9.7 illustrates common steps in a sales letter. This type of letter is highly individualized, and one desirable goal is often to create a unique appearance. Thus, sales letters vary tremendously in the ways they are written and formatted. However, they all share the persuasive principles outlined in the formula. Two sample sales letters are included in Exhibits 9.F and 9.G. Note how each letter adapts the formula.

```
                                        Vanden Cosmetics
                                        38 Park Plaza
                                        New York, NY 10019




May 4, 19XX

Ms. Elizabeth Carmichael
726 Montclaire Dr.
Austin, Texas  76908

Dear Ms. Carmichael:

Vanden Cosmetics is renowned for its commitment to provide women
around the world with the finest quality of skin care products.
We continue that commitment with the creation of ELIXIR, our
scientifically formulated moisturizing skin treatment.

Every woman wants to look her very best.  Every woman wants a
soft, fresh complexion.  ELIXIR can give you the look you want.
Beautiful, vital skin.  Radiant skin.

ELIXIR has collagen protein, which enhances your skin's natural
moisture layer.  It is fragrance-free and hypoallergenic for
sensitive skin.  A special sunscreen helps block harmful rays.
This ultralight moisturizing treatment is perfect under makeup
or as a nighttime treatment.

ELIXIR is now being offered at finer department stores at a
special introductory price of $35 for two ounces.  It is also
available in a four-ounce size.  Take advantage of this special
offer.  Go ahead . . . indulge yourself.  Beautiful skin awaits
you.

Vanden Cosmetics . . . committed to beautiful skin.


Mary E. Whiteley
Mary E. Whiteley
Sales Manager
```

EXHIBIT 9.G   Sales Letter to an Individual

Introduction:	Grab attention for the product.
	Create a sense of need in the reader.
	Promise benefits to the reader.
	State the general purpose of the letter.
Body:	Provide details about the features of the product.
	Explain benefits to the reader.
	Establish your credibility as a seller.
	Compare your product to that of competitors.
	Anticipate and overcome any objections.
Conclusion:	Provide action steps on how to acquire the product.
	End with a strong appeal to act now.

FIGURE 9.7   Formula for Sales Letters

The sales letter requires special skill and much practice in order to be distinctive and effective. Notice how sales materials are constructed when you receive them in the mail. The envelope and enclosures are often used to enhance the sales message. Develop your own sense of the most effective format, attention getters, evidence, and action steps. You may discover a dynamic new skill in yourself that can benefit you in your career.

Persuasive Announcements

Chapter 8, on informative letters, discussed announcements for business events. Some announcement letters are purely informative, but others not only announce the event but also try to persuade the reader to attend or support the event in some way. Such persuasive announcements are sometimes called solicitations or invitations. As with the informative announcement, the persuasive one should focus attention on the event and motivate the reader to action.

The opening of the announcement should emphasize the name of the event to grab attention. If the reader will benefit in some way from the event, these benefits can be highlighted as well. The announcement should provide all necessary details about the event in order to anticipate any questions the reader might have. The specific features of the event and the benefits that the features will create should be explained in detail. Finally, readers should be given all necessary details in order to perform the desired action. Dates, times, places, admission fees, and other details should be included so that the reader will be thoroughly prepared to act in the desired manner. Figure 9.8 outlines the common formula for a persuasive announcement.

The key to effective announcements is to explain fully the benefits to readers. Try to understand readers' points of view. Why should they attend? What can they gain? What do they have to lose? What will take place? These questions exist in the minds of your readers, so you should satisfy any questions your announcements will provoke. The more completely you explain the features and benefits of the event to readers, the more convincing you will be. Exhibit 9.H illustrates a persuasive announcement.

Introduction:	Focus on the event being announced.
	State an attention-grabbing benefit.
	State the purpose of the announcement.
Body:	Explain pertinent details about the event.
	Explain benefits in detail.
	Anticipate any objections and overcome them.
Conclusion:	Explain action steps for participation.
	End on a positive, optimistic note.

FIGURE 9.8   Formula for Persuasive Announcements

November 30, 19XX

Jansen Gifts, Inc.
40 Landon Street
Gladden, MI 49035
(812) 315-8877

Mr. George Peters
1243 Alden Road
Bemming, CA 94189

Dear Mr. Peters,

    Congratulations on becoming a Jansen consultant! Now that you have chosen this great oppurtunity, please allow us to help you. We encourage you to attend our Jansen quarterly sales meeting. These meetings are vital to your success in our company because they furnish you with important sales strategies, testimonial insights, and background about our business. Blaine Howard, author of <u>Success in Selling</u>, will be our guest speaker.

    The main emphasis of these meetings is to expose you to new product lines and information about the company to furthur your sales success. Our high performers will testify and encourage you with their victory stories, and Blaine Howard will explain the sales principles he has learned over the years. His book will also be given out free and awards will be delivered to top achievers. It has been encouraging to hear the positive feedback from consultants who have attended these meetings. One of our top sales people said her sales doubled after she received a tip from one of her fellow consultants.

    Please post a note on your calendar concerning this meeting. It will be December 15, 19XX, at 7:00 p.m., in the conference room at the Sheritan Hotel (please notice the enclosed map). Refreshments will be served afterward, and admission is free. We highly recommend this meeting and would enjoy getting to know you better.

Yours truly,

Grant Bruneau

Grant Bruneau
Vice President of Sales

Enclosure

EXHIBIT 9.H   Persuasive Announcement

Persuasive business letters demand a keen ability to understand the reader and appeal to the reader's needs, interests, and values. The strategy, based on grabbing interest, convincing with evidence, and motivating action, works in many persuasive situations. These principles also apply to many other forms of communication: application letters, résumés, interviews, and public speeches. By developing a sensitivity to persuasive techniques in letters, you can become more influential in many business situations.

EXERCISE 9.1
Writing a Claim Letter

Directions: Write a persuasive letter to a real person from whom you would like some form of compensation or consideration: a refund, a reimbursement, an additional service at no cost, a repeat service at no cost, a reconsideration of a decision already made, another chance to do something, or an exception to a stated policy. Use the formula and suggestions presented in this chapter to organize and construct your letter.

_____

_____

_____

_____

_____

_____

_____

_____

_____

_____

_____

_____

_____

_____

_____

_____

_____

_____

_____

_____

_____

_____

EXERCISE 9.2
Evaluating a Sales Letter

Directions: This exercise is designed to improve your ability to analyze sales appeals. Select a sales letter that is mailed to your home, or find an example of a sales letter in a magazine. Attach the letter to this page. Mark on the sample letter the location of each type of sales appeal listed below. Then evaluate the effectiveness of the letter by encircling the appropriate ranking—low, medium, or high—for each sales appeal. Be prepared to provide explanations for your rankings.

1. Attention-getting:
   (Does the letter focus interest
   and attention early?)   Low   Medium   High

2. Need creation:
   (Does the letter create a sense of
   need or problem in the reader?)   Low   Medium   High

3. Clear purpose:
   (Is the product identified clearly?)   Low   Medium   High

4. Features:
   (Are the features explained fully?)   Low   Medium   High

5. Benefits:
   (Are the benefits to the reader
   clarified and emphasized?)   Low   Medium   High

6. Credibility:
   (Does the writer offer credibility factors?) Low   Medium   High

7. Comparison to competitors:
   (Is the product or seller compared
   to the competition?)   Low   Medium   High

8. Objections anticipated and overcome: Low   Medium   High
   (Are objections dealt with fully?)

9. Action steps: (Does the reader know exactly what to do to get the product?)	Low	Medium	High
10. Envelope/enclosures: (Is the sales message supported?)	Low	Medium	High
Overall evaluation:	Low	Medium	High

EXERCISE 9.3
Writing a Sales Letter

Directions: Do you have something you would like to sell, such as an unused item collecting dust in the basement or a service you can provide for a fee? If you do not have a real item for sale, pretend that you do. Compose a sales letter to someone who might be interested in buying your product or service. Use the guidelines suggested in the formula for sales letters presented in this chapter.

_____

_____

_____

_____

_____

_____

_____

_____

_____

_____

_____

_____

_____

_____

_____

_____

_____

_____

_____

_____

_____

_____

EXERCISE 9.4
Writing a Persuasive Announcement

Directions: Compose a persuasive announcement for one of the following events. Create any details you need to make the letter convincing. Address the letter to a group that might be interested in purchasing the offered product or service.

1. You are president of the local Toastmasters Club, a volunteer group that meets once a week for two hours to practice public speaking skills. Your group holds social events and sponsors speakers in contests and tournaments. Your club now has 40 members, and you are holding an orientation meeting to attract new members. The annual membership fee is $10.00.

2. You work as a manager in a store that sells skiing equipment. The owner of the store wants to hold an open house for first-time buyers of skiing equipment. It will be an educational and entertaining event with free refreshments, live entertainment and dancing, skiing films, and coaching by ski instructors. Ski equipment, instruction, and travel packages will also be for sale at special prices.

3. You work for a local hospital. Your hospital has several openings for nurse volunteers. You are asked to plan an evening orientation meeting in which you will explain the nurse volunteer program and encourage people to join. Write a letter to students at a local high school encouraging them to attend the orientation meeting.

ACTION ASSIGNMENT

9

Persuasive Letters

1. Make copies of the sales letter you composed for Exercise 9.3 and distribute them to your classmates. Read and critique each letter on the basis of the guidelines suggested in this chapter. Does the letter make a convincing case for selling the product?

2. Make copies of the persuasive announcement you composed for Exercise 9.4. Form a group of five people and distribute these copies to each group member. Read and critique each announcement on the basis of the guidelines suggested in this chapter. Does the announcement make a convincing case for its purpose?

3. Find a letter to the editor in a local newspaper that you feel is particularly ineffective in communicating its message. (These letters are usually found on the editorial page.) Analyze the letter by answering the following questions:

   What is the purpose of the letter?
   To whom is the letter written?
   Why does the letter not accomplish its purpose?
   Does the letter use inappropriate language or weak arguments?

4. Write a letter to the editor of a local newspaper (either a city or a school paper) in which you express you opinion about some issue. (You may wish to address the same issue as was discussed in the ineffective letter you analyzed in Action Assignment 3.)

5. Assume that you are the collection officer for a local business. You have a customer who has not paid for merchandise that has already been delivered. Invent whatever details necessary to compose an effective letter that will persuade the customer to pay his bill. Write a series of three letters that address the following situations:

   The customer's payment is one month overdue.
   The customer's payment is two months overdue.
   The customer's payment is three months overdue.

10
Tactful Letters

The most difficult letters to write are those in which you must refuse a request, report bad news, or otherwise disappoint the reader. In these situations, your task is to maintain a positive feeling with the reader but still convey the information that threatens your relationship. This balance requires tact, courtesy, and diplomacy.

This chapter investigates two of these writing situations: the letter refusing a request and the letter reporting disappointing news. The key to writing such letters lies in the use of specific strategies for creating trust and maintaining positive relationship in the face of bad news. These strategies are also covered in this chapter.

The Diplomatic Strategy: Be Tactful, Be Positive

When faced with the need to write a bad-news letter, you must choose between a direct and an indirect approach. The direct approach is best when the person making the request expects the refusal or at least knows that it is a strong possibility. In such a situation, you are merely confirming what the reader already suspected but was hoping might not be the case. It is more courteous to report the refusal early in your letter rather than later. If you are going to refuse someone, it is inconsiderate to make the receiver read an entire page before getting to the point. In contrast, the indirect approach is usually more effective when the person making the request expects an affirmative answer and will be upset by the bad news. In this situation, you should offer your explanation for the refusal before you actually state it. These two approaches are discussed in greater detail in the following section, on letters refusing requests.

When presenting a disappointment, you should not be blunt about breaking the news. Start the letter with positive relationship factors, and state the disappointment in the most favorable terms possible. The goal of the tactful letter is twofold: both to report the bad news and to maintain

Show appreciation for the reader's interest.

Thank the reader for the initial contact.

Show your concern for the reader's concern.

Demonstrate your understanding of the reader's position.

Agree with the reader about something you feel in common.

Refer to prior, more pleasant dealings you have had.

Express your desire to maintain a positive relationship.

FIGURE 10.1 Positive-Relationship Factors for Tactful Letters

positive relationship with the reader. Thus, you should begin the letter positively and maintain a positive tone throughout. Figure 10.1 lists several devices you can use to create and maintain a positive tone in a tactful letter.

The purpose of the relationship building at the beginning of the letter is to warn the reader subtly that his or her request is not going to be granted automatically. When granting a request, writers often state the good news immediately. By delaying the reporting of your news, you give your reader time to anticipate a problem.

Once you have established a positive tone in your letter, you should state the news. Announce the refusal or disappointment, but state it in positive terms. Do not use negative or loaded terms about the request or the condition of the person making the request. Likewise, do not offer trite or insincere expressions of apology. Figure 10.2 suggests common trite phrases that you should avoid.

Your statement of your decision should state your reasons for the refusal or the disappointment in positive terms that are objective and clear. Take care to be objective in the language you use to explain your reasons. If you have good reasons for making your refusal, the reader should accept them gracefully. The explanation tells the reader about your situation and asks for understanding in accepting your refusal. If you have any helpful alternatives to suggest to the reader, these can follow the explanation for your refusal.

The positive tone should be maintained through the close of the disappointment letter. Once you have created a positive relationship, stated the refusal in positive terms, and offered your explanation, do not undo your good work with a weak ending. Refer again to the positive relationship you created at the opening of the letter. Look toward an optimistic future. Do not end on a negative note by repeating the refusal—once is enough. Likewise, do

"It is my sad duty to inform you that . . ."

"I regret to inform you that . . ."

"I am sorry, but I must say that . . ."

"There is nothing I can do . . ."

"I hope you can understand, but . . ."

"If there were anything I could do, I would, but . . ."

"We have tried everything, but . . ."

FIGURE 10.2 Trite Phrases to Avoid in Bad-News Letters

not end with clichés or insincere attempts to make the reader feel better. Be firm in your decision, and do not imply that you may rethink your decision later. Finally, do not apologize for your decision. Leave the reader feeling that your decision is a necessary one and that you want to maintain a good relationship in the future.

Letters Refusing Requests

When you must refuse a request from someone, you can use either the direct or the indirect approach. The direct approach is more appropriate when you know that the person making the request is aware that a refusal is possible. The indirect approach is preferable when the news will come as an unpleasant surprise to the reader. In both cases, you want to begin the letter with positive relationship building and end on a positive tone. The major difference between the two lies in the order in which the elements of the body of the letter are presented.

THE DIRECT APPROACH

To use the direct approach, you should first state the refusal and then offer your explanation. This approach makes the reader feel that you are being straightforward and honest in your answer. Figure 10.3 lists the steps to follow when using the indirect approach to refuse a request. Two sample letters of refusal are given in Exhibits 10.A and 10.B.

When stating your reasons for the refusal, be sure not to imply any criticism of the reader for having made the request, even if you think it was inappropriate. Review the list of common presumptuous phrases in Chapter 8. You should avoid them when making your explanations in tactful letters.

When making a refusal, you are under no obligation to help the reader solve the problem posed by the request. In situations where you want to offer assistance, you can make suggestions, tell the reader that you are available for consultation, or help the reader find another solution to his or her need. Going this extra step is an excellent relationship-building device. While you may not be able to give the reader what has been requested, you are being as

---

Introduction: Refer to the request.
Establish positive relationship.

Body: State the refusal.
Offer your reasons for the refusal.

Conclusion: State your interest in future dealing.
End on a positive, cordial note.

FIGURE 10.3   Formula for Letters Directly Refusing Requests

LAWNDALE CORPORATION

1811 Reading Avenue, Allentown, PA ● 214/633-7200

December 15, 19XX

Mr. Timothy James
The Bear Creek Group
168 Lafayette Way
Woodland Hills, PA 16211

Dear Mr. James:

Thank you for your interest in Lawndale Corporation as a source
for financial assistance in your upcoming "Believers" seminar.
We have reviewed your correspondence and cannot, unfortunately,
honor your request.

It is Lawndale's policy to refrain from becoming involved with
projects that may be construed as an endorsement or promotion of
any given religious persuasion. This is an issue we feel is
better left up to the individual, without corporate influence.
Since the "Believers" seminar directly represents a particular
religious belief, Lawndale will have to decline your request.

Lawndale does pride itself in contributing toward a variety of
projects. We feel that it is our responsibility to offer
assistance in events that benefit our community. If, in the
future, your organization wishes to promote alternate types of
community events, Lawndale would be pleased to consider a
donation.

We wish you success in your current endeavor. Once again, thank
you for considering Lawndale.

Sincerely,

Steven Faria

Steven Faria
Public Relations Director
Centralized Activities

SF:sd

EXHIBIT 10.A Direct Letter of Refusal

helpful as possible. Most readers will appreciate this effort, and you will gain
credibility for your future dealings with the reader.

THE INDIRECT APPROACH

In situations where the refusal is unexpected by the reader, you may wish to
put your explanation before the refusal itself. When a refusal is likely to be
met with heated emotion, placing the reasons first ensures that the reader
will be somewhat prepared for the refusal and helps defuse a strong emotional reaction. As with the direct approach, your language should be positive throughout the letter. Figure 10.4 outlines the indirect approach. Two
sample letters using this approach are presented in Exhibits 10.C and 10.D.

TM CORPORATION
45 Prospect Avenue
San Francisco, California 94123
(415) 555-1234

December 10, 19XX

Ms. Rebecca Morgan
DynaSales, Inc.
4040 East Street
New York, NY 10027

Dear Ms. Morgan:

I was pleased to receive your letter requesting the services of TM Corporation. Your favorable comments were greatly appreciated.

Unfortunately, we cannot provide the services that DynaSales requires at this time. We have recently reached agreement with a major contractor that will require all our resources. We have established a high standard of customer service over the past ten years, and we are unwilling to compromise these standards. It would be a disservice to you if we were to accept your offer and then be unable to support your needs.

Our contractual commitments will expire in May 19XX. We would be available to discuss your needs at that time. If your needs require immediate attention, I would recommend that you get in touch with Mr. William Kavanagh at Kavanagh & Sons. Mr. Kavanagh has performed services for TM Corporation in the past, and his company does excellent work.

I thank you for considering TM Corporation. I hope you will keep us in mind in the future. Please let me know if I can be of further assistance.

Sincerely,

Mark H. Morris
President

EXHIBIT 10.B   Direct Letter of Refusal

Introduction:	Refer to the request.
	Build positive relationship.
Body:	Provide reasons for your decision.
	State the refusal.
Conclusion:	Reaffirm positive relationship.
	End on a positive, cordial note.

FIGURE 10.4   Formula for Letters Indirectly Refusing Requests

```
Kinzler Hardware Supply Co.
935 Bridge Street
Oakland, CA  94603
(415) 1234




December 10, 19XX

Mr. Tim Rose
550 E. 42nd Street
Oakland, CA  94610

Dear Mr. Rose:

Thank you for your letter concerning the Smithson plumbing fix-
tures you purchased from our store last September 14.  You are a
valued customer, and we appreciate your business.  We strive to
provide you with the best products at the best price.

As exclusive dealers of Smithson fixtures, we work closely with
Smithson to ensure customer satisfaction.  In your case, A
Smithson engineer reviewed the problems you encountered when you
attempted to install their fixtures and concluded that improper
installation was the cause of the failure of the equipment.  In
addition, the fixtures were damaged beyond repair and cannot be
reinstalled.

Because of these findings, I cannot credit your account for the
cost of the Smithson fixtures you purchased.  Smithson has
offered to custom design new fixtures for you at a discounted
rate.  I am sure you will be satisfied with their solution to
your problem.

Thank you for choosing Kinzler Hardware for your plumbing needs.
Please write me if you need further assistance.

Sincerely,

Mark H. Morris

Mark H. Morris
Store Manager
```

EXHIBIT 10.C Indirect Letter of Refusal

Letters Reporting Disappointing News

In some business situations, you may need to reveal unwelcome news. For example, you may have to report price increases, pending legal action, cessation of services, or cutbacks of availability. As with the refusal of requests, your two purposes are to announce the bad news while maintaining a positive relationship with the reader.

Many of the same strategies work in both the disappointing-news letter and the refusal letter. You should be direct in reporting the news and maintain a positive tone throughout the letter. Provide a complete explanation for

```
                                          Plaza Camera Center
                                          84 Crow Canyon Place
                                          San Ramon, CA 94583




                                          December 9, 19XX

Ms. Shannon Antrim
132 Diablo View Terrace
San Ramon, CA 94583

Dear Ms. Antrim:

We have received your request for a refund of the purchase price
of the Gibson 35mm camera you recently purchased at our San Ramon
store.  You stated the product you purchased is difficult to use,
and you were not fully advised about the difficulty of operation
before you purchased the camera.

We appreciate your decision to purchase your camera at our store.
It is our desire to provide the maximum amount of satisfaction to
all of our customers.  We provide a written policy at the time of
purchase indicating that cash refunds will be made within 30 days
of purchase if the product purchased is defective.  Since the
problem is not one of the product being defective, we are unable
to offer you a cash refund.  However, we would like to offer you
complimentary lessons on the operation of the camera.  We are
sure you will be satisfied with the camera once you have received
instruction in its use.

We hope that this offer will be an acceptable alternative to your
request.  We are looking forward to hearing from you.  Please
present this letter at our San Ramon store or call for an
appointment to arrange your free lessons.

Sincerely,

Marilyn Ghiorso

Marilyn Ghiorso
Store Manager
```

EXHIBIT 10.D Indirect Letter of Refusal

the disappointing news. If at all possible, provide alternative solutions and suggest action steps that will help the reader adjust to the news. You may wish to make yourself available to the reader to answer questions or to provide more explanation.

The key to writing effective and supportive letters reporting disappointing news is to see the announcement from the readers' perspective. How are they likely to respond to the news? What questions will they probably ask? What information will they need to understand the news? What will they probably want to do in response to the news? The answers to these questions will guide you in determining what to include in your letter. Figure 10.5 outlines the steps in writing letters reporting disappointing news. Two sample letters in Exhibits 10.E and 10.F illustrate the use of this formula.

RICHARDSON INC.

201 Industrial Boulevard, Santa Rosa, California 92139 ● 707/683-3012

December 15, 19XX

Ms. Valerie Newhouse, President
Concepts in Interiors, Inc.
451 East Jefferson Boulevard
Woodside, NY 06701

Subject: Discontinuance of Richardson "Opus" line

Dear Ms. Newhouse:

Richardson Inc. has a longstanding policy of communicating, in advance, all changes in product availability. This communication provides you with our Discontinuance Strategy for the Richardson "Opus" line of linoleum floor coverings. Please share this information with the appropriate people in your organization.

The "Opus" line of linoleum will be available through July of next year. Please note, however, that our order-acceptance "window" for the "Opus" line will close March 31. Therefore, if you have continuing requirements for the above-mentioned line of flooring, we recommend that you place your final orders within the next 120 days. Due to manufacturing lead times and commitments, all orders will be non-cancellable. Orders received after March 31 cannot be honored.

Richardson continually works to maintain communication with our customers. In following our policy of timely product news announcements, this document provides a planning period of 120 days and a deliverable horizon of eight months in support of your final "Opus" flooring requirements.

We are grateful for your past business and are hopeful that we will be a successful part of your future product family.

Sincerely,

Steven Faria

Steven Faria
Vice President
Interior Covering Division

EXHIBIT 10.E   Letter of Reporting Disappointing News

Introduction: Establish positive relationship.

Body: State the disappointing news.
                  Provide any necessary explanation.
                  Suggest alternative solutions (if applicable).

Conclusion: Reaffirm positive relationship.
                  End on a positive, cordial note.

**FIGURE 10.5   Formula for Letters Reporting
Disappointing News**

```
                                        Longview Paper Products
                                        23 Franklin Circle
                                        Livermore, CA 94550




                                        December 9, 19XX

Mr. William Larsen
Valley Community Hospital
15 Logan Street
Manteca, CA  95877

Dear Mr. Larsen:

We appreciate the long relationship we have had with Valley
Hospital.  You are a reliable customer, and we value the
opportunity we have had to provide you with your special-order
file folders.

Unfortunatley, a sharp rise in costs has forced us to reevaluate
the ordering and price structures we can offer you.  Effective
February 1, 19XX, we must make the following changes:

           1)  An increase in the minimum quanity required per
               order from 5,000 to 10,000 file folders
           2)  An increase in the price per folder from $.40 to
               $.45

As you know, your file folders require a premium-grade paper
product and manual assembly.  In recent months we have
experienced an increased cost for the raw materials and an
increase in the hourly rate we pay our assemblers.  The above
quantity and price increases will help us achieve an economy in
our purchasing of the raw products and allow us to cover
additional labor costs. We hope that the increased minimum-order
policy will allow you to reduce your ordering and shipping costs.
We will still offer you the same quality product.

Once again, we have appreciated your long relationship with our
company and wish to remain your exclusive supplier.  Please call
me with any questions or concerns.

Sincerely,

Marilyn Ghiorso

Marilyn Ghiorso
Sales Representative
```

EXHIBIT 10.F   Letter Reporting Disappointing News

Letters of refusal and disappointment are not easy to write. They demand all your powers of tact and diplomacy to keep the positive regard of your reader. This challenge can be met successfully, however, by using the suggestions provided in this chapter. Bad news need not mean the end of a good working relationship. It often forms the basis for working with your reader to overcome present adversity and to forge an even stronger relationship.

EXERCISE 10.1
Changing from a Negative to a Positive Tone

Directions: One of the keys to writing effective disappointment letters is using a positive tone. The following sentences are negative in tone. Without changing the meaning of the sentence, recast each into positive language.

1. You do not meet our admission standards.

_____

_____

2. You completed this form wrong. Please do it again.

_____

_____

3. Your action caused us to lose a $10,000 sale.

_____

_____

4. Mr. Smith said that you were rude and insulting to him.

_____

_____

5. This is the fourth time I have had to tell you that you cannot take your vacation in May.

_____

_____

_____

6. Do not attempt to get into the building before 8:00 a.m.

_____

_____

7. Can't you see why people interpret that behavior as offensive?

_____

_____

8. I don't want you to order pizza for the secretaries ever again. They got melted cheese all over the computer manuals.

_____

_____

_____

EXERCISE 10.2
Correcting a Letter of Refusal

Directions: Below is a letter of refusal that ignores many of the suggestions made in this chapter. Identify the principle that is violated in each of the following sentences, and rewrite the sentence so that it communicates more effectively with the reader.

Bernie Allbloom
64 Harrison Way
Biltmore, KY 49586

October 9, 19XX

Harry Wheeler
Kelly Greenhouse
2435 Flower Way
Biltmore, KY 49587

Dear Harry:

(1) Thanks for asking, but unfortunately, I cannot grant your request for credit at my flower shop.

(2) I have heard from several people that your checks bounce regularly.

(3) As you already know, I do not offer credit to anyone at my shop.

(4) We always aim to please, but in this situation I cannot help you.

(5) Obvioulsy, I do not have a large enough clientele to carry accounts.

(6) I might be tempted to change my policy, but I doubt it.

(7) Thanks for your patronage in the past, and stop by again real soon.

Using your rewritten sentences, compose a letter from Bernie to Harry in which he announces the disappointing news that he cannot extend credit. You may wish to add comments beyond those in the seven sentences above, and do not feel that you have to include all seven.

Bernie Allbloom
64 Harrison Way
Biltmore, KY 49586

October 2, 19XX

Harry Wheeler
Kelly Greenhouse
2435 Flower Way
Biltmore, KY 49587

Dear Harry:

_____

_____

_____

_____

_____

_____

_____

_____

_____

_____

_____

_____

_____

_____

_____

_____

EXERCISE 10.3
Composing a Letter of Refusal

Directions: Compose a letter of refusal for one of the following situations:

A friend asks to borrow your car for a three-day trip.
A co-worker asks you to cover for him during a vacation.
A customer asks to return a pair of shoes that do not fit.
A friend asks to borrow $200 for a month.

Invent any specific details you need to create a relationship with the reader and to give a complete explanation of your refusal.

_____

_____

_____

_____

_____

_____

_____

_____

_____

_____

_____

_____

_____

_____

_____

_____

_____

_____

_____

_____

Tactful Letters

1. Make copies of the tactful letter you composed for Exercise 10.3. Form a group of five people and distribute the copies to group members. Read and critique each letter on the basis of the guidelines suggested in this chapter.

2. Rewrite the letter you composed for Exercise 10.3 using a different approach. That is, if you used a direct approach originally, rewrite the letter using an indirect approach, and vice versa. Compare the two letters. Is one more appropriate than the other? Be prepared to discuss your opinion.

3. Imagine that you are the owner of a business. You have interviewed two people for a position as sales clerk, and you intend to hire one. Write a letter to the person whom you will not be hiring and inform him or her of your decision. Invent any details necessary to justify your decision.

11
Short Reports

Every business uses reports to transmit information, analyze situations, and find solutions to problems. There are literally hundreds of types of reports. Each company has unique needs and develops its own special formats and styles of reports to meet these needs. As an aspiring business worker, it is important that you be familiar with the common types of reports and be able to use the report format effectively. The following list summarizes a few of the types of situations you may encounter and need to report on:

Drawing attention to a problem/situation.
Researching the history of a problem/situation.
Analyzing the causes of a problem/situation.
Proposing a solution to a problem/situation.
Reporting on business activities over a certain time period.
Accounting for your time or expenses.
Requesting reimbursement for expenses incurred on the job.
Planning a project.
Estimating costs, materials, and personnel needs for a project.
Reporting on the progress of a project.
Summarizing the results of a project.
Reporting on a policy, procedure, or set of rules.
Proposing to change a policy, procedure, or rule.
Recording the action of a meeting, a conversation, or event.

You will be required to write reports, so it is a vital business skill to develop. While the contents of reports may vary tremendously, certain underlying principles are common to all types of reports. By understanding the basic logic of reports, you can use them more effectively in your career area.

Types of Reports

While there are many unique names for reports, they can logically be thought of in four basic categories—according to function, content, time, and format.

The *functional* classification of a report tells you what it does: transmits information, analyzes data, makes recommendations, or proposes the implementation of specific plans. Informative reports are generally called research documents. Analytical reports discuss evaluations, experiments, or investigations. Recommendation reports draw conclusions from data and suggest general courses of action for the future. Proposals suggest specific courses of action and often include budget forecasts, work schedules, and other implementation elements.

Another way to think about reports is by their *content*. Thus, there are sales, management, financial, accounting, credit, tax, research and development, and other types of reports that come from various units in an organization.

Reports can also be classified by the *time* at which they are written. Planning reports are written in the initial stages of a project. Progress reports provide current information about the development of the project. Periodic reports are produced at regular intervals, while special reports respond to a unique need and are not necessarily repeated. Final reports summarize the results of a project once it is completed.

The final method for classifying reports is by the *format* used. Reports are sometimes made on specially created forms that categorize the data to be reported. You can also create a report using a letter or memo format—these are usually called short, or informal, reports. The formal report is a longer, more complex document that is traditionally divided into sections for easier reading.

These categories overlap to some degree. For example, you might encounter a research report, created for the sales department and recommending a certain action, that is written in a short, informal memo format. Since there is such variety in the types of reports, it is important that you familiarize yourself with the reports that will be used in your profession. Do some research into the types of reports you will be expected to write in your chosen field. Find examples, if possible, of types of reports that you may encounter in the future. This chapter and the following one will deal with the basic elements of reports, but you must supplement this information with the unique expectations of your field. This chapter discusses the short report. The next chapter describes the longer formal report.

Planning Reports

A report resembles every other form of written communication in that good planning is essential to its effectiveness. As with letters and memos, you need to analyze thoroughly the situation you will write about in the report. Figure 11.1 lists items to consider when planning a report.

What is the purpose of the report—to inform, analyze, recommend, or implement?

Who will read the report?

What are the pertinent interests and values of the readers?

Is there any action that may be taken on the basis of the report?

What situation/problem does the report address?

What is the history of the situation?

How much information, background, or analysis should the report include?

Which format would be most effective for the report?

How formal in format, tone, and style should the report be?

FIGURE 11.1 Planning Considerations for Reports

You should consider the purpose of a report carefully, since multiple purposes are often involved. Many reports are assigned to be written as part of a job responsibility. Thus, one of the purposes may be merely to meet this requirement. You might also write a report because you feel the situation requires some future action. Reports can identify vital problems and generate early solutions. In addition, reports demonstrate your competence as a writer and problem solver on the job. Thus, you can emphasize your ideas and abilities through your reports.

A thorough analysis of the audience helps to determine how much readers already know, what they need from the report, what attitudes they may have toward your ideas, and other factors that affect your writing. Before writing a report, you may need to gather some feedback about its topic, scope, length, and materials you should include.

If the report addresses a problem, you need to understand the history, causes, effects, and potential solutions to the problem before you propose a solution of your own. Again, talking about your ideas with informed sources as you plan the report will provide you with valuable feedback that may prevent you from making some tactical error in the report itself.

A final consideration in planning is to determine how formal the report needs to be. Short reports are usually informal. They include first-person and second-person pronouns ("I," "me," "my," "you," "we," "our") in discussing issues, and writers include more personal opinions. The informal approach makes the short report more personal and direct. Longer formal reports generally use only the third person ("the writer," "the investigating team," "the company"), and opinions are rarely offered. Writers of formal reports draw conclusions only after presenting substantial evidence. The formal report sounds more objective and professional in some people's minds. Currently, the trend is away from formal language and third-person usage, even in formal reports. You need to be sensitive, however, to the expectations of the readers and critics of the report you write when making decisions about the level of formality you will use.

Organizing Short Reports

A short report is a brief document, usually one to five double-spaced typed pages. It is often written in either a letter or memo format. The short report also uses headings to divide and organize the parts of the report. The use of headings makes the report logical in development and easier to read. The reader sees at a glance the contents of the report and can select which part to read in whatever order desired. For example, if a reader wants to read only the recommendations or wants to read them first, the division of the report by headings allows him or her to find them immediately.

Since there are so many types of short reports, this section covers only a few of the more common organizational patterns. You should adapt these patterns to your needs in specific situations. Depending on your specific purposes, you may need fewer or more headings than the sample outlines show in order to organize the parts of your report.

The *informative report* merely collects and summarizes data. In its simplest form, the informative report includes an introduction, body, and conclusion. The introduction states the purpose of the report and provides some background on the issue about which the report is written. If a unique procedure is used to gather the information, this detail may be included in the introduction as well. The body contains the findings of the research—the facts and statistics that fulfill the information needs of the reader. The conclusion usually summarizes the main points.

In some cases, you may wish to interpret the information you have found in your research. The *analytical report* expands on the informative pattern and allows you to draw conclusions on the basis of the information you present. Figure 11.2 outlines a common organizational pattern for analytical reports.

When preparing an analytical report, it is important to make a distinction between conclusions and recommendations. Conclusions are generalizations drawn from the facts that your research has uncovered. Recommendations are suggestions for action to be taken. Recommendations are based on conclusions: because you conclude that certain conditions exist, you recommend that certain actions should be taken. An analytical report need not have recommendations, since the analysis can end with the discussion of the findings and your conclusions. The analytical report can take a further step, however, and end with suggestions for action. When it does so, it overlaps

Introduction:	Purpose of the report.
	Background of the issue.
	Procedure used in the report (optional).
Body:	Findings
	Discussion of the findings.
Conclusion:	Conclusions.
	Recommendations (optional).

FIGURE 11.2 Formula for Analytical Reports

Introduction: Purpose of the report.

Body: Nature and scope of the problem.
Probable causes of the problem.
Criteria for a workable solution.
Possible solution.

Conclusion: Best solution (conclusions).
Implementation plan for the solution (optional).

FIGURE 11.3   Formula for Problem-Solving Reports

with the *recommendation report*. Other types of recommendation reports include the problem-solving report, the progress report, the periodic report, and the proposal.

The *problem-solving report* investigates the causes, effects, and possible solutions for a problem. Effective problem-solving reports follow the formula given in Figure 11.3. The problem-solving report can address several purposes: to propose a set of possible solutions, to propose a single best solution, or to offer a plan for implementing a solution. Thus, the exact structure of the report will depend on your purpose.

The *progress report* is used to clarify the status of a project and to recommend alterations needed to meet the objectives or timetable of the project. Progress reports identify problems early so that the project is less likely to be sidetracked by unexpected developments. Figure 11.4 outlines typical elements of the progress report.

The *periodic report* is similar to the progress report, but it is used in regular, ongoing work environments. For example, the departments of a company are often required to make periodic reports every week, month, quarter, or year. Since ongoing work may not be as schedule-driven as a special project, the findings do not include projected due dates. Figure 11.5 presents the formula for the typical periodic report.

The *proposal* is a type of report that outlines specific steps for solving a problem or meeting a need. It often uses elements of other types of reports for identifying the problem, analyzing its causes and effects, establishing criteria for a solution, and reviewing solutions that have already been tried. The key feature of the proposal is its detailed recommendation section, which outlines specific plans, schedules, personnel assignments, and costs for the implementation of a solution. Some companies use proposals to generate

Introduction: Brief statement of purpose or background.

Body: Current status of the project.
Work ahead of schedule.
Work behind schedule.
Problems encountered.

Conclusion: Recommendations.

FIGURE 11.4   Formula for Progress Reports

Introduction:	Brief orientation.
Body:	Current status of work.
	Significant developments since last report.
	Problems.
Conclusion:	Recommendations.

FIGURE 11.5 Formula for Periodic Reports

business: they identify problems and propose that they be hired to solve them. When a proposal is used in this way, it usually contains a section on the background and credibility of the writer who proposes the solution. Figure 11.6 lists the elements of a proposal.

There are two keys to organizing a short report. First, you must understand the overall structure of the purpose of the report and select headings that logically help you accomplish your purpose. The organizational pattern of a report should make sense to the reader; otherwise, you will confuse readers and fail to persuade them to accept your ideas. You must have a clear picture of the entire report and organize it for efficient reading.

The second key to organizing a report is to consider the impact of the order in which you place information. Place the most interesting and necessary facts first. Readers need not wade through unnecessary details if you know that what they want most are the conclusions or the recommendations of the report. Many reports place the summary, the conclusions, or the recommendations first and then provide the background, procedures or findings. Analyze your readers carefully, and structure your report to match their needs and interests. The result will be a more useful document that satisfies readers.

Short reports demonstrate your skills as both a valuable employee and a good writer. You demonstrate your analytical abilities, your skill in identifying and solving problems, and your initiative in proposing solutions. Moreover, a well-written report is excellent documentation of your communication skills. The short report is a valuable tool to both your career and your employer. By developing skill with this tool, you will do much to enhance your worth as an employee.

Introduction:	Purpose of the proposal.
Body:	Background of the problem situation.
	Criteria for a solution.
	Proposed solution.
	—Schedule for implementation
	—Personnel assignments
	—Budget
	Background of the proposers (optional).
Conclusion:	Contact step.

FIGURE 11.6 Formula for Proposals

EXERCISE 11.1
Organizing a Short Report

Directions: Imagine that you are in one of the following situations. List the steps you would use to organize a short report, in a brief, one-page preliminary outline.

Situation #1: The Analytical Report

You were an intern in a large accounting firm for the summer. When you return to school in the fall, the dean of the Business School asks you to write a short report evaluating your experience. The dean wishes to collect several such reports and publish them as a small handbook to encourage other students to take internships and to give them some advice on what to expect.

Situation #2: The Problem-Solving Report

You work in a sales department with five other people. You sell magazine subscriptions by phone to the general public. Your office has no receptionist. Incoming calls are answered by anyone who is free at the moment. This results in delays in answering calls and in time wasted by the sales staff providing answers to general questions that could be more efficiently handled by a secretary. You want to propose to your sales manager that a receptionist be hired to handle incoming calls.

Situation 3: The Recommendation Report

You work as an assistant manager in the credit office of a retail firm. You notice that most people in the office are dissatisfied with only one hour for lunch. Sixty minutes is not enough time to leave the building and purchase their lunches, as most would prefer to do. You want to propose to your boss a 90-minute lunch period that people could take if they make up the extra 30 minutes by coming in earlier or leaving later.

EXERCISE 11.2
Writing a Short Report

Directions: Write a short (four- or five-page) informative or recommendation report on one of the following topics.

Dealing with Absenteeism
Improving the Maintenance System
Advantages of Long-term Planning
Reducing Employee Turnover
Adopting an Incentive Pay System
Instituting a Flexible-Schedule Work System
The Values of Cooperative Education
The Advantages of an Internship Program
A Plan for Reducing Littering
The Need for a Training Program
Instituting a Child Care Plan
Developing an In-House Day Care Center
Adopting an Employee Health Plan
Improving Customer Relations
The Need for a New Course in Our School
Improving Food Service in the Office (or Dormitory)
A Plan for a More Effective Registration System

11
Short Reports

1. Interview a person who is currently employed in your future career area. Ask about the role of report writing in that industry:

   What types of reports are commonly used?
   What reports does this person write?
   What reports does this person read?
   What makes for effective report writing in that industry?

2. Ask the person you interviewed if you can read a typical short report used in that industry. As you read the report, critique it in terms of the guidelines suggested in this chapter.

12
Formal Reports

Formal reports provide information and investigate problems by using formal language and well-defined formats. The topics covered in formal reports are often the same as those in short reports, discussed in Chapter 11. Formal reports can inform, persuade, make recommendations, and provide a detailed plan for action. The major difference between the short report and the formal report is the depth of analysis and the resulting length. The formal report can vary from around ten to hundreds of pages.

Because of the length of the formal report, readers need assistance to digest the material. Thus, report writers offer a formal, logical organizational framework so that the report is easier to read. Many readers are too busy to read an entire report. They need the report to be clearly divided, logically organized, and summarized so that they can select the most useful parts to read. If the summaries do not satisfy readers' immediate needs, then the other parts of the report should be clearly labeled with subheadings so that readers can analyze them in greater detail.

This chapter discusses the parts of formal reports and various techniques for organizing the content of a report. With these techniques, you can organize information and present it in an especially readable manner.

The Parts of Formal Reports

Formal reports are traditionally divided into the parts listed in Figure 12.1. Not all reports have each of these sections, and some reports may add innovative elements that are not included on the list. The criteria for deciding which parts to include in a report depend on your assessment of the reader's needs and the most logical way of organizing the information you have to present. Select those parts which contain the information most necessary to your purpose.

Cover/binding.

Title page.

Letter of authorization.

Letter of transmittal (cover letter).

Table of contents.

List of Illustrations.

Summary (executive summary, synopsis, abstract).

Body of the report.

Glossary.

Appendix.

Footnotes.

Bibliography.

Index.

FIGURE 12.1 Parts of Formal Reports

There are similarities in format between the short report and the long report. As you can see from Figure 12.1, the formal report has a large number of parts. The body of a short report may be organized in the same manner as the formal report. The formal report may have more analysis, a greater number of findings, or more recommendations, but the purpose and basic organizational structure of the two types of reports are similar. Since the formal report includes much more data, the writer offers additional structural signposts to help the reader digest the information.

The *cover* or *binding* of a formal report holds the report together, protects the pages, and provides an attractive package. A company's logo can be stamped on the cover to personalize the report or make it look more professional.

The *title page* includes the title of the report, the name and position of the writer of the report, the person to whom the report is delivered, and the date of submission. The title of the report should contain key words indicating the topic areas covered in the report and the general purpose of the report. Avoid overly clever, literary, humorous, or mysterious titles, which may confuse or mislead the reader about the report's contents.

The *letter of authorization* is a copy of the original letter authorizing the report. It is often from the person to whom the report is delivered. Including the authorization justifies the time and effort spent in preparing the report, reminds the reader of the original purpose in requesting the report, and demonstrates the report's attempt to meet the needs expressed in the letter.

The *letter of transmittal*, or *cover letter*, is a personal message from the writer of the report to the reader. It provides an overview of the contents of the report and prepares the reader to be receptive toward the report. Figure 12.2 lists the typical contents of letters of transmittal.

The letter of transmittal is often the first thing the reader will see in a report, so you should select the contents carefully. If the findings of the report are straightforward and expected, then the transmittal can be a brief summary of the entire report. If, however, the report findings are likely to be controversial or upsetting, then you should include only a few details about

Introduction:	Establish positive relationship with the reader.
	Announce that the report is enclosed.
Body:	Summarize the major conclusions.
	Briefly review the major recommendations.
Conclusion:	Invite further communication if necessary.
	Offer a positive, cordial close.

FIGURE 12.2   Formula for Letters of Transmittal

the report's contents in the letter and encourage the reader to analyze the complete report. Likewise, if you expect the reader to disagree with the findings, you can establish your credibility in detail in the opening letter. If you have any personal comments to the reader that will assist him or her in understanding the contents of the report, these comments should be made in the cover letter.

The *table of contents* provides the reader with a list of the headings used in the report and the page numbers on which the sections begin. The table of contents can be as detailed as you feel is necessary, including only the major section headings or the subheadings used for smaller organizational units as well. The report should be paginated with arabic numerals (1, 2, 3, 4, etc.) starting with the body of the report. Use lower-case roman numerals (i, ii, iii, iv, etc.) for the introductory material: title page, introductory letters, table of contents, and tables of figures.

The *list of illustrations* indicates where graphic elements—figures, charts, graphs, photographs, and other visual materials—can be found in the body of the report. This list helps the reader find this information quickly.

The *summary* is a brief—one page or less—condensation of the report. The purpose of the summary is to give the busy reader a quick overview of the entire content. The summary should include the purpose, the methodology, the main conclusions, and the principal recommendations of the report. If the reader wants more detail, he or she can learn from the table of contents where to find the information in the body of the report.

The *body of the report* can be organized in many ways, depending on your purpose. Use the organizational pattern that you think is the most appropriate way to structure the information you have to present. Chapter 11 suggested several organizational patterns for reports. Review these patterns and use them for formal reports when they suit your purpose. The formal report often elaborates on these basic patterns and develops the introduction, findings, and conclusion sections more fully. Figure 12.3 lists sample headings that you can use in structuring a formal report.

The report should be organized so that the reader clearly understands the method you used in writing the report. As a writer, you want the reader to understand at all times where the report is going. You should state your overall purpose at the beginning of the report, and each element in the body should be logically subordinated to that ultimate purpose. The reader should finish the report satisfied that the purpose has been achieved.

A *glossary* is sometimes added at the end of a report to define any new or unusual terms that you use in the body. The reader can refer to the glossary if there is any confusion about the meaning of a word or abbreviation.

Introduction:

Origin of the Report	Overview
History of the Issue	Background Information
Subject and Purpose	What Is the Situation?
Purpose of the Report	What Is the Problem?
The Problem	Review of the Literature
Definition of the Problem	Rationale
The Situation	Research Methodology
Statement of the Problem	Definitions

Body:

Explanation of the Causes	Recommended Solution
Specific Complaints	Supporting Reasons
Who Is Affected?	Benefits
What Happened	Advantages
What Was Observed	Disadvantages
Description	The Basic Plan
Analysis	Technical Plan
Results of the Study	Management Plan
Discussion of the Findings	Implementation Plan
Other Solutions Considered	What Should We Do?
Other Options	What Can We Do?

Conclusion:

Conclusions	Evaluation
Recommendations	Suggestions
Summary	Recommended Action
Implications	Where Do We Go from Here?

FIGURE 12.3   Sample Headings for Formal Reports

An *appendix* contains bulky amounts of raw data that would clutter the body of the report and make it difficult to read. When dealing with large amounts of facts and figures, it is usual to discuss only general details in the body and to refer the reader to the appendices for more specific details.

The *bibliography* cites all the published sources used in the preparation of the report. You should include the authors and titles of works you consulted, places of publication, publishers, dates of publication, and page references—usually in that order. A thorough bibliography is a valuable tool for other people who wish to research your subject further.

Footnotes are citations for the direct quotation of data or original ideas from other people's works. Failure to give credit for a direct quotation from someone else's writing is plagiarism, an illegal activity if the work is copyrighted and an unethical act even if it is not.

An *index* lists the page references for key terms, names, and ideas you use throughout your report. The reader can use the index to locate your discussion of a particular idea in the text of the report. Indexes are used only in extremely long reports and in books.

Techniques for Organizing Formal Reports

As the writer of a formal report, you must make choices about the number of parts to use, the pattern of organization, the data to include, and the management of large amounts of information. When preparing the report, do not forget the elements of good writing that have been discussed earlier in this text: clarity of purpose, accuracy of facts and writing mechanics, completeness of coverage, appropriateness of style, and dynamism. The formal report is similar to any other piece of business writing in its demands for good grammar, punctuation, and readability. The following suggestions will help you polish your formal report.

START WITH A CLEAR PURPOSE

As you begin to prepare the report, make sure you fully understand your purpose as a writer and the expectations of your readers. Analyze the audience carefully and gather as much advance feedback as you can to ensure that your report will be focused and complete. State your purpose early in the report so that the reader knows what you intend to do. This early warning prevents the reader from having expectations different from those you intend to fulfill.

CHOOSE AN ORGANIZATIONAL PATTERN

Consider several ways of organizing the material you have to present. Weight the advantages and disadvantages of each pattern and select the one that presents your data in the most interesting and effective way. Too often writers do not realize that a different order of presentation or a different way of organizing can have great impact on clarity and readability.

PUT THE MOST IMPORTANT INFORMATION FIRST

Analyze carefully the information you have to present. What is most important to the reader? What is most critical for the reader to understand? What will help the reader in understanding the rest of the report? The answers to these questions point to the information that should probably be placed near the beginning of the report so that the reader is oriented and prepared to understand your findings. You can place key elements in the letter of transmittal, in the executive summary, or in the opening paragraphs of the body of the report. Help the reader understand the major points of the report by placing the crucial, "bottom line" elements in prominent places unless you have a specific reason for deemphasizing them.

USE HEADINGS TO DIVIDE THE REPORT

The most effective technique for organizing a report is to use headings. Analyze your data and divide it into logical sections. Label each part with a heading that describes the contents of that section. The pattern of the headings helps the reader understand the overall scheme of your report, and the headings break up large blocks of text with white space that makes for easier reading.

USE VISUAL DEVICES FOR LARGE AMOUNTS OF DATA

When dealing with significant amounts of numerical or statistical data, long lists, or visual details, you can make your report easier to read by using visual aids. Graphs, such as line, bar, and pie graphs, organize numerical data. Charts explain the parts of a process or an organization. Diagrams are a visual representation of information. Figure 12.4 illustrates several types of visual aids that you can incorporate into reports.

When you add visual elements to your reports, label each one with a descriptive word such as "Figure" or "Table." Number the figures consecutively from the beginning of the report to the end. Provide a title for each figure that describes its content or major idea. If you have many figures, you can provide a guide to them with a separate table of figures in the report's table of contents.

CHECK YOUR REPORT FOR ACCURACY

Once you have completed the report, proofread it for accuracy and clarity, as you would any piece of business writing. You may wish to divide a longer report among co-workers for proofreading. Check that page numbers are accurate, internal references are clear, all parts are assembled in order, and all intended elements are included. In a large and complex writing project like a formal report, it is easy to neglect the proofreading stage. Much of the work you have done in the report to increase your credibility, however, can quickly be undone by errors or oversights that could easily be corrected at the proofreading stage. Proofread carefully.

The formal report is a challenge for the business writer. It demands skill in being able to select, organize, and present large amounts of information in a coherent and interesting way. By following the guidelines that this chapter has presented, you should be able to select the elements that best suit your purpose and organize them for maximum comprehension.

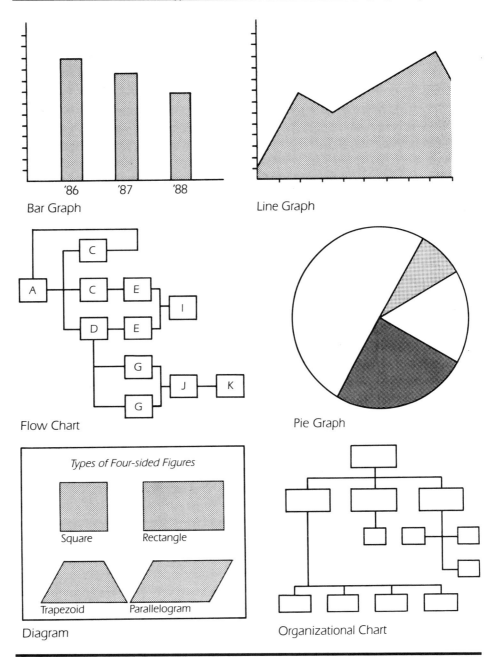

FIGURE 12.4 Visual Aids for Reports

EXERCISE 12.1
Organizing a Formal Report

Directions: The typical elements of a formal report are included below in jumbled order. Cut along the lines and rearrange them in the order that you feel most effectively accomplishes the report's purpose.

Appendix A	List of tables	Possible causes
Letter of transmittal	Recommendations	Benefits of the proposed solution
Other solutions attempted	Table of contents	The proposed solution
Implementation plan	Title page	Disadvantages of the proposed solution
Executive summary	Background of the problem	Schedule, budget, and staffing needs

EXERCISE 12.2
Critiquing a Formal-Report Outline

Directions: Bob Dill works at an auto insurance company as a claims adjuster. The company's current filing system is alphabetical by name of client. Each time a client makes a claim, the paperwork is filed by the client's last name. This system has resulted in an extremely uneven workload distribution among employees, since each adjuster is assigned to handle three letters of the alphabet. The adjuster who is responsible for clients R-S-T has a much larger work load than the one who has clients X-Y-Z.

Bob wrote a formal report in which he analyzed the problems with the current filing system and proposed a new plan that would organize claims numerically by the date of their submission. Each adjuster could then be assigned an equal number of cases. The outline of Bob's report is given below.

Critique the organizational structure of Bob's outline. How might he have organized it more logically?

BOB'S OUTLINE	YOUR IMPROVED OUTLINE
Title Page: A Plan for Reorganizing the Office Filing System	_____
Table of Contents	_____
A Note to the Reader	_____
What Other Offices Are Doing	_____
Why We Have an Alphabetical System	_____
Benefits of a Numerical System	_____
What Is Wrong with the Present System	_____
What We Ought to Do	_____
Recommendations	_____
Summary	_____
Appendix A: The Present Filing Plan	_____
Appendix B: The Proposed Plan for a New Numerical Filing System	_____

EXERCISE 12.3
Writing an Outline for a Formal Report

Directions: Select one of the following topics and compose an outline for a formal report that would deal with the issue.

The Company Profile of a Potential Employer
Analysis of a Current Work Problem
Instituting a Performance Appraisal System
Developing a Fitness Plan
A Plan for an Inventory Control System
The Need for Telephone System Improvements
A Plan for Redesigning the Workspace
Banking System Improvements
Developing a Fringe Benefits Package
A Plan to Increase Retail Sales
Improving Telephone Techniques
The Need to Replace Machinery
An Employee Stock Ownership Plan
Needed Change in Production Procedures
Improving Worker Morale
Instituting a Quality-Circle System
Reasons for Purchasing a Mobile Telephone System

ACTION ASSIGNMENT

12
Formal Reports

1. Visit a department within your city or county government—such as health, transportation, planning, or education—or visit the mayor's office. Explain that you are a student in a business communications class and that you have been assigned to analyze a formal report. Ask to buy or borrow a copy of a short formal report (under 30 pages) written by a consultant. Critique the report on the basis of the guidelines suggested in this chapter:

   Is the cover letter used effectively?
   Is the table of contents clear?
   Is an introductory summary used?
   Is the report clearly organized?
   Is the report clearly written?
   How does the writer use visual aids in the report?
   What appendices are used in the report?

2. Obtain a copy of the annual report of a large corporation or other business. Annual reports are usually available in large libraries (ask the reference librarian for their location), in student placement services, or directly from the company. Analyze the report on the basis of the guidelines suggested in this chapter.

unit III

EMPLOYMENT AND INTERVIEWING SKILLS: JOB SEARCH, APPLICATIONS, RÉSUMÉS, AND INTERVIEWING

Job-Search Skills

Your communication skills will be tested to their fullest when it comes time to locate and apply for a job. While many people may be qualified for a position, an employer must somehow choose among several applicants. The ability to communicate your skills and abilities in writing and interviewing often makes the difference between being selected and being rejected for a job. This unit explores these job-search communication skills: application letters, résumés, letters of recommendation, information-gathering interviews, and employment interviews.

Before you can prepare or write these types of communications for the job search, you need to do serious career planning. Many students and job-seekers often face difficulty in preparing for a job search. Have you ever been stymied by any of these concerns?

"I really don't know what I want to do."
"I don't have any experience."
"I don't have some of the skills the employers say they want."
"I don't know what my skills are."
"I can't seem to find any attractive job openings."
"Why would someone want to hire me?"

These attitudes frequently keep people from applying for jobs they could easily attain, and, worse yet, they lead to a great deal of fear and frustration in the job search. If you are serious about achieving your full potential as a worker and in getting a job that you enjoy, you must first address the concerns in this list.

Many people find the career search intimidating, but their fears can be overcome by simple career planning. The following chapter investigates the preliminary planning necessary to complete these crucial career-search steps:

Determine your career goals.
Identify your skills and abilities.
Find job leads.
Plan the job-search strategy.

With good planning, you will discover and develop a satisfying and exciting career. An additional benefit in learning these skills is that you will be better prepared to advance in your career once you land your first job. Studies show that Americans change jobs on the average of once every three years, and they change career paths twice in their lifetimes.[1] Each of these changes requires a job search. By thoroughly learning job-search skills at the beginning of your career, you will be better prepared when the next job search becomes necessary. It will be easier to plan and manage, and you should be even more successful at it.

Determining Your Career Goals

The single greatest career concern for most people is that they are not clear about their goals or what they want to do with their work lives. This lack of clarity makes it very difficult for them to find a job, because they do not know where to begin to look for job openings. If a position becomes available, the person without clear career goals often lacks confidence and enthusiasm about going after the job. These attitudes lessen the chances of being an attractive candidate. Even when people know the type of job they want, they may not have considered fully where the job leads and how it can be used as a stepping stone to even greater career fulfillment.

In clarifying your career goals, begin by identifying the activities you enjoy. Let us say, for example, that you are an accounting major (or English, or physical education, or whatever) or that you currently have a job as a retail clerk (or waiter, or manager, or whatever). Why do you have that major or job? Do you enjoy the activities involved in it? If you do not, then the chances are low that you are going to be happy with a job that demands those activities. If you are an accounting major but you do not enjoy your accounting classes, then is it realistic to think that you will enjoy an accounting job any better?

So what *do* you enjoy? How do you spend your free time? What do you enjoy most in school? What do you enjoy most about your current job? What areas would you like to know more about but have never explored? The answer to each of these questions will lead you toward many different career possibilities. Every interest you enjoy is associated with many potential careers. Have you ever considered those as possible career paths?

Many people overlook the obvious answer to their lack of a career goal: do what you enjoy and make a job out of it. If a person loves dogs more than anything else in the world, then why should he or she become an accountant if that is not going to be a satisfying job? Of course, there are many ways to combine interests. The person with the accounting major could become an accountant for a large dog kennel or some other canine business. Another combination might be to work part-time as an accountant in a small firm and start a dog-breeding business on the side. Since accounting is a fine career path which many people do enjoy, perhaps a person with an interest in dogs could develop a short-term career in accounting until a dog-related business becomes feasible.

There are infinite ways in which new and exciting careers can be found or created. Unfortunately, many people rely only on traditional career paths that other people have chosen for them. Analyzing yourself is the best way to find *your* career path. A useful tool for this analysis is the "Career Search Inventory" developed by Richard Bolles.[2] A similar career-search tool is in Exercise 13.1 at the end of this chapter. Step One of this exercise will help you identify possible careers by analyzing how you spend your time. By analyzing what you do at home, at school, and at work, you can find the activities you are successful at and enjoy doing. This self-knowledge, more than any other preparation, will help you determine your career goals. If you have any trouble completing Step One, you may wish to see a career counselor, who can give you personal attention in determining your interests and skills.

You have to be prepared to reconsider career goals occasionally, because your interests and abilities may change as you are exposed to new information and experiences. Throughout your professional life you should constantly be aware of how your interests change; new career opportunities may be just around the corner. Career counselors can help you clarify and identify your interests and abilities. Your school or local community health center may offer useful career-guidance programs.

In general, the more time you invest in thoroughly analyzing your goals, the better the results. Give serious thought to what you want out of a career, where the career will take you, and why you want that career. Even if you are committed to a certain career path at present, keeping an open mind about possible changes may lead to new opportunities. A clear direction at the start of your career will keep you on a sure and satisfying path to your desired ends. Remaining flexible will help you as your career progresses.

Determining Your Skills and Abilities

In general, there are two approaches to getting a job: active and passive. These two approaches are summarized in Figure 13.1. Which one characterizes you?

The Active Approach	vs.	The Passive Approach
I want to develop my own interests.	or	I am willing to do what somebody else wants.
I want to develop my own skills.	or	I just want to use the skills I have.
I want to move up.	or	I just want to get by.
I want to create a career.	or	I just want to find a job.
I see myself as a "rising star" and a professional.	or	I just hold a job.
I can motivate myself.	or	I need other people in order to be motivated.
I am an active career-path finder.	or	I am a passive career-path follower.

FIGURE 13.1 Two Approaches to Getting a Job

It is much easier to start a career search if you develop the attitudes of an active career finder and professional. If you are interested in your career, if you see yourself as a professional, and if you are optimistic about your chances, then many more opportunities will come your way—because you will make your own opportunities. Finding a job is hard work, but the effort will result in a satisfying and rewarding career.

The path to being a professional rather than just a "jobholder" can begin at any time in your career. Do you belong to your profession's organizations so that you know people and feel at home in the profession? Do you read professional newsletters and journals so that you know what is going on in your profession? Do you attend professional meetings? Do you talk to others about professional problems and solutions? Do you work on projects that will advance your standing in the profession? These techniques will give you a sense of professionalism and will provide contacts and knowledge that will be extremely useful when the time comes to look for a job.

Having a self-motivated attitude about your job search makes it much easier to determine your skills and abilities. Passive jobseekers usually see skills and abilities only as a "minimum requirement" to getting a job. Active jobseekers see the job as an "opportunity" to use their skills and to develop new ones. Any prospective employer wants an applicant to arrive with skills useful to the tasks of the job. But most jobs require that a worker be able to learn new skills easily and quickly. Thus, most employers will look for much more than just the "minimum required skills" necessary to do a job. They want an employee who is eager and willing to learn new skills and one who can develop additional ones.

An employer looks for three basic groups of traits in a prospective employee: skills, knowledge, and abilities. A *skill* is a task behavior, such as manual dexterity, physical strength, typing, organizing an office, managing a work group, or researching a report. *Knowledge* is the possession of useful information, such as where resources are located in a library, who the key people in an industry are, how to do a certain process, or what the relevant facts about a certain subject are. *Abilities* are the psychological characteristics that make skills and knowledge useful, such as being logical, prompt, detail-oriented, patient, assertive, energetic, or cheerful. These three groups of desirable traits are often called *transferable skills* because they can be taken with you from one job to the next. They are also transferable because they can come from other life experiences besides the job.

Every person has hundreds of skills that will be useful in a new job. Your task as a jobhunter is to identify what skills the employer needs and then show that you have them. You may have some work-related skills that a prior job gave you, but do not overlook transferable skills that you have gained at school or through your personal interests. This advice is particularly important for people who feel that they do not have any "experience." Everyone has ample experience—the task is to show and explain how your experience has given you transferable skills that will fill the needs of a future employer.

Steps Two and Three of Exercise 13.1 assist you in identifying your transferable skills, knowledge, and abilities. A good way to identify your transferable skills is to enumerate your achievements in the three aspects of your life: home, work, and school. Step Two asks you to write down your achievements from different periods of your life. An achievement statement is an objective, honest, and factual account of something you are proud of having done. You need not have won an award or trophy for an activity in order to list it as an achievement, nor does anyone else need to know of it—but you need to be aware of your achievements. This list of achievements will become the elements you use later to build your résumé, application letter, and interview. Step Three asks you to identify the skills, knowledge, or ability it took to accomplish each achievement. Employers want to know about your skills, knowledge, and abilities. By identifying your achievements and the skills it took to accomplish them, you acquire good evidence of your transferable or applicable skills. It is essential to examine your skills, knowledge, and abilities because you need to be able to talk comfortably and confidently about them.

When you find a job you want, you need to analyze the job in terms of the skills, knowledge, and abilities it would take to do the job well. Go beyond just the minimum requirements and ask, What would it take to do an excellent job? If significant numbers of your skills and abilities match the skills and abilities needed to do a job, then you have a good chance of getting that job. It does not matter if your skills and abilities were developed in a slightly different context. As long as you can present yourself as a person having solid experience, including a set of skills and abilities that the employer wants, then you have a chance of getting the job. Often an employer values an applicant who has a positive attitude about working far more than an applicant who merely has the right set of skills, so do not underestimate your chances if you do not have direct experience for a position.

Listed in Figure 13.2 are typical job-related transferable skills. As you analyze your experience in Steps Two and Three of Exercise 13.1, take care to include these skills if you have them.

While it is important to identify your abilities, the traits essential for different jobs will differ. When you look for a job, develop a precise list of your pertinent, transferable skills, knowledge, and abilities that qualify you for the job. This list will help you both in targeting the kinds of jobs you want and in developing skills for a future potential employer. Exercise 13.2 at the

Managing	Supervising	Coordinating
Evaluating	Planning	Scheduling
Organizing	Delegating	Establishing priorities
Budgeting	Accounting	Auditing
Appraising	Researching	Analyzing
Persuading	Reasoning	Selling
Recruiting	Negotiating	Writing
Motivating	Operating	Assembling
Shipping	Interviewing	Investigating
Gathering data	Critiquing	Listening
Understanding	Assisting	Instructing
Innovating	Being creative	Imagining
Performing	Advising	Informing
Training	Encouraging	Explaining
Inventing	Facilitating	Arranging
Classifying	Processing	Recording
Bookkeeping	Record keeping	Administering

FIGURE 13.2 Common Transferable Skills

end of this chapter guides you in analyzing a particular career. Your analysis can be aided by doing some research in the following career-information resources, which are available in most libraries:

Dictionary of Occupational Titles: contains descriptions of job titles in the United States and is subdivided by occupational areas.

Occupational Outlook Handbook: contains job descriptions, salary expectations, employment prospects for the future, and addresses for requesting further information.

Jobs Almanac: contains more extensive and interesting information than the above two books, including more current career areas, current salary levels, and a more complete analysis of professional-level jobs.

Finding Job Leads

Now that you know the kind of job you want and the skills and abilities you have to bring to that job, the next task is to locate a job opening. Many people automatically assume that the classified advertisement section of the local newspaper is the place to find a job. That is a very dangerous assumption, since it is estimated that 90 percent of available jobs are never advertised but instead are filled through personal contacts.[3] Help-wanted ads can be useful for certain types of jobs, but the careful jobseeker should also develop personal contacts within a prospective employment market in order to be in the right place at the right time. Analyzing and responding to want ads will be discussed in greater detail in Chapter 14. This chapter focuses on the "hidden job market," the 90 percent of available jobs that must be unearthed by the active jobseeker.

There are many useful techniques for finding job leads in the hidden job market. Getting involved in professional activities puts you in an advantageous position for learning about job openings and meeting people in social and business contexts who know of job openings. Many schools provide students with professional introductions to businesses: internships, cooperative education opportunities, special projects in business settings, and student chapters of professional organizations. All these activities provide excellent ways of making business contacts. On-campus interviews help you meet local business representatives. Volunteer activities in your community often put you into contact with business people, and various civic organizations create a meeting place for young professionals and business leaders. If you are already employed in your career area, take care to meet people, to go to industry events, and to learn your way around your business area.

Sometimes you will have to take the initiative and introduce yourself to total strangers—an activity termed "cold calling" in sales. If you have to use cold calling in order to meet people in your profession, Chapter 17, on information-gathering interviews, will be useful in providing a technique for acquainting yourself with prospective employers. You can get to know strangers within your profession if you take the time to prepare and conduct meaningful interviews. You can also gather useful information about your career area and specific companies that interest you.

Since the hidden job market depends entirely on personal contacts, you need to develop a network of acquaintances who can funnel information to you about job leads. Exercise 13.3 at the end of this chapter is a networking chart that you can use to prepare for your job search. You need to alert everyone you know to the fact that you are looking for a job. Be prepared to explain the specific kind of job you want. Through your network you can gather much more information about job leads than you can obtain on your own. Friends or people you meet who work in interesting companies can spot openings for you. They can also introduce you to business contacts who may help you with information-gathering interviews.

One final technique for finding job leads, particularly when you know the specific company where you want to work, is to go to the target job site and do some investigating. You may be able to set up some information-gathering interviews, find notices of job openings on bulletin boards, or meet people in the cafeteria who are willing to share information about job prospects within the company. Most people are glad to be helpful if you give them the chance. By putting yourself in the right place at the right time, you may find an opening. Of course, you want to abide by standards of decorum and integrity when job hunting, so avoid being overly pushy or obnoxious when investigating. An active job search, however, will yield far greater results than a passive one. Be prepared for some refusals to share information, because people in business may not always be able to take the time to help you. Ultimately, your job search will succeed if you are diligent.

Exercise 13.4 provides a worksheet for discovering information about job leads. You may think it is early to begin exploring actual job openings; but the more information you gather early in the job search, the more you will know when you actually begin looking for a job. Identifying and exploring job leads, even when you are not currently looking for a job, gives you practice in developing your network, using your information-gathering skills, and exploring new career options. Using the list of possible career areas identified at the end of Exercise 13.1, analyze the sources of information for finding job leads in those areas. If you are actually looking for a job, use the worksheet to explore specific openings in the area you seek.

Planning Job-Search Strategies

For an efficient job search, you need an overall strategy. A combination of self-analysis, writing application letters and résumés, information-gathering interviews, and employment interviews is the best approach to use in finding a job. The remaining chapters in this unit are designed to develop your skills in each of these job-search activities.

You need to prepare each part of the strategy carefully. The first task, which you have already begun in this chapter, is to determine exactly what you want to do. You may have several different job targets, or you may have only one. Analyze the transferable skills, knowledge, and abilities you have for each one. Know your accomplishments and be ready to show an employer how you will be an excellent worker.

As you find each job opening, analyze it for the skills and abilities the employer will want—not only those stated in the want ad or job description but also those which are unstated. Chapters 14 and 15 will help you identify your target jobs and write effective application letters and résumés. Chapter 16 discusses the value of letters of reference to support your job applications. Information-gathering interviews, discussed in Chapter 17, are useful in gathering additional information in any phase of the job search. Chapters 18 and 19 help you to anticipate the kinds of questions that you will face and to prepare a strong presentation of your most valuable skills and abilities in a job interview.

Coordinate all aspects of the job search so that you give as much helpful information as possible to the employer. Do not duplicate in the application letter the information presented in the résumé. Likewise, in an interview do not merely repeat the contents of the application letter. Prepare each unit of the job search as a separate but coordinated activity. Consider what would best be said in each part: the letter, the résumé, and the interview. By coordinating the individual tactical units, you will make your overall strategy stronger.

Looking for a job is a full-time job in itself. If you are unemployed, you should set up a schedule to keep yourself busy looking for a job at least four hours a day. Search for job leads. Keep careful records of names, addresses, and telephone numbers. Schedule information-gathering interviews. Seek help from job-placement services and other career resources. Read books on jobseeking skills. Talk to the people in your network. They will encourage you and keep you active in your search. By staying active, you will keep yourself motivated and encouraged. Jobseeking is hard work, but the time and energy you invest in it will pay off. You will get the job you want, and you will set your career on a successful course.

NOTES

1. See Richard A. Bolles, *What Color Is Your Parachute? A Practical Manual for Job Hunters* (Belmont, Calif.: Wadsworth, 1986), and Richard A. Bolles, *The Three Boxes of Life* (Berkeley, Calif.: Ten Speed Press, 1985). An expanded version of the Career Search Inventory is available from Ten Speed Press for $2.00. Write P.O. Box 379, Walnut Creek, CA 94596.
2. Bolles, *The Three Boxes of Life.*
3. See Carl R. Boll, *Executive Jobs Unlimited* (New York: Macmillan, 1979).

RESOURCES

Bolles, Richard A. *What Color Is Your Parachute? A Practical Manual for Job Hunters.* (Belmont, Calif.: Wadsworth, 1986.)

This book is the "bible" of job-search techniques. It is extremely helpful for career planning and for using the information-gathering interview. It has an excellent bibliography and special sections on jobhunting for women, members of minorities, and handicapped people.

Bolles, Richard A. *The Three Boxes of Life*. Berkeley, Calif.: Ten Speed Press, 1985.

This book is very useful for analyzing the three aspects of life: home, school, and work.

Figler, Howard. *The Complete Job Search Handbook*. New York: Holt, Rinehart and Winston, 1980.

This is a very useful book for all aspects of the job-search process, especially for people who are shy or have limited jobhunting experience.

Irish, Richard K. *Go Hire Yourself an Employer*. Garden City, N.Y.: Anchor Books, 1978.

This book explains the philosophy that puts the applicant, not the employer, in the driver's seat. It is very good at explaining the necessity of "enjoyment" as a hiring criterion.

Mencke, Reed, and Ronald L. Hummel. *Career Planning for the 80s*. Monterey, Calif.: Brooks/Cole, 1984.

This book provides a good overview of all aspects of the job-search process. Written in workbook form, it has a highly practical section on career planning.

EXERCISE 13.1
Your Career Inventory

The following outline guides you in developing a career inventory—a self-analysis by which you will discover your interests, skills, knowledge, and abilities. This exercise will help you in determining which career areas to explore, what to include in résumés and applications, and how to present yourself as a skilled and valuable employee in interviews.

Work through the three steps: experiences, achievements, and skills. Fill in as many blanks as you can recall. As time passes, more experiences may come to you, so be prepared to add other elements as you recall them. There are no "right" answers. The inventory is based entirely on your experience. The more thorough you are in completing it, the more useful the inventory will be in planning the résumé, the application, and the interview. You may need to supplement the pages provided here with additional sheets of paper.

STEP ONE: ANALYZING YOUR LIFE EXPERIENCES

Directions: List below the major ways in which you have spent your time in three areas: home, school, and work. Include things that are relevant to your career search (such as skills you have developed, knowledge you have gained, or abilities it takes to do these things). Also include things that may not have any apparent career application but which you enjoy or spend a lot of time with.

A. Home Life

Chores: 1. _____

2. _____

3. _____

4. _____

Duties: 1. _____

2. _____

3. _____

4. _____

Volunteer work: 1. _____

2. _____

3. _____

Activities/crafts: 1. _____

2. _____

3. _____

Interests/hobbies: 1. _____

2. _____

3. _____

B. School Life

Major courses: 1. _____

2. _____

3. _____

4. _____

Special projects: 1. _____

2. _____

3. _____

4. _____

Activities: 1. _____

2. _____

3. _____

4. _____

Leadership positions: 1. _____

2. _____

3. _____

4. _____

Awards and honors: 1. _____

2. _____

3. _____

C. Work Life
   Position #1:

   Duties/responsibilities: _____

   _____

   Promotions/raises: _____

   _____

   Special skills/training: _____

   _____

   Position #2:

   Duties/responsibilities: _____

   _____

   Promotions/raises: _____

   _____

   Special skills/training: _____

   _____

   Position #3:

   Duties/responsibilities: _____

   _____

   Promotions/raises: _____

   _____

   Special skills/training: _____

   _____

D. Insight:
   On the basis of the analysis of how you spend your time, list ten career areas in which you could spend time doing activities you enjoy. For example, if you enjoy remodeling your house, how might that become a career? If one of your work responsibilities is ordering stock, how might that be worked into a career area? Notice particularly how interests and skills could be combined in unique ways.

1. _____

   _____

2. _____

   _____

3. _____

   _____

4. _____

   _____

5. _____

   _____

6. _____

   _____

7. _____

   _____

8. _____

   _____

9. _____

   _____

10. _____

   _____

STEP TWO: UNCOVERING YOUR ACHIEVEMENTS

Directions: Review your experiences and reflect for a moment on areas of success and accomplishment. Make a list of the twenty most important achievements you feel you have made in your life, no matter which area they were in—home, school, or work. You may not have received an award or public recognition for these achievements, but they are the ones that make you feel proud.

1. _____
2. _____
3. _____
4. _____
5. _____
6. _____
7. _____
8. _____
9. _____
10. _____
11. _____
12. _____
13. _____
14. _____
15. _____
16. _____
17. _____
18. _____
19. _____
20. _____

STEP THREE: IDENTIFYING YOUR SKILLS, KNOWLEDGE, AND ABILITIES

Directions: From your list of twenty achievements, select the ten most important ones and analyze for the skill, knowledge, or ability that it took to accomplish each. Be exhaustive in listing what it took to achieve each success. This list will serve as the basis for your strongest "selling points" when you write the résumé and application letter and prepare for the interview.

ACHIEVEMENT

1. _____

   Skills: _____

   _____

   Knowledge: _____

   _____

   Abilities: _____

   _____

2. _____

   Skills: _____

   _____

   Knowledge: _____

   _____

   Abilities: _____

   _____

3. _____

   Skills: _____

   _____

   Knowledge: _____

   _____

   Abilities: _____

   _____

4. _____

Skills: _____

_____

Knowledge: _____

_____

Abilities: _____

_____

5. _____

Skills: _____

_____

Knowledge: _____

_____

Abilities: _____

_____

6. _____

Skills: _____

_____

Knowledge: _____

_____

Abilities: _____

_____

7. _____

Skills: _____

_____

Knowledge: _____

_____

Abilities: _____

_____

8. _____

Skills: _____

_____

Knowledge: _____

_____

Abilities: _____

_____

9. _____

Skills: _____

_____

Knowledge: _____

_____

Abilities: _____

_____

10. _____

Skills: _____

_____

Knowledge: _____

_____

Abilities: _____

_____

EXERCISE 13.2
Analyzing Your Career Path

Directions: Select a general career area or a specific job you might like to attain in the future. Determine what skills (task-related behaviors), knowledge (sets of information), and abilities (personality factors) are necessary to perform well in that job or career area. Conduct your analysis by answering the following questions.

The job/career area that interests me: _____

What skills are necessary in the job?

_____

_____

_____

_____

What knowledge is necessary in the job?

_____

_____

_____

_____

What abilities are necessary in the job?

_____

_____

_____

_____

EXERCISE 13.3
Networking Worksheet

Directions: With the following grid, identify people who are already in your network. Be as thorough as you can in listing whom you know and how they may help you find a job lead.

Relatives	Friends
Friends of relatives	Friends of friends
Past employers	Past business associates
Doctor, dentist, etc.	Lawyer, banker, etc.

College acquaintances	Teachers, professors
Politicians, public officials	Insurance, real estate agents
Business owners	Clergy, church members
Trade union, professional association members	Other

EXERCISE 13.4
Identifying Job Leads

Directions: This exercise is designed to help you find job leads once you know the type of job you want. In the spaces provided, list the names of people whom you already know or whom you need to meet who can offer you information about job openings. Once you have made this list, identify the people who would be most likely to help you. This becomes your working contact sheet of people you should make an effort to meet, interview, and get to know.

The job you want: _____

People who already hold this job:

_____

_____

_____

People in professional organizations who know about this job:

_____

_____

_____

Professors or teachers who know about this job:

_____

_____

_____

People in related jobs or companies who know about this job:

_____

_____

_____

EXERCISE 13.5
Writing Your "Dream Job" Want Ad

Directions: Using the self-analysis of your interests, skills, knowledge, and abilities that you have done in this chapter, compose a want ad for the job that you would desire if anything were possible. Do not limit yourself to a job for which you already have the skills or even to a job that exists. Invent a job, if you like, in which you could best pursue your interests, use the skills you enjoy, and develop the knowledge you find most interesting.

STEP ONE: COMPOSE THE WANT AD

_____

_____

_____

_____

_____

_____

_____

_____

_____

_____

STEP TWO: MAKE IT A REALITY

Directions: Analyze your ad for transferable skills. What skills, knowledge, and abilities do you already have that would qualify you for this job? What do you need to develop? Do you think you can reach this potential? What will it take to achieve this potential?

14
Application Letters

In applying for a job, you may be required to submit an application letter. Even when one is not required, writing an application letter is a useful strategy to supplement the information presented in a résumé or an interview. This chapter discusses the two types of application letters, and outlines specific steps for writing them. By tailoring your application letter, you will appear to be the "ideal candidate" to the employer.

The application letter accomplishes several goals in the job-search process. It reviews and stresses your major skills, interests, and accomplishments. It also illustrates your command of the English language and your skill as a communicator. Finally, the application letter provides an opportunity for you to communicate your personality to the employer. Most résumés contain only technical details about jobs held, skills used, and educational records. Rarely does a sense of the "real person" come through in a résumé. Thus, the application letter reinforces the technical details of the résumé while revealing your personality: your confidence, your sense of achievement, your interests, and your insight into the nature of the job for which you are applying.

Some announcements of job openings request only a résumé. In such cases, you need to decide whether a letter of application should accompany your résumé. By submitting a letter of application, you can communicate twice with the reader. The résumé contains your employment and educational history, while the letter of application offers an opportunity to supplement the résumé and provide additional reasons that the prospective employer should grant you an interview.

You can use two major types of application letters when applying for jobs: the broadcast letter and the tailored letter.

Broadcast Application Letters

A broadcast application letter is designed for mass mailing to several potential employers for a specific type of job. For example, if you want a job as a staff accountant in a small to medium-sized business, you might mail copies of the same letter to 100 different businesses that might be hiring. Because the letter will have so many different readers, it has to be general in its description of your skills and interests. The broadcast letter is most effective when you seek a specific type of job. The more standard the requirements of the job, the greater the likelihood that you can represent yourself well in a general description of your skills and abilities. As a result, the broadcast letter is best for clearly defined, traditional job categories. It is not effective for uniquely tailored or unusual jobs that demand an uncommon combination of skills.

The broadcast letter should be targeted at potential decision makers. You need to research the names and addresses of executives in the target companies who could hire you for the position you seek. Your letter has a greater chance of success if it is read by a decision maker. For that reason, having the name of a person is very important in addressing the letter. Sending a broadcast letter to the "Vice President of Finance" or "Financial Officer" will probably only get it filed in the wastebasket. Time spent in researching names will ensure a more favorable reading. You can identify recipients either by making information-gathering telephone calls or by consulting business directories in the library.

When you use the broadcast approach, the number of job leads you generate depends on the number of letters you send. The more letters you send, the greater is the chance of a response. It is not uncommon for people to send up to 300 letters at a time to different potential employers. It may be more effective, however, to target the companies and decision makers carefully in order not to waste your time and money with mass mailings. Some authors cite a standard response of up to 5 percent for well-constructed broadcast letters.[1] The more accurately the letters are targeted, the greater the chance of a positive response.

The broadcast letter should consist of dynamic attention-getting devices to make the reader consider you for a position. The best strategy for the letter is to get it into the hands of someone who is hiring *today* and who would thus be likely to respond to an application received "out of the blue." You therefore want to present your skills as completely and as dynamically as possible in order to prompt readers to action.

The best opening for a broadcast letter is to refer to the needs of the readers. Are they looking for someone with special skills to fulfill a vital function in their company? A confident claim that you can perform this function must be substantiated with proof. Use factual, specific statements about your abilities to show your record of achievements in the past. The reader is more likely to read further if your accomplishments match what he or she is looking for. You also need to communicate that you understand the job for which you are applying. Cover each of the skills and abilities required in the position with proof that you have experience and accomplishments in each area. You can include a résumé with the technical details of your employment history, or you may want only to spark the reader's interest by suggesting that you will gladly supply the résumé if desired. The broadcast letter should conclude with a request for an interview or for telephone contact to discuss your qualifications in more detail.

Once you mail the broadcast letters, you should keep by your telephone an accurate list of where you mailed them. If you get a call from a potential

Introduction:	Create interest by referring to reader's needs.
	Grab attention with a bold statement of an accomplishment.
	Ask for an opportunity to introduce yourself as an applicant.
Body:	Review your experience and background.
	Use accomplishment statements to demonstrate your skills and abilities.
Conclusion:	Request an interview to discuss your qualifications in more detail.

FIGURE 14.1   Formula for Broadcast Application Letters

employer, you want to be able to recognize the name of the executive and the company quickly so that you can give special attention to the telephone contact. You can also make follow-up telephone calls to potential employers and ask if they have received your letter. You can then prompt them to action by asking if there are any positions available for which you might qualify. This request may lead to an interview.

A general format for broadcast application letters is provided in Figure 14.1. Review the steps of this type of application letter. A sample broadcast letter is given in Exhibit 14.A. Note how the sample illustrates the various strategies and suggests ways of personalizing the broadcast letter.

You cannot be assured of getting a response to a broadcast letter. Some company officials are overwhelmed by broadcast letters during the May to July hiring season. You must be prepared to receive no responses and be ready to use more targeted job searching if the broadcast letter does not succeed.

Targeted Application Letters

The most common type of application letter is one targeted at a specific job opening. Applicants normally use this letter to respond to a want ad or an announcement of a specific position or an opening identified by a network contact. You also can use it to write to a specific person for whom you would like to work and who may be seeking an employee. With some background research you can pinpoint the exact requirements for a job and write your application to match those needs.

The targeted application is most effective when it covers all the desired qualifications for a position. Want ads or job postings often do not include all the requirements for a job. A telephone call for information about the qualifications or for clarification of the duties may net some valuable information for your letter. By visiting the job site (if the address is listed in the job posting), you can see the working conditions and your potential co-workers. If possible, arrange a preliminary information-gathering interview with the decision maker or some other employees from the company. You can gather information about the duties and responsibilities required in the job and about the qualities desired in an ideal applicant. This information will help you write an application letter tailored to the employers. Like the broadcast letter, the targeted letter should be addressed to a specific person. Identify the name of the hiring executive if at all possible.

```
                                        James Mc Gregor
                                        54 Hilary Way
                                        Bluffton, MO  56894
                                        (405) 487-2034

                                        June 14, 19XX




John Agnoson, Vice President
Amory Products
9583 Sunset Blvd.
Los Angeles, CA  92837

Dear Mr. Agnoson:

Are you looking for a salesman who can increase net sales up to
100 percent in his first year?  That is what I did last year with
Alyson Industries--your major competitor.  I want to leave my
present position because of the company's upcoming reorganiza-
tion, and I can bring the same skills and determination to work
for you.

I have been extremely happy with my position at Alyson, but I
seek a position where I can have the room to grow in my career.
I enjoy sales, and I want to be able to use my skills for an
employer who wants to succeed as much as I do.

I have held two other sales positions--both of which were quite
successful--and I am thoroughly acquainted with the people in our
industry nationwide.  I have an undergraduate degree in marketing
from Southwest Missouri State University.

If you would like more information about my background, I would
be pleased to send you a resume.  You can also call me at the
above number at any time.  I hope we can be of benefit to each
other.

Sincerely,


James McGregor
```

EXHIBIT 14.A   Broadcast Application Letter

The first paragraph should establish a positive relationship with the reader and explain your purpose. If you have made prior contact with the hiring agent, refer to this contact in the opening of the letter. By referring to this contact (a speech you heard, an interview you held, or a discussion you had), you create a sense of personal relationship with the reader. If you are writing "out of the blue," explain where you learned of the position and try to establish some sense of relationship with the reader in the opening paragraph: your admiration for the company, any contact you have had with the company or its products, people whom you know in common with the reader, or the name of someone who suggested that you apply for the job. Make it very clear in the opening paragraph that you wish to apply for a specific position.

The second paragraph of the application should explain your general qualifications for the position: your education, prior work experience, and the skills you bring to the job. When discussing your education or work history, do not merely repeat what is in your résumé. Explain unique features of your education, special skills that would benefit the employer, special coursework that developed skills useful on the job, and other relevant data. Also include personal opinions or experiences that make your education memorable to the reader: a high grade-point average, self-financing of your education, internships, or special extracurricular activities that make you a particularly suitable candidate.

When discussing your work experience, include specific examples of your skills and abilities as evidence that you have them. Do not just claim that you can do something or that you have certain traits. Use specific instances and accomplishment statements to demonstrate that you understand what it takes to do a good job and that you have done a good job for other employers in the past. Likewise, you should include only those skills and experiences pertinent to the job in question. Omit any irrelevant or distracting details, and do not draw attention to any deficiencies you may have. Always state your skills positively. If you do not meet one of the qualifications, do not point that out to the reader; instead, explain that you do have related skills. By analyzing what the employer wants in an employee, you can select the most relevant and interesting details from your background that enhance your application.

The third paragraph of the targeted application is the hardest to write, but the most important: its purpose is to distinguish your application from all the other letters. Chances are great that many applicants will have the same general qualifications. What will make one person—you—stand out from the rest? You can achieve distinction by pointing out your unique abilities. Perhaps you have an unusual combination of skills and experiences that might be especially useful in the position you seek. If you have outstanding achievements in your past employment, explain these in detail. Even if you feel that you do not have special skills or outstanding achievements in your past employment, you can demonstrate your potential as an employee by exhibiting a unique understanding of the job. Describe why you want to work for this particular company and what contributions you could make to the firm. Include examples of your personality traits that would make you a valuable employee and a strong contributor to the company. In essence, the third paragraph should set you apart from the crowd and answer the reader's question, "Why should I hire this person instead of someone else?"

I financed my college education by working part-time during six out of eight semesters.

I developed good client relations at my job. As a result, I received several written recommendations from clients.

I saved my company more than $30,000 by designing and implementing a new inventory system.

I received a promotion for identifying the need for a new computer accounting system, for selecting, ordering, and installing it, and for training other workers to use it.

I won a Salesperson of the Month award by increasing sales by 25 percent.

I researched and wrote a report on the marketing needs of a local nonprofit organization. The group implemented the recommendations.

FIGURE 14.2 Sample Accomplishment Statements

The second and third paragraphs of your application letter should contain several dramatic accomplishment statements describing your specific skills and abilities. These statements support your claims about yourself and demonstrate your value as an employee. Exercise 14.1 at the end of this chapter will help you discover and write these accomplishment statements. Much like the achievement statements discussed in the last chapter, accomplishment statements are objective, factual accounts of something you are proud of having done—but they relate directly to a particular job for which you are applying. Describe your accomplishments in specific, measurable terms, if at all possible. Sample accomplishment statements are presented in Figure 14.2.

The final paragraph of an application letter should note that your résumé is enclosed and request an interview in which your qualifications can be discussed in detail. You need to decide how aggressive you want to be in approaching the potential employer. You may want to tell the reader that you will call to arrange an interview. In some cases, you may not know the address of the company, or the want ad may not identify the employer by name. In these cases you will have to wait for the reader to call you. If you know the name and address of the employer, however, a call to arrange an interview demonstrates that you have a strong interest in the job and are assertive in accomplishing what you want—traits valued in most employment situations.

A good jobhunting tactic is to follow up the application letter with a telephone call three or four days later to be sure the application has been received. This call may afford you the opportunity to talk directly to the decision maker and to have a brief personal interview to supplement the application. If you use this technique, be prepared to have a screening interview immediately on the telephone. Have your qualifications and accomplishment statements well in mind.

When you send a targeted application letter, do not merely duplicate the information in your résumé. Instead, the application letter should highlight certain aspects of your skills and experiences—the ones that will probably be most valuable to the employer. You should amplify the education and work histories in the résumé by going into greater detail about your abilities and accomplishments. Add a personal touch in the letter—your interest in the particular employer, your positive job-related personality traits, and a sense

Introduction:	Refer to previous contact with the reader or company.
	Establish positive relationship with the reader.
	Refer to the reader's needs for an employee.
	Grab attention with an accomplishment statement.
	State the purpose of the letter.
Body:	Present your general qualifications.
	Describe your education and training.
	Refer to past employment experience.
	Explain your skills and abilities.
	Document your abilities with specific examples.
	Include accomplishments to show competence.
	Refer to outstanding abilities or skills.
	Highlight outstanding accomplishments.
	Demonstrate your insight into the job.
	Explain unique personality traits that make you the most qualified applicant.
Conclusion:	Refer the reader to the enclosed résumé for more details.
	Restate your interest in the position.
	Request an interview to discuss your qualifications.

FIGURE 14.3 **Format for Targeted Application Letters**

of confidence and positive outlook. The letter and résumé should be designed to work hand-in-hand to give a total picture of your employment and educational background as well as your personality.

If you apply for a job with only an application letter, you should include more specific details about your employment and education, since you cannot refer to an enclosed résumé. In this case, the application performs the tasks of both résumé and letter.

Figure 14.3 outlines the format for a targeted application letter. Give particular attention to the strategies of the opening and closing paragraphs; these are the most difficult for most writers.

Strategies for Application Letters

Two common problems encountered in writing application letters are a lack of work experience and a lack of related work experience. If you have only an educational background and no practical work experience, you need to describe your education in terms the employer will appreciate. If you did class projects, reports, or exercises that dealt with work-related topics, then you do have experience. If you performed a simulated audit in a class, that activity is probably similar to an actual audit. Since audits vary from company to company, your experience is just as valuable as that of someone who would be applying from a different company. It is very important that you do not label yourself as a "no experience" applicant. You do have experience—it is just in an academic setting. Your task is to explain how you have transferable skills that will benefit the employer. If you remain confident of your skills, then you should be able to convince an employer that you can do the job.

Do include your return address.

Do include a daytime telephone number.

Do address the letter to a specific person, if at all possible.

Do use a letter-quality printer.

Do try to limit your résumé to one page unless it is appropriate in the profession to use a longer one.

Don't use a trite opening line (for example, "I am looking for an exciting, challenging job in _____ with growth opportunities").

Don't use the pronoun "I" too much—use "you" more often.

Do apply for a specific job—don't express a general interest.

Do explain how you found out about the job opening.

Don't make vague, unsupported claims about yourself—provide evidence to prove your claims.

Do talk more about what you can do for them than what they can do for you.

Do provide only the most outstanding and interesting details—don't get trivial.

Don't be apologetic, stuffy, or formal—be confident.

Don't be overly confident or boastful—it will sound pompous.

Don't use the word "anxious"—you usually are, and that works against you.

Do call and see if your application has been received and if the prospective employer is interested—don't sit and wait for an answer.

FIGURE 14.4 Do's and Don'ts for Application Letters

The same principle applies if you have experience unrelated to the job for which you apply. If you have the skills required to do the job, then it should not matter where you acquired those skills. Your task as an applicant is to present your background in such a way that the reader sees how your skills apply directly to the position you want. You may have to explain to the prospective employer how your seemingly unrelated experience actually gave you many related and necessary skills that will benefit the company.

Several glaring errors occasionally find their way into application letters. Figure 14.4 lists important "do's and don'ts" for writing application letters. Avoid pitfalls by referring to this checklist as you compose your application letter.

A final bit of advice for writing any kind of application is to critique your own writing from the viewpoint of the prospective employer. The tone of the application letter should say, "What can I (the applicant) do for you (the employer)?" Too many times applicants are overly concerned about what the employer can do for them—provide benefits, upward mobility, prestige, a pleasant work environment, or a challenging job. Always keep the reader's needs uppermost in your mind. Demonstrate that you understand the employer's needs and that you want to satisfy those needs. This attitude makes your letter distinctive and attractive to the potential employer.

Two sample targeted application letters are shown in Exhibits 14.B and 14.C. Note how they incorporate the suggestions presented in this chapter.

4096 Alta Way
Ridgemont, MI   59385
(402) 884-3328

April 14, 19XX

Mr. Edward L. Cash
Teleflex Network Systems
3059 Machine Court
Edgewood, MI   52948

Dear Mr. Cash:

Mr. Gerry Hacket, manager of Special Engineering Services at
Tele-Network, Inc., suggested that I write you. He believes I am
particularly qualified for a position in your Leadership
Development Program because of my active role in analyzing
telecommunications networks at my current job at Tele-Network.

Next June, I will graduate from Michigan State with a M.S. in
communications engineering. I have been employed at TNI for six
years. As a result, I am familiar with analyzing and installing
systems, and keeping downtime to a minimum. I have worked up
through the ranks, starting on the line and finally being
promoted last year to Assistant Manager.

Besides my technical qualifications, I feel that my strengths as
an employee lie in motivating others. This past year I started
informal suggestions and brainstorming sessions at lunchtime for
the people in my unit. People were so animated by our
discussions, we began to meet on a weekly basis. I thrive on
motivating others to achieve their goals, and I am interested in
your management development program because of its reputation for
producing outstanding managers.

The enclosed resume contains details of my professional
experience and educational background. I would appreciate your
giving me the opportunity to discuss my qualifications in person.
I will call you in the next week to arrange an appointment at
your convenience.

Sincerely,

Dennis A. Towers

EXHIBIT 14.B   Targeted Application Letter

```
39405 Birken Way
Losralto, MA  04395
(705) 243-5987




April 13, 19XX

Ms. Cora Peppers, Employment Officer
Elver's Department Stores
14th and Main Streets
Meladon, NH  02938

Ms. Peppers:

Are you looking for an aggressive, well-educated, mature indi-
vidual with experience in retail sales?  My retail sales training
and experience can be of value to Elver's in the position you
advertised in the Boston Globe last Sunday.  I wish to apply for
the job of Sales Representative.

I have a college degree in business management, but I feel that
experience has been my best teacher.  I have more than four years
of experience in retail sales, and I am knowledgeable in all
aspects of retail department store sales.  From my job as Lead
Salesperson at Stapelton's store in Newbury, I have learned
skills that do not come from a textbook.  I have stong communica-
tion skills, and delegating ability has been part of each job I
have held.  I know about Elver's commitment to quality and
exceptional customer service.  I would be proud to be a part of
your team, and I can meet the sales goals you set.

My basic qualifications are summarized in the enclosed resume.  I
will call you to arrange an interview in which we can explore how
I might be of service to Elver's.  I can be reached at the number
in my resume at any time.  I am very interested in this position,
and look forward to meeting you.

Regards,



Elaine Nance

P.S.  Marion Elmon, my advisor, sends her regards and asks that I
tell you she recommends me highly for this position.
```

EXHIBIT 14.C Targeted Application Letter

NOTE

1. Carl R. Boll, *Executive Jobs Unlimited* (New York: Macmillan, 1979), p. 25.

RESOURCES

Boll, Carl R. *Executive Jobs Unlimited.* New York: Macmillan, 1979.
This book contains excellent chapters on the broadcast application letter, with specific suggestions and examples for various industries.

Murphy, Herta A., and Charles E. Peck. *Effective Business Communications.* New York: McGraw-Hill, 1980.
While most textbooks on business communications have chapters on application letters, this one is particularly useful. It has many helpful examples of letters in different styles.

EXERCISE 14.1
How to Read a Help-Wanted Ad

Directions: Help-wanted ads are often not as specific or complete as they might be. The wary applicant has to analyze a want ad closely in order to determine the skills and abilities desired by the employer. Complete the following worksheet. It guides you through an analysis of the want-ad below.

WANTED: ASSISTANT MANAGER

Local wholesaler seeks intense, responsible person for Pricing and Purchasing Dept. Will work directly with sales and suppliers. Heavy phone interaction. Must be detail-oriented, with good typing skills. Ten-key by touch. Data entry experience a plus. Salary plus medical and dental. Please submit résumé to P.O. Box 5483, Capital City. Attn: Roberta Travis.

---

1. What specific skills are required in the ad?

_____

_____

_____

_____

_____

_____

2. What knowledge does the job require?

_____

_____

_____

_____

_____

_____

3. What abilities (personality traits) are required in the ad? How could an applicant demonstrate them?

_____

_____

_____

_____

_____

_____

4. What specific tasks will the job involve?

_____

_____

_____

_____

_____

_____

5. What tasks are likely to be required in the job but are not identified in the ad?

_____

_____

_____

_____

_____

_____

6. What additional information would you want before you could determine whether you were interested in obtaining this job?

_____

_____

_____

_____

EXERCISE 14.2
Writing Accomplishment Statements

Directions: Identify a job that you would like to hold in the future. List your accomplishments that have transferable skills relevant to that job. (You may want to look at Exercise 15.1 in Chapter 15 for examples of other accomplishment statements.) Analyze each accomplishment statement for the skill, knowledge, or ability that you used in achieving your success. Include specific numerical data when possible.

EXAMPLE: "I was editor of the Accounting Association newsletter."

SKILLS: Scheduling writers' assignments, meeting publishing deadlines, editing and proofreading copy, and duplicating 500 copies per month.

KNOWLEDGE: Word processing, newsletter design.

ABILITIES: Managing volunteer staff, motivating others to meet deadlines, assigning duties, budgeting, scheduling, encouraging and training new writers, coordinating duplication time and resources with Business Department staff.

The job I would like: _____

Accomplishment #1:

Skills: _____

_____

Knowledge: _____

_____

Abilities: _____

_____

Accomplishment #2:

Skills: _____

_____

Knowledge: _____

_____

Abilities: _____

_____

Accomplishment #3:

Skills: _____

_____

Knowledge: _____

_____

Abilities: _____

_____

Accomplishment #4:

Skills: _____

_____

Knowledge: _____

_____

Abilities: _____

_____

Accomplishment #5:

Skills: _____

_____

Knowledge: _____

_____

Abilities: _____

_____

Accomplishment #6:

Skills: _____

_____

Knowledge: _____

_____

Abilities: _____

_____

EXERCISE 14.3
Application Letter Worksheet

Directions: Clip a want ad or a job description for a position you might consider in the future. Plan a letter of application targeted at the want ad. Make sure you include each of the required skills and abilities in your letter that are stated in the ad. Attach the want ad or job description to this page.

Job Description/Want-Ad Analysis

Skills required for the job:

_____

_____

_____

_____

_____

Knowledge required for the job:

_____

_____

_____

_____

_____

Desirable abilities for the job:

_____

_____

_____

_____

_____

Significant accomplishments relevant to the job:

_____

_____

_____

_____

_____

_____

Application Letter Planning

Opening Strategies:

(Previous contact) _____

_____

_____

(How I learned of job opening) _____

_____

_____

(Accomplishment statement) _____

_____

_____

(Reader's need) _____

_____

_____

(Purpose of letter) _____

_____

_____

General Qualifications I Have for the Job:

(Work experience) _____

_____

_____

(Specific skills) _____

_____

_____

(Knowledge) _____

_____

_____

(Educational background) _____

_____

_____

Special Qualifications and Outstanding Achievements I Have:

(Outstanding skills) _____

_____

_____

(Significant accomplishments) _____

_____

_____

(How I can benefit the company) _____ _____

_____

_____

(Personal reasons for wanting to work for this company) _____

_____

_____

Closing Strategies:

(Reference to enclosed résumé) _____

_____

_____

(Statement of interest in the job) _____

_____

_____

(Request for an interview) _____

_____

_____

(How I can be reached/how I will get in touch with them) _____

_____

_____

Special Postscript: _____

_____

_____

ACTION ASSIGNMENT

14
Application Letters

1. Make copies of the letter of application you composed in Exercise 14.3 and of the job description or help-wanted ad on which you targeted the letter. Distribute these copies to your classmates. The class should read and critique one another's letters on the basis of the guidelines suggested in this chapter, and answer the following questions:

   What is your general feeling about the applicant from the information provided in the letter?

   What three adjectives would describe the applicant?

   Would this letter make you want to see the applicant's résumé or arrange an interview with the applicant?

   What are the strengths of the letter?

   What areas of weakness in the letter need to be addressed?

   How might the letter be improved?

2. Compose a letter of application and show it to a person who is employed. Ask for their honest appraisal of your letter on the basis of their experience in the business world.

15
Résumés

Your résumé plays an important role in your job search. A carefully constructed résumé creates a strong, positive first impression with a prospective employer. Although you can pay someone to create an impressive-looking résumé for you, it is important to know how to build a résumé from the ground up. Résumés are highly personal and rarely satisfactory when someone else creates them. This chapter gives you the skills to write your own résumé and to use it successfully in your job search.

A résumé briefly summarizes your work history, education, skills, or other information that might be useful to a potential employer. When applying for a job, people are often asked to submit a résumé so that the employer can screen the applicants and select only the most likely prospects to interview. Thus, the résumé should be constructed to increase your chances of being asked for a personal interview. Once in the interview, you and the employer can examine your credentials in greater detail. Sometimes a hiring decision may be made from the information in a résumé, so you want to present a full set of qualifications in your résumé; but more often the résumé only qualifies you for an interview.

This chapter looks at various myths about résumés, the types of résumé formats you can use, the elements that you should include in constructing an effective résumé, techniques for writing a résumé, and strategies for using your résumé. Several examples of effective résumés are included throughout the chapter.

Myths About Using Résumés

Several misleading assumptions prevent people from using résumés effectively. By understanding the best use of résumés, you can anticipate how they will be read by future employers, and you can determine how to write a more effective one. Do you hold any of the following assumptions about résumés?

MYTH #1: A GOOD RÉSUMÉ WILL GET YOU A GOOD JOB

A good résumé may get you an interview, but you still have to prove to the interviewer that you are the person for the job. Your résumé cannot give a prospective employer all the information necessary to make a hiring decision. Careful employers will want to see an applicant in person, discuss job qualifications in greater detail, and in general get to know an applicant before hiring him or her. So all the résumé will do is qualify you for an interview. Once you have the interview, it is up to you to present yourself in the best possible way. You will be hired on the basis of the interview—not on the basis of your résumé. A good résumé will give a good first impression, but it is only a small part of the job-search process.

MYTH #2: ONCE YOU HAVE A GOOD RÉSUMÉ, IT NEVER CHANGES

A résumé should be a dynamic document, adapted and changed with use. A common weakness in résumés is their lack of adaptation to specific situations. You must analyze an employer and the job being applied for so that you can include relevant and applicable information in your résumé. Why include the fact that you have experience flying airplanes when you apply for an office position? It may be interesting information, but if it is totally irrelevant to the job, then you should not highlight it in your résumé. Each time you prepare a job application, you should carefully tailor your résumé to fit that position. Of course, if you are using a broadcast approach, applying to many companies for the same type of job, then one résumé may be prepared so as to fit many different situations. However, the best approach is to re-write, or at least reorganize, your résumé for each job application.

MYTH #3: I CAN'T WRITE A RÉSUMÉ IF I DON'T HAVE EXPERIENCE

Everyone has experience of some kind—school experience, personal experience, sharing in the experiences of others. If you have never been employed, you can still use the kind of experience you do have to create an interesting and effective résumé. You have skills and abilities useful to a potential employer. Most employers look for skills more than for specific job experience, so do not put yourself into a hole by thinking that you are less qualified or that you cannot write an effective résumé because you have little or no work history.

MYTH #4: A GOOD RÉSUMÉ SHOULD BE PREPARED BY A PROFESSIONAL

Some people spend great sums of money to have their résumés professionally prepared and printed. The finished product may be very good, but what do you do the next time you have to look for a job—pay someone else to write another résumé? It is far better for you to learn the principles of résumé writing so that you can respond to new opportunities as they arise. Your ability to write an effective résumé does much more than merely present your skills. A well-written résumé shows that you know how to condense information, organize it clearly, present it attractively, and write persuasively—all very important business communication skills. Take pride in the résumé you construct yourself. In the process of writing it, you will become more confident about the interview. Because you have reviewed your abilities and described them in positive, specific ways, you will be ready to answer questions that arise from the résumé. You will also be able to prepare tailored résumés for different kinds of positions.

Types of Résumés

Any résumé should contain a brief description of your education and work history and should highlight your strongest qualifications. However, there are several different types of résumés you can use to present your experience and skills. Each type has certain strengths and weaknesses. In order to select the résumé most useful for your purposes, you should review the different types of résumés and consider the advantages and disadvantages of each choice.

THE CHRONOLOGICAL RÉSUMÉ

The traditional and most frequently used type of résumé is the *chronological résumé*. This résumé lists the applicant's employment history in chronological order, usually with the most recent job first. This type of résumé is most suitable for traditional or conservative professions that expect a commitment to a definite career path. The chronological résumé also works best for the applicant who has a steady work history and a record of advancement from one job to the next. The strength of the chronological résumé is that it demonstrates your background and experience within a definite career area. This résumé is not very effective for people who have no work history or who have a history of jobs that are unrelated to the target position. The sample chronological résumés in Exhibits 15.A and 15.B illustrate the effective use of this résumé in two different situations.

```
                          CAROLYN R. ROME
                         1775 Alpine Way, #343
                          Scranton, PA  18519
                           (717) 552-8832
OBJECTIVE

   Accountant, specializing in auditing

WORK EXPERIENCE

   City of Scranton, Scranton, Pennsylvania - July 1979 to Present
   Legal Secretary II - to Deputy City Attorney

      ° Prepare resolutions, ordinances, board letters and litigation reports for
        City Supervisor's meetings

      ° Assign numbers to all City ordinances; responsible for having all
        ordinanaces published in an official newspaper of the City of Scranton

      ° Transmit certified copies of ordinances and other legal documents to City
        Clerk and County Recorder for recording and filing

      ° Law Library duties:  ordering legal publications, keeping law library
        updated with books and supplements

      ° Miscellaneous duties:  answering phones, filing, typing letters, ordering
        office Supplies, handling payments of bills

   John Karr, Scranton, Pennsylvania - March 1978 to May 1979
   Assistant Bookkeeper

      ° Balanced and posted journals
      ° Typed, filed, and recorded invoices
      ° Calculated, proofed, and verified purchase orders

   Kibben-Young Insurance, Taylor, Pennsylvania - June 1977 to March 1978
   Assistant Bookkeeper

      ° Verified and mailed monthly statements to customers
      ° Posted entries to journal
      ° Verified all figures from journals, purchase orders, and invoices
      ° Filed invoices

EDUCATION

   B.S., Accounting, Pennsylvania State University, Scranton, 1983

OUTSTANDING ACHIEVEMENTS

   Dean's Honor Roll, Pennsylvania State University, 1981 and 1983
   Central Bank Achievement Award in the field of business - 1977
   Beverly W. Wyman Business Scholarship - 1977

REFERENCES:  Available upon request
```

EXHIBIT 15.A Chronological Résumé

```
JAMES E. DUNN
48301 Salton Drive
Orland, CA  95693                                                    (916) 396-5827
```

CAREER
OBJECTIVE: Sales Representative position, with the opportunity to advance
                  to sales management.

SUMMARY OF
EXPERIENCE: Through academic study and job experience, have developed
                  abilities and understanding of management, economics,
                  interpersonal communication, research, computer skills, and
                  planning.

EDUCATION: B. S., Business Administration, option in Marketing,
                  California State University, Chico (1985).

COURSE
HIGHLIGHTS: Financial Management, Sales Management, Accounting Control,
                  Sales Analysis, Marketing Management, Computer Science

                  All education obtained while working and completely self-
                  financed.

WORK EXPERIENCE:

6/81 to
Present   Journeyman Clerk, WALMART STORES, INC., Chico, CA

                       Presently responsible for the preparation and merchandising
                       of Household and Perishable products. Provide customer
                       service, take inventories, order products, and create promo-
                       tional displays. Develop training programs to increase
                       skills of new Household apprentices.

7/75 to
9/80   Assistant Supervisor, K & M FARMS, Nord, CA

                       Responsible for setting my own time schedules. Supervised
                       farm crews (up to 15 people). Reduced costs by maintenance
                       of tomato harvesters and tractors. Increased profits by the
                       construction of a new barn and stable. Managed plowing and
                       planting of crops and assisted in shipping of finished goods.

COLLEGE
ACTIVITIES: American Marketing Association member, small-business
                  consultant, and intramural basketball.

REFERENCES: Available upon request.

EXHIBIT 15.B Chronological Résumé

THE SKILLS (OR FUNCTIONAL) RÉSUMÉ

The *skills (or functional) résumé* suits people who have no job experience, who are changing career paths, or who are returning to work after a long absence. The skills résumé organizes your work history under your skill areas or functional areas in which you have abilities. For example, if you are applying for a position as a manager, you might organize a résumé into the most important management skill areas: communication skills, organization skills, and

RANDALL DALE MORGAN

Rural Route 5, Box 345
Marion, Illinois 62959
(618) 993-4139

Areas of Competence

         Writing Skills: Composition: articles, manuals, news releases
                           Newsletter publication
                           Resume writing and business writing training
                           Editing

        Media Relations: Radio writing and production
                           Television production and direction
                           Audiovisual training
                           Public speaking: director of speakers bureau

      Office Management: Scheduling and time budgeting
                           Light bookkeeping
                           Typing (60 wmp)
                           Office machines: word processing, ten-key

Professional Experience

              1983-84: Williamson County Division of Mental Health
                         - radio scriptwriting and production team

                        Harry Martin Court Reporting, Inc.
                         - office assistant

              1980-83: The Obelisk, student newspaper editor, copy writer,
                         and graphics coordinator.

Education: 1983: B.S., double major in Communication and Education,
                         Southern Illinois University, Carbondale

References: Available upon request

EXHIBIT 15.C Skills Résumé

```
                        SHIRLEY A. Q. WONG

        664 Pacific Avenue #4              Home: (213) 445-7128
        Venice, CA 90291                   Work: (818) 333-5665
        _____

                           Qualifications

Analytic and Planning Skills:
        o Management system consultant in a 14-branch corporation
        o Responsible for redesigning the management systems for the head office
          and all subsidiary offices
        o Revised existing system of the company, located errors, and devised
          remedial systems
        o Designed and instituted a new management system, which increased
          managerial efficiency by 20 percent


Accounting and Control Systems:

        o Accounting control clerk in a CPA firm that practices public tax
          accounting
        o Thorough knowledge of and experience with payroll services
        o Maintained control system for entire firm with increased accuracy and
          efficiency


Trilingual Skills:

        o Lived in Hong Kong for 14 years and Japan for 5 years
        o Speak fluent Chinese and Japanese
        o Speak fluent English


                            Employers

Management system consultant at BioTech, Inc., Pasadena, CA 1982 to present

Accounting control clerk, at Ace Accounting, Santa Monica, CA, 1980 to 1982


                            Education

B.S., Los Angeles College.  Majors:  Management Information Systems and
Accounting,  1985

A.S., DeAnza College.  Major:  Accounting, 1980


                             Honors

Academic honors with GPA above 3.5 were awarded every term in college

           References and further information provided on request
```

EXHIBIT 15.D   Skills Résumé

financial skills. Then under each of these three headings, you list your experience and accomplishment statements. This type of résumé is most useful for showing how transferable skills from unrelated jobs or school experiences have prepared you for the job under consideration. It also demonstrates your creativity and your understanding of the job by emphasizing your skills and abilities. Two samples skills résumés are shown in Exhibits 15.C and 15.D.

THE COMBINATION RÉSUMÉ

A third type of résumé is the *combination résumé*, which combines the traditional and the functional approaches. This résumé capitalizes upon the advantages of the other two by listing your work experience and demonstrating your skills under your listing of each job you have held. In essence, you demonstrate that you have held related work positions and that you have developed and used valuable skills in each job. This résumé is most suitable for highly qualified applicants with broad experience who need to present the most relevant aspects of their work histories. Exhibits 15.E and 15.F offer sample combination résumés.

WILLIAM ROPPEL

ADDRES: 5800 Jasmine Avenue, Savannah, GA 31404   (912) 863-3906

PROFESSIONAL EXPERIENCE

    MATERIALS MANAGER, Department of Chemistry, Armstrong State College,
    Savannah, GA (February 1933 to present) (912) 442-8921

    Purchasing
    ◦ Manage procurement with 19,000 orders of $25 million annually
    ◦ Guide the unit in aggressive purchasing

    Receiving
    ◦ Plan and coordinate the unit's strategies to accommodate new demands
      while maintaining the current level of service
    ◦ Represent the department to college administration and vendors to
      obtain best delivery conditions

    Managing Stores
    ◦ Oversee the stores system having an annual sales exceeding $500,000
    ◦ Direct inventory control, billing, forecasting, and sales

    Supervising
    ◦ Three supervisors, seven full-time employees, and six student assistants
    ◦ Conduct annual performance evaluations and salary recommendations

    Other Activities
    ◦ Develop and implement the college's computerized purchasing-receiving-
      invoicing system
    ◦ Interact with the colleges business offices to keep operations within
      established budgets
    ◦ Extensive computer experience: IMB IX and AT; software (data bases,
      word processors, spreadsheets, etc.); Mainframe Armstrong UNIX, Ingres
      data base and related utilities

STOCKROOM SUPERVISOR. Department of Microbiology, Purdue University, West
Lafayette, IN 47907 (November 1977 to January 1983)

    ◦ Stockroom inventory forecasting, billing, and account maintenance for a
      computerized $150,000 inventory
    ◦ Safety and spill control, departmental receiving, chemical waste
      handling, operation of the HPLC column packer, and departmental liaison
      for vendors

EDUCATION

    M.B.A. Savannah State College (degree to be granted spring of this year)
    B.S. Biochemistry - Purdue University, 1977
    A.S. Northwestern Indiana Junior College, 1975

REFERENCES AND RECOMMENDATIONS

    Available upon request

EXHIBIT 15.E   Combination Résumé

```
                    CATHERINE J. DILLINGHAM
                       3145 Manoa Valey Road
                       Honolulu, HI  96821


       EDUCATION

            B.S., Business Administration, University of Hawaii (June 1987).
            Options:  Marketing and Advertising.  Minor: Sociology.  Grade point
            average:  3.28


       EMPLOYMENT

            Lead sales person, Liberty House Department Store, Ala Moana Center,
            Honolulu, HI   (November 1983 to present)

                 * Responsible for selling merchandise
                 * Design merchandising displays
                 * Coordinate sales staff
                 * Negotiate with dissatisfied customers
                 * Assist in training of new hires in department


       COMMUNICATION SKILLS

                 * Tutor in scholastic studies, including math and sciences
                 * Enlisted participants for annual school blood drive
                 * Mediator with students and administration


       LEADERSHIP AND ORGANIZATION SKILLS

            Key salesperson to coordinate opening of the new Liberty House at
            Ala Moana:

                 * Directed other workers in stock set-up and sales floors
                 * Evaluated the strengths and weaknesses of proposed setups
                 * Assisted executives in formulating system to ensure uniformity of
                   stockrooms throughout the chain


       HONORS

                 * Graduated cum laude from Kaneohe High School
                 * Received Outstanding Achievement Awards in drawing (1986 and 1987),
                   painting (1985 and 1986), and mathematics (1985), University of
                   Hawaii


       REFERENCES

            Available upon request
```

EXHIBIT 15.F Combination Résumé

THE TARGETED RÉSUMÉ

The three types of résumés presented thus far—the chronological, the skills, and the combination—differ in the way in which information is organized on the page. The fourth type of résumé—the *targeted résumé*—makes each of these three forms even more effective. Some people feel that a résumé should reflect all elements of their past, but the targeted résumé includes only those elements most relevant to the target position. Thus, certain jobs you have had may be omitted because they are irrelevant or because the skills you used in that position are covered under some other job heading. The writer of the targeted résumé analyzes the target job and focuses the résumé to fit the job description and the needs of the interviewer as closely as possible. This approach creates the strongest possible résumé. Any of the other three types of résumés can be strengthened by using the targeted approach.

In selecting the type of résumé you will use, consider your situation. Weigh the advantages of each type and consider how each format can present your qualifications most effectively. You may want to experiment by trying to write a résumé in each of the three styles and using a general or targeted version. Get feedback from your contacts on which résumé best reflects your abilities. Knowing your options and becoming more comfortable with different ways of presenting your qualifications helps you select the most appropriate résumé for each job-search situation.

Figure 15.1 reviews the characteristics of the four types of résumés and the situations in which you should consider using each type.

The Chronological Résumé

Lists jobs you have held in chronological order, with the most recent job first.

Emphasizes a steady work history and advancement.

Presents a suitable image for traditional or conservative professions.

Shows commitment to a definite career path.

Demonstrates your background and experience within a chosen field.

The Skills (or Functional) Résumé

Organizes your qualifications under skill areas or functions you can perform.

Lists examples of your accomplishments in each area.

Emphasizes skill and ability and compensates for lack of traditional experience.

Relates transferable skills from unrelated job or school experience to the current job opening.

Suits people lacking job experience, changing career paths, or returning to work after absences.

The Combination Résumé

Includes both work history and skill descriptions.

Combines strongest features of chronological and skill résumés.

Maximizes advantages of chronological and skills résumé formats.

The Targeted Résumé

Lists experience, skills, and abilities most relevant to a position.

Emphasizes your ability to analyze the job and your experience in doing what is required.

Focuses skills of highly qualified candidates with a broad background of experience.

Demonstrates job insight and understanding.

FIGURE 15.1 Four Common Types of Résumés

Identifying information:	Your complete name (omit nicknames).
	Your complete address (with ZIP code).
	Your home and office telephone (with area code).
	Message service (if available).
Education:	Degrees you hold (with date awarded).
	Schools attended.
	Special emphasis (major, option).
	Special coursework or projects.
	Awards or honors.
Work history:	Positions held (emphasize job title).
	Name of company (with city and state).
	Dates of employment (month and year).
	Description of job responsibilities.
	Accomplishments while on the job.
	Special work-related training.
Additional information:	Volunteer work, military service.
	Awards and honors.
Reference statement:	"References available upon request"
	(List names, business addresses, and business telephone numbers of references on a separate sheet, to be sent if requested).

FIGURE 15.2 Items to Include in Your Résumé

What to Include in Your Résumé

Regardless of the type of résumé you select, certain information must always be included. Figure 15.2 lists the basic components of any résumé. Different types of résumés determine where you place the information on the page, but you should include the details listed in Figure 15.2 unless you have a specific reason for omitting one of them.

You can include a number of optional elements in your résumé if you want to emphasize certain aspects of your record or if you have extra space. Figure 15.3 lists some of these other considerations.

Different experts will give you different advice about what to include in a résumé, so you need to decide for yourself which information best presents your qualifications. Clearly, however, certain elements are critical: your name, your address, your phone number, and your most relevant experience. Beyond those factors, anything else can be and has been effective for different applicants. However, a few things are almost universally avoided in résumés. You should *not* include the things listed in Figure 15.4.

Career objective: Use this if you are in a traditional career path and want to demonstrate commitment to a long-term career goal.

Employment objective: Use this if you know exactly the type of job you want and wish to target your résumé to that specific job.

Summary statement: Use this to provide a brief personal philosophy or a summary of your strongest qualifications.

Special skills/abilities: Use this to highlight special knowledge (e.g., foreign language), skills (e.g., computer literacy), training (e.g., first aid certification), or abilities (e.g., newsletter production).

Activities: Use this to emphasize community involvement, campus leadership, and a people-oriented background.

Interests: Use this to give some personality to your résumé; be specific and appropriate in selecting interest areas.

Professional affiliations: Use this to demonstrate your knowledge of the field and your commitment to the profession.

Personal information: Include only necessary job-related information (e.g., willingness to relocate, job-related interests)

FIGURE 15.3 Optional Elements for Your Résumé

In general, avoid including any information that could be misinterpreted. Readers of résumés have only the information on the page to know you by, so you should not include anything that might create a negative impression. Anticipate your readers' prejudices, and omit anything that might be used to disqualify you. You can always add more information about yourself during the interview.

Brightly colored paper or overly dramatic typesetting (unless applying for a dramatic or creative position).

Photos (unless applying for an acting role, a modeling job, and the like).

High school affiliations (unless important to the interviewer).

Political affiliations (unless you are applying for a political position or you know the politics of the interviewer).

Religious affiliation (unless this works to your advantage).

Marital status or children (unless the job has to do with family-oriented goods or services).

Physical details (height, weight, sex, handicap).

Dangerous interests—skydiving, ice climbing, and the like (unless appropriate to the position).

FIGURE 15.4 What *Not* to Include in Your Résumé

Techniques for Writing Your Résumé

Once you have selected the most appropriate type of résumé and the elements you want to include, the next step is to construct your résumé so that it is easy to read, relevant, interesting, and attractive. Even the most highly qualified candidate may create a poor impression if his or her résumé is disorganized, full of irrelevant and distracting details, sloppy in appearance, or plagued by typing and spelling errors. As you prepare your résumé, use the following suggestions to make the best first impression.

To make your résumé easy to read, organize it clearly and logically. Some employers give only brief attention to a résumé if they are scanning hundreds of them at a time. One study at a California university reported that on-campus company recruiters spend only approximately 40 seconds scanning a résumé.[1] To be effective, then, your résumé must grab attention immediately. A clear organizational pattern helps you capture the reader's attention and entices him or her to read more. Use headings to label clearly the different parts of the résumé. Carefully select a consistent system of capitalization, underlining, and indentation to emphasize key words and items. Do not try to pack too much information onto a single page; instead, use plenty of white space to separate the sections, so as to give the reader some "breathing room" between the items.

In selecting elements to include in the résumé, be as brief as possible while still including all relevant information that might interest the reader. Some authors suggest a one-page limit to résumés, but the length of a résumé depends on how much you have to say about yourself. A highly qualified candidate for a traditional professional position may have quite a lengthy résumé. A résumé for an entry-level position should be shorter and more to the point. You must determine which of your experiences, skills, and abilities are most relevant. Remember that the real purpose of the résumé is just to get an interview. You can provide much more detail once you meet the potential employer in person, so include only enough information to make the employer want to hear more about you. Analyze the job description closely and make each of the elements you include in your résumé fit some need of the employer. Do not include details merely because they seem important to you. Look at your résumé from the employer's point of view, and select materials that will be important to him or her.

When summarizing your skills and abilities, use interesting and lively language. Under each of the headings in your résumé—whether you use the chronological, skills, combination, or targeted approach—describe accomplishments that *prove* you have the abilities you say you have. Load your résumé with accomplishment statements from the list you prepared in Chapter 14. Show the prospective employer that you can accomplish things, save money, be creative, work hard, or whatever he or she most wants from an applicant. Exercise 15.2 at the end of this chapter helps you analyze your current work position in order to identify statements that prove your work skills.

When describing your accomplishments and abilities, use vivid and active verbs. Start each phrase with a verb that dynamically describes what you have done. Use the list of verbs in Figure 15.5 to start your descriptions of experience and skills.[2]

accomplished	distributed	invented	recorded
achieved	eliminated	investigated	recruited
activated	enlarged	launched	reduced
adapted	equipped	led	reinforced
administered	established	maintained	reorganized
analyzed	evaluated	managed	researched
approved	examined	motivated	revamped
arranged	expanded	negotiated	reviewed
built	expedited	organized	revised
completed	founded	originated	scheduled
conceived	funded	participated	serviced
conducted	generated	performed	sold
controlled	guided	planned	solved
coordinated	implemented	presented	streamlined
created	improved	produced	structured
delegated	increased	programmed	supervised
delivered	influenced	proposed	supported
demonstrated	initiated	provided	taught
designed	instituted	raised	trained
developed	instructed	recommended	wrote
directed			

FIGURE 15.5 Action Words to Include in Your Résumé

You want your résumé to be attractive. Look at other people's résumés for layout ideas. Experiment with ways to design your résumé in an attractive and interesting style. Select a heading that emphasizes your name and looks bright and professional. Consider employing a typesetting service to provide heading labels or to typeset the entire résumé. Some employers resist résumés that look "too polished," so do not overdo the graphics. A clean typed copy may demonstrate your abilities more directly than an extravagant, professionally prepared masterpiece.

Once you complete the first draft of your résumé, carefully proofread it several times to catch any typographical or spelling errors. Asking a friend to proofread it may save you money and embarrassment in the long run. Make copies of your résumé in case you need it again or for reference. Have your résumé copied onto a high-quality (25 percent bond) paper by a professional copier. Copy centers in most cities provide this service for a reasonable price.

Strategies for Using Your Résumé

There are many different sources of advice about how to use your résumé once it is written. Some authors suggest never showing a prospective employer your résumé until you have had an information-gathering interview, so that you know how to target it precisely. While that sounds like useful advice, many occasions require you to submit a résumé without knowing exactly what the job description entails. In general, you should target your résumé to the specific needs and interests of the interviewer as well as you can, no matter which type of résumé you are using. Any type of résumé can be targeted to suit the needs of the prospective employer. The more you look at your résumé from the employer's viewpoint, the more effectively you can present your qualifications. The best course of action is to gather as much information as you can about the prospective job before composing the résumé.

Another helpful strategy in creating your résumé is to start a "résumé pool" of ideas about what to include, copies of your past résumés or other people's resumes, and lists of accomplishment statements that may be useful in later résumé-building sessions. The hours you spend composing your résumé will pay off in a better job and a more fulfilling career for you. Look upon your résumé preparation as time invested in your career. The hardest work, of course, is writing your first résumé. Once that task is accomplished, however, later versions will be easier, since you will have a solid foundation to build on.

NOTES

1. Developed by Career Placement Service, California State University, Hayward.
2. Developed by Career Placement Service, California State University, Hayward.

RESOURCES

Biegeleisen, J. I. *Job Résumés: How to Write Them, How to Present Them, Preparing for Interviews.* New York: Grosset & Dunlap, 1969.
   This is an old manual, but it provides many useful examples and suggestions for strategy in using your résumé.

Jackson, Tom. *The Perfect Résumé.* Garden City, N.Y.: Anchor Books, 1981.
   This workbook is an excellent aid in planning and constructing résumés of various types.

EXERCISE 15.1
Correcting a Poor Résumé

Directions: The résumé below has several problems. What would you change? Write your comments and corrections in the spaces provided.

```
RESUME                                                    John Smith

                        354 Sampson Street
                        Alta Mesa, New Mexico

Career objective:   To prove that I can be a top-notch retail manager and to
                    really get ahead in my profession.

Education:          B.S. Degree in Business Admin: Retailing (June, 1983)
                    San Luis Obispo State University
                         GPA:  2.3
                         Honors: None
                         Activities: TAU Fraternity Pledge Chairman
                                     Manager, SLOSU Basketball Team
                                     Intramurals Football Team (four years)
                                     Chairman:  TAU Ice Cream Social

                    Graduated:  Alta Mesa High School (June 1979)

Work history:       STOCK CLERK: Value Grocery,            (Aug. 80-June 83)
                              San Luis Obispo, CA
                    I just stocked shelves, did general maintenance around
                    the store, had to manage ordering produce and set up
                    displays.  I also oversaw hiring new staff and training
                    them.  Did budgets.  Managed store in owner's absence--
                    once for three months

                    PIZZA DELIVERY MAN: Red Dog Pizza Parlor,(Aug. 79-June 80)
                                  San Luis Obispo, CA

                    Delivered pizza.

                    NEWSPAPER DELIVERY BOY:  Alta Mesa Times,      (1975-79)
                                             Alta Mesa, New Mexico
                    Delivered papers.

                    RETAILING INTERN: Macy's              (Summers: 1980-83)
                                  New York City

                    I worked in each of the retailing departments:  pur-
                    chasing, stock management, customer relations, billing,
                    floor sales, management (planning budgets).

Interests:          Sports, TAU Alumni Group, talking to people

REFERENCES AVAILABLE UPON REQUEST
```

Critique Sheet

Overall appearance and accuracy:

_____

_____

Headings:

_____

_____

_____

Career objective:

_____

_____

_____

Education:

_____

_____

_____

Work history:

_____

_____

_____

Interests:

_____

_____

_____

Clubs/professional activities:

_____

_____

_____

Other elements you might include:

_____

_____

_____

EXERCISE 15.2
Identifying Your Current Job Skills

Directions: This exercise is designed to help you identify the skills, knowledge, and abilities you use in your current job and to write about them in a way that would interest a potential employer. Analyze your current job by dividing it into 30-minute segments; for example, if you work from 1:00 until 5:00, you will have eight time periods. For each time period, note the specific type of skill you performed. You may use several skills in each period, so make separate entries for each skill. Write a short sentence that describes your use of this skill. Use a vivid verb from the list in Figure 15.5 in this chapter.

This exercise only begins to analyze your skills on the job, since it is limited to just one day. Consider other skills you use on your current job or skills you have developed on other jobs. These will be important elements to include in your résumé.

Your current job: _____

Time period: Skills used:

_____   _____

                      _____

_____   _____

                      _____

_____   _____

                      _____

_____   _____

                      _____

_____   _____

                      _____

_____   _____

                      _____

_____   _____

                      _____

Time period: Skills used:

_____   _____

_____   _____

                   _____

_____   _____

                   _____

_____   _____

                   _____

_____   _____

                   _____

_____   _____

                   _____

_____   _____

                   _____

_____   _____

                   _____

_____   _____

                   _____

_____   _____

                   _____

_____   _____

                   _____

_____   _____

EXERCISE 15.3
Preparing Your Résumé

Directions: This worksheet helps you prepare the elements of your personal résumé. The best way to use this exercise is to target a specific position. Having a target makes it easier for you to determine which format to use and which elements to include. You may wish to use the same job description you used in Chapter 14, when you analyzed the want ad and wrote the application letter. Prepare the elements of your résumé by filling in the categories provided.

IDENTIFYING INFORMATION

Name: _____

Address: _____

_____

Home Telephone: _____ Work Telephone: _____

Answering Machine: _____

EDUCATION

Degree: _____

School: _____ Date: _____

Degree: _____

School: _____ Date: _____

Special Coursework: _____

_____

_____

_____

_____

_____

Special Projects: _____

_____

_____

_____

_____

_____

WORK HISTORY

Position #1:

Company: _____ Dates: _____

Job responsibilities: _____

_____

_____

_____

_____

_____

1. Skill used: _____

2. Skill used: _____

3. Skill used: _____

Accomplishments:

1. _____

2. _____

Position #2:

Company: _____ Dates: _____

Job responsibilities: _____

_____

_____

_____

_____

_____

1. Skill used: _____

2. Skill used: _____

3. Skill used: _____

Accomplishments:

1. _____

2. _____

Position #3:

Company: _____ Dates: _____

Job responsibilities: _____

_____

_____

_____

_____

_____

1. Skill used: _____

2. Skill used: _____

3. Skill used: _____

Accomplishments:

1. _____

2. _____

SPECIAL SKILLS

1. _____
2. _____
3. _____
4. _____
5. _____

AWARDS/HONORS

1. _____
2. _____
3. _____
4. _____
5. _____

PROFESSIONAL ACTIVITIES/CLUBS

1. _____
2. _____
3. _____
4. _____
5. _____

INTERESTS

1. _____
2. _____
3. _____
4. _____
5. _____

ACTION ASSIGNMENT

15

Résumés

1. Locate a collection of student résumés. Often a campus placement service or business school keeps a file of student résumés for reference purposes. Analyze this collection for ideas on formatting your own résumé, items to include in your résumé, and ways of organizing your résumé.

2. Make copies of the résumé you prepared in Exercise 15.3 and distribute them to your classmates. Read and critique one another's résumés on the basis of the guidelines provided in this chapter.

3. Rewrite your résumé using a different format. For example, if you originally wrote it using a chronological format, rewrite it using a skills format (or vice versa). Compare the two résumés. Which format reflects your qualifications more effectively?

4. Imagine that it is five years in the future. Write the résumé you would like to have five years from now. As realistically as possible, invent the qualifications, experiences, skills, and accomplishments you hope to gain during the next five years. Have fun with this assignment and stretch your horizons.

16

Letters of Reference

In many job-application situations you may be asked to supply *references*—the names and addresses of people who can testify to your abilities as a worker. It is best to be prepared well in advance for this request, since assembling names, addresses, and telephone numbers takes time and research. Likewise, it takes time to check with each person you wish to use as a reference in order to make sure that she or he has some idea of what you would like the letter to include and is willing to write it. Develop your references early in the job search so that you will have the list ready at a moment's notice to provide prospective employers with the information needed. Your promptness will make a favorable impression and help you to secure the job you want.

There has been some criticism of the use of references and letters of reference in recent years.[1] A growing trend has been for letters of reference to be uncritically positive, full of exaggerated praise, and vague to the point of puffery. Many employers complain that letters of reference are worse than useless—they are actually misleading or deceptive. Despite this skepticism, employers still need some way of verifying an applicant's abilities at work. Many employers find it worth their time to consult former employers of applicants. You can assist prospective employers in this task by preparing a list of references who can give an accurate and honest report about your abilities as a worker. If you are forthright in presenting yourself in the job search, the prospective employer will admire your sense of candor and professionalism.

There are several ways in which references are used. Sometimes references are asked for with the job application, either in the form of names, addresses, and telephone numbers of references or in the form of a request for letters of reference. More commonly, references are asked for at the close of a selection interview. An employer usually waits to check references as one of the last steps before hiring because of the time involved in reaching references by letter or phone to verify your abilities. Whichever method is requested, you should be prepared with good references who can attest in specific and pertinent terms to your value as an employee.

This chapter details how to select references and how to write the two basic forms of letters of reference—the general and the specific. The general letter of reference, often tritely begun with "to whom it may concern," describes a person's abilities in a fairly general way. Comments can be specific and precise, but they are not targeted at the needs of a specific employer or position. The general letter of reference is usually written as documentation—comments for the record, which will be used at a later date. The specific letter of reference targets its comments toward the tasks and responsibilities unique to a particular job. It is usually written on behalf of a person applying for a specific job opening. The specific letter of reference is a stronger one, but it takes much more time to research and prepare.

Building a Reference Pool

The best way to prepare your references is to build a "reference pool"—a set of people who have expressed a willingness to serve as references for you. Your pool should be broadly based so that you can select the most relevant references for a specific situation. Different people may know you in different ways, so you need to select references according to the kind of information they can disclose about you. Just as you build a résumé to target your skills and abilities toward a specific job, you should target your references to provide information that helps you secure the job you want.

Include in your reference pool people who can testify to your qualities as a worker. Former employers can verify your experience, skills, abilities, accomplishments, personal characteristics while on the job, and other work-related traits. Teachers with whom you have worked closely can testify to your knowledge, special research, personal characteristics as a student, and traits related to your school experience. Professional or well-known people who know you add credibility and impressiveness when they talk about your abilities. Personal friends can serve as references, but employers often perceive their opinion as biased. In general, you should select the most relevant work-related references for a position you seek. By looking at the references from the prospective employer's point of view, you can determine who will be the most useful, relevant, and impressive. The following list provides suggestions about the characteristics of people who might serve as good references:

Someone who has known you in a specific work situation.
Someone who has known you for a long time.
Someone who likes you and the work you have done.
Someone who can provide specific comments about your work.
Someone who writes well and is willing to act as a reference.

You should accumulate your references during the time you work with people. If you return two or three years later to ask an employer or a teacher for a reference, the person may have forgotten who you are and how you performed for them. It is important to place people in the reference pool as soon as they have something to say about you that will be useful in the future. If you wish to include an employer, ask him or her for a general letter of reference when you leave the position. If you want professors to act as references, ask at the conclusion of your study with them or upon your graduation from the school. By asking for a general letter of reference while your abilities remain fresh in their minds, you make it possible for your references to offer more precise information. Be sure to record references' addresses and telephone numbers, so that you will have them on file for future use.

Requesting Letters of Reference

Specific strategies are involved in using letters of reference. You will recall that general letters are written with no specific target in mind. In some instances, you may want to use general letters of reference when applying for a specific job—particularly if your recommendations are strong and especially relevant for the desired position. In this case, merely photocopy the letter and include it in your application.

In most cases, however, general letters of reference are too general to be of much use in the targeted-application procedure. Either they do not give information about specific skills you need, or they include irrelevant details that do not apply to the position you seek. In this instance, you may wish to ask the reference to write a more specific letter of reference for you. Include with your request a copy of the previously written general letter of reference, and supplement it with the details of how you would like the letter to be targeted more precisely toward the job you seek. The general letter jogs the reference's memory of you and provides the basis for expanding to a more specific letter.

When requesting a general letter of reference, you should provide details of what you want included in the letter. Be specific in asking for details that you think will be most useful to you in later job searches. If you know that certain tasks you did, skills you developed, or traits you possess are going to be relevant in later jobs, then be sure to mention them in your request for a general letter. Figure 16.1 contains the key points in requesting a general letter of reference.

Introduction: Establish positive relationship with the reader.
Refer to previous contact you have had with the reader.
Express thanks for the reader's help or support.
State purpose of your letter: to request a letter of reference.

Body: Explain the probable future use of the letter.
Provide suggestions about what might be included: tasks performed, skills demonstrated, knowledge gained, responsibilities held, outstanding accomplishments, personal traits demonstrated.

Conclusion: Thank the reader for providing this service.
Ask whether you may request a more specific reference in the future.
Close on a positive, optimistic note.

FIGURE 16.1 Formula for Requesting General Letters of Reference

Some people may not wish to take the time to write a letter, or they may feel that they cannot give you a useful recommendation. If you have performed well for them, however, most people are willing to write an honest and useful letter of reference. Of course, you should select references who have a positive attitude toward you.

Letters of reference are often protected by confidentiality, so you may not know what is included in a letter you have requested. It is probably a good idea to verify that your prospective reference will give you a positive letter before you have him or her include it in an application file, put it on record in a placement file, or send it to a prospective employer.

The format for a request for a specific letter of recommendation is similar to that for a general letter. The opening and closing paragraphs are almost identical. One difference is that the possible future request in the conclusion is omitted. The major difference lies in the middle paragraphs. You should explain the details of the job you seek so that the reference understands the target. You should then suggest specific comments about your skills and abilities that are especially pertinent to the position you desire. If the person has already written a general letter of reference, then the new task is to add more specific targeted comments and to delete any irrelevant ones. If the request for a specific letter of reference is your first contact with the reference, then explain in greater detail what you would like included in the letter.

Sample requests for a letter of reference are provided in Exhibits 16.A and 16.B. Notice how the requests follow the format suggested in Figure 16.1.

You should anticipate that the potential employer may get in touch with your references directly. Direct contact is an increasingly common practice among employers. If you request that someone serve as a reference, you should advise the person that he or she may be approached directly and suggest certain items that he or she could stress on your behalf.

```
Mavis Olson
44 Larkin Street
Van Nys, AL  37283

June 4, 19XX

Dr. James Quinn
History Department
Southern Alabama University
Winne, AL  39403

Dr. Quinn:

As the school year draws to a close, I am reminded of the several
excellent classes I have had at Southern.  Your American History
course was among the finest courses I had, and I would like to
express my appreciation for the work you put into your lectures,
for your helpfulness, and for your interest in your students'
welfare.

I will be leaving Southern at the end of fall term when I
graduate.  I plan to pursue a career in radio broadcasting, and I
would like to find a position as a newscaster.  I would appre-
ciate greatly a general letter of reference from you, if you feel
that you could recommend me for such a position.

Broadcasting jobs are rare, and I will be challenged to find a
position.  Your letter would be helpful in supporting my claims
about my background and abilities.  You may recall the paper that
I did for you on the use of radio by early twentieth-century
politicians.  You said at the time that it was one of the finest
pieces of student scholarship you had seen this year.  Likewise,
I scored well on your exams, and you commented on my enthusiasm
and participation in the class.  These comments, when put in
business terms such as determination and good communication
skills, would help me, I know, in my job search.

I appreciate your taking the time to perform this service for me.
You can address the letter to "Prospective Employer," and I will
include it in my application file with the school's placement
service.  May I write you again if I need a reference directed
toward a specific employer?

Again, my thanks for your excellent course and for this service.
I will carry with me fond memories of Southern and its excellent
staff.

Sincerely,


Mavis Olson
```

EXHIBIT 16.A Letter Requesting a General Letter of Reference

```
Mavis Olson
4405 Peach Street
Mobile, AL  39485


December 2, 19XX

Dr. James Quinn
History Department
Southern Alabama University
Winne, AL  39403

Dear Dr. Quinn:

Your American History class in the summer of 19XX was a highlight
of my college career.  I still appreciate your excellent work in
preparing such an exciting class.

To refresh your memory, I am enclosing the general letter of
reference you wrote upon my graduation.  It was quite useful in
helping me secure my first job in a radio station.  I am now
writing radio play scripts, specializing in educational topics.
I am applying for a job with the Alabama Historical Society,
where I would research and write radio play scripts concerning
early Alabama pioneers.  I would appreciate a more specific
letter of reference for this position if you would be willing to
write one.

This position requires historical research, clear writing, the
ability to work with a team of writers, and a general enjoyment
of historical research.  From the comments in your previous
letter, I think you can vouch for me in each of these four areas.
I have enclosed a current resume to bring you up to date on my
career.  You will note several credits writing for the University
radio station and WFGR in Mobile the past two years.  Because of
your keen interest in Senator Artess Haxley, I am also enclosing
a copy of the script on his life that I finished last month.

If you are willing to write this letter, please address it to Mr.
Kyle Andersen, c/o the Alabama Historical Society in Mobile.  I
believe that you are familiar with the organization and might
even know Mr. Andersen.

I know I would enjoy this job, because I enjoy writing historical
pieces a great deal.  I owe you much of the credit for developing
both my interests and my skills in history.  If I can answer any
questions or provide any more information, please write or call
me.  I will let you know whether or not I get the position.

Warm regards,



Mavis Olson
```

EXHIBIT 16.B   Request for a Specific Letter of Reference

Writing Letters of Reference

At some point in your career, you may be asked to write letters of recommendation for other people. In some instances people serving as your references may ask you to write a letter of reference for yourself that they can merely sign. For these reasons, you need to know how to prepare letters of reference.

Keep these concerns in mind when you compose letters of reference:

Be pertinent. Include only relevant details about the job at hand. Analyze the target position and include comments that the reader will find useful and practical in making a hiring decision for that job.

Be specific. Include examples of the applicant's skills, abilities, or traits. Do not merely say that the applicant is an "excellent worker." Give specific examples and facts that support this opinion.

Be reasonable. Use superlatives and extravagant praise sparingly. Giving too glowing a recommendation undercuts the impression of objectivity that you want to convey and renders the recommendation suspicious or worthless to the reader.

Be tactful. If you must include negative comments (and consider their relevance before you do), phrase them as positively as possible. Be honest and fair. A specific description of the behavior on which your opinion is based is better than loaded judgments and vague labels. You must be judicious when including negative remarks, because letters you write may or may not be kept confidential. Providing false or misleading information may be interpreted as libel in a court of law. Comments that could be construed as discriminatory may also create legal difficulties. Some writers find it easier to refuse a request than to write an unfavorable letter of recommendation. Others feel that it is only fair to warn employers about the drawbacks of prospective employees. Whichever course you select, you should carefully consider the truth, the relevance, the objectivity, and the legality of your negative comments. Most negative remarks can be made in a positive way, and the wary prospective employer will be able to "read between the lines" of tactful criticism. Another possibility is to show your letter to the person asking for the reference before you mail it, to give him or her the opportunity to withdraw the request.

The format for a letter of reference is provided in Figure 16.2. This format can be used for either general or specific letters of reference. While there is great diversity in how such letters are worded, most letters of reference include the elements shown in the figure.

Sample letters of reference are given in Exhibits 16.C and 16.D. Notice how the writers make their recommendations relevant, support their claims with details, address weaknesses tactfully, and avoid making extravagant claims.

Introduction:	State the purpose of the letter.
	Identify yourself.
	Explain your relationship to the applicant—specific period of acquaintance, positions held, and degree of involvement.
Body:	Explain the applicant's duties and responsibilities when working with you.
	Give details of the applicant's skills and abilities, providing specific examples to demonstrate each claim.
	Answer any direct questions asked about the applicant.
Conclusion:	State your availability for direct telephone contact for other information (often optionally used for negative comments).
	Offer a candid assessment of the candidate's overall suitability for the job.

FIGURE 16.2 Formula for Writing Letters of Reference

Dr. James E. Morran
Management Department
Alcott College
Reading, MA 03927

May 20, 19XX

Joan Biddingly
Amfact Information and Computer Services
4059 Broadway
Boston, MA 04938

Dear Ms. Biddingly:

Mary Hart has requested that I write a letter of recommendation
to support her application to your company. I understand she is
applying for the position of sales executive. I can recommend
her highly, and I am sure she will do an outstanding job for your
firm.

I know Mary from the several classes she took from me while at
Alcott. She was an outstanding student, both in the grades she
received for the courses and in the enthusiasm and interest she
took in the subject. She was one of the few students who regularly sought me out during office hours to probe the course
material more carefully and to develop a deeper understanding of
the subject. She volunteered on several occasions to do extra
research for assignments to improve her classwork.

On a personal level, Mary was easy to work with and a pleasure to
instruct. She took feedback and corrective advice very well.
She was always open to suggestions on ways to improve her classwork, and she sought out that advice from me. She was also quite
vocal with her opinions in classroom discussion, and several
students commented to me that she had provided assistance to them
with assignments. Her participation in class was always balanced
and mature, and she demonstrated a thorough understanding of the
issues we discussed.

As far as sales skills are concerned, Mary developed a sales
training program for one course I taught, and she was an excellent speaker in a Sales Presentation course. She is dynamic,
enthusiastic, and a determined worker, and has great promise in
professional sales.

I think Mary would be an excellent addition to any sales force,
and I recommend her without reservation for the position. If I
can provide any additional information about her qualifications,
please do not hesitate to write me at the above address.

Regards,

James Morran

EXHIBIT 16.C   Letter of Reference

```
                          ALL-DAY CLEANING
594 Hillsdale Way                        Montgomery, AL 39208
Office:  (809) 493-2849                  Emergency:  (809) 493-9374



                                                March 4, 19XX


Kay Wiegel, Admissions Advisor
Emerson Business School
Tyup, New York  10293

Dear Ms. Wiegel:

Mark Hartford is an applicant to your M.B.A. program and he has
requested that I write a letter of recommendation.  I wish to
support his application to your program and provide some evidence
of his qualifications as an aspiring professional businessman.

Mark was employed at my cleaning service for four years as a
manager during the time he was an undergraduate at Davidson
College.  He worked approximately 15 hours a week while he
maintained a full load of courses at school.  He handled these
responsibilities admirably, though at times he was hard-pressed
to satisfy all the demands on his time.

As a manager, he was responsible for scheduling workloads for
cleaning crews, maintaining and preparing equipment, ordering
supplies, and managing work crews.  At times, he assisted in
recruiting and interviewing job applicants.

Throughout the four years, Mark showed continual improvement in
his ability to manage his work areas.  He gradually developed
more skills in managing the work crews, and he assumed more
independence as a manager.  At times, Mark needed assistance in
balancing the demands of both school and work, but he responded
well to suggestions and was always eager to make the extra effort
to perform well.  While the time demands prevented him from
committing as much time to his schoolwork as I know he would have
liked to give, his work for me never suffered.  He was always on
time, willing to stay late if necessary, and level-headed in the
face of any problems that arose.

Now that Mark has decided to return to school full-time to get
an M.B.A., I think he will make an excellent and dedicated
student.  I recommend him heartily and completely to you.

Sincerely,


Clayton Morrison, Pres.
All-Day Cleaners
```

EXHIBIT 16.D   Letter of Reference

EXERCISE 16.1
Correcting a Poor Letter of Reference

Directions: The following sentences are from a letter of reference written by Sam, a former employer of Jim, the applicant for a position as a librarian's aide. Each sentence contains an error in technique for writing effective letters of reference. In the space provided, identify the error, and rewrite the sentence so that it is more effective.

1. "I don't know much about Jim, but I'll tell you what I do know."

   Error: _____

   Rewrite: _____

   _____

   _____

2. "Jim and I worked together a lot."

   Error: _____

   Rewrite: _____

   _____

   _____

3. "Jim's outstanding trait is his love of jogging."

   Error: _____

   Rewrite: _____

   _____

   _____

4. "Jim is probably the best library worker in the country."

   Error: _____

   Rewrite: _____

   _____

   _____

5. "Jim doesn't have any experience as a librarian, but he does have some experience in bookkeeping and filing."

Error: _____

Rewrite: _____

_____

_____

6. "Jim has the ability to learn quickly and to do a good job."

Error: _____

Rewrite: _____

_____

_____

7. "Jim was always late for work."

Error: _____

Rewrite: _____

_____

_____

8. "Overall, Jim is everything you could possibly want in a librarian's aide."

Error: _____

Rewrite: _____

_____

_____

EXERCISE 16.2
Assembling Your Reference Pool

Directions: In order to develop your own reference pool, complete the following form. From your work experience, school experience, and personal source, list the people whom you would like to be able to ask to serve as references for you. Assemble their business addresses and telephone numbers. For each person, list what he or she knows about your skills, abilities, and traits.

EMPLOYMENT REFERENCES

1. Name: _____

   Title: _____

   Business address: _____

   _____

   Business telephone: _____

   Abilities this person can verify: _____

   _____

   _____

   _____

   _____

2. Name: _____

   Title: _____

   Business address: _____

   _____

   Business telephone: _____

   Abilities this person can verify: _____

   _____

   _____

   _____

   _____

3. Name: _____

   Title: _____

   Business address: _____

   _____

   Business telephone: _____

   Abilities this person can verify: _____

   _____

   _____

   _____

   _____

ACADEMIC REFERENCES

1. Name: _____

   Title: _____

   Business address: _____

   _____

   Business telephone: _____

   Abilities this person can verify: _____

   _____

   _____

   _____

   _____

2. Name: _____

   Title: _____

   Business address: _____

   _____

   Business telephone: _____

   Abilities this person can verify: _____

   _____

   _____

   _____

   _____

3. Name: _____

   Title: _____

   Business address: _____

   _____

   Business telephone: _____

   Abilities this person can verify: _____

   _____

   _____

   _____

   _____

PERSONAL REFERENCES

1. Name: _____

   Title: _____

   Business address: _____

   _____

Business telephone: _____

Abilities this person can verify: _____

_____

_____

_____

_____

2. Name: _____

Title: _____

Business address: _____

_____

Business telephone: _____

Abilities this person can verify: _____

_____

_____

_____

_____

3. Name: _____

Title: _____

Business address: _____

_____

Business telephone: _____

Abilities this person can verify: _____

_____

_____

_____

_____

EXERCISE 16.3
Writing a Letter Requesting a Specific Letter of Reference

Directions: The worksheet below is designed to assist you in planning a letter in which you request a letter of reference from one of the people in your reference pool. Assume that you are applying for a specific position and that you would like the reference to be targeted to the job you identify. Once you have planned the letter, prepare a typed version of it.

Inside address: _____

_____

_____

_____

Opening paragraph:

(recall positive relationship) _____

_____

_____

_____

(thanks for reader's help or support) _____

_____

_____

_____

(purpose of letter) _____

_____

_____

_____

Middle paragraphs:

(nature of the job) _____

_____

_____

_____

(specific skills, abilities, and traits needed on the job) _____

_____

_____

_____

_____

(suggestions of points the letter of reference might include) _____

_____

_____

_____

_____

Closing paragraph:

(thanks for this service) _____

_____

_____

_____

(positive, optimistic close) _____

_____

_____

_____

EXERCISE 16.4
Writing a Letter of Reference

Directions: Assume that you have asked a professor to write a general letter of reference for you. The response of the professor was that you should write the letter, which he or she will then sign. In the spaces provided below, plan the letter of reference about yourself that you would write. Once it is planned, type a completed version.

Return address: _____

_____

Salutation: _____

_____

Opening paragraph:

(purpose of the letter) _____

_____

_____

_____

(identification of the writer) _____

_____

_____

_____

(writer's relationship to applicant) _____

_____

_____

_____

Middle paragraphs:

(applicant's duties/responsibilities) _____

_____

_____

_____

_____

(details about the applicant)

(skills) _____

_____

_____

_____

(abilities) _____

_____

_____

_____

(special knowledge) _____

_____

_____

_____

(personality traits) _____

_____

_____

_____

Closing paragraph:

(candid but tactful statement of overall assessment) _____

_____

_____

_____

_____

ACTION ASSIGNMENT

16

Letters of Reference

1. Make copies of the letter of reference you wrote in Exercise 16.4. Form a group of five people and distribute these copies to your group members. Read and critique one another's letters on the basis of the guidelines provided in this chapter.

2. Select a partner for this assignment whom you know fairly well. Write a general letter of reference for each other that each of you might use in future jobhunting situations.

17
The Information-Gathering Interview

Information is vital to the career search. You have already investigated and determined your interests and skills in the career inventory and self-analysis in Chapter 13. You have also developed networking as a useful tool for finding job leads. The information-gathering interview is another technique you may wish to learn before you take part in a selection interview, in which you meet the potential employer and review your qualifications.

The information-gathering interview is excellent preparation for the selection interview. Once you find an opening for a position you want, you need to gather information about the requirements for being hired and the actual working conditions. This information provides valuable clues for planning the selection interview. It also will help you decide whether you want the job if it is offered to you. This chapter looks at the ways in which you can use the information-gathering interview, suggestions for planning the interview, and useful techniques for conducting one.

Uses of the Information-Gathering Interview

Interviews to gather information are useful at various stages of the career-search process. The following list illustrates several ways in which the information-gathering interview may be helpful.

1. *Clarifying career goals.* If you are uncertain about the type of job you want, interviews with counselors, instructors, or professionals whose opinions you trust may help you discover interesting career paths.
2. *Getting to know a profession.* You may have a general idea of the professional area you want but not know specific details about the types of available jobs, new developments in the profession, or other opportunities By interviewing people in a specific professional area, you get a better overall picture of its potential for you.

3. *Getting to know a job.* You can interview people who actually hold positions similar to those which interest you. You can determine the tasks the job involves and the working conditions at specific companies, and you can generally get to "know the ropes" of a specific position by interviewing someone who holds the same type of job.

4. *Investigating a job opening.* Once you find a job opening that interests you, gathering information helps you target your application and résumé. Some job listings are vaguely stated. By talking to someone who knows the job, you gain a clearer picture of what the employer seeks in an ideal candidate. This information helps you present your qualifications in a more focused manner.

5. *Doing general research.* Beyond the specific needs of gathering information about a career search, the information-gathering interview is also useful for any type of research. If you are planning to give a speech, write a report, or prepare an analysis, the information-gathering interview enables you to acquire in-depth and current information, a personal view of the facts, and contacts who may be useful in later stages of your career.

Planning the Interview

Planning is the key to effective interviews. Careful planning ensures that you are interviewing the right person, that you use your time efficiently, that you have planned questions to stay on track, and that you are thorough. The following suggestions offer steps to use in planning an information-gathering interview. Use them as a checklist when you plan.

DETERMINE YOUR PURPOSE

What kind of information are you seeking? If you have only a vague idea of what you are looking for, then you are likely to end up wasting the valuable time of the person you interview. Carefully consider your purpose in advance. Clarify to yourself, either by discussing it with a friend or by thinking it through on your own, the specific kinds of information you want, the number of topics you can cover in a reasonable amount of time, and the specific areas you want to cover in the interview. This forethought forms the basis for a stronger, more efficient interview.

DETERMINE THE BEST SOURCES OF INFORMATION

Once you know what information you need, then consider who could provide you with it. You should interview people who are experienced in the field that interests you, who might share some valuable insights in that area, and who are willing to take the time to talk to you. Your network may lead you to some helpful people. Good sources of information are instructors, former employers, and professional contacts you have already made. You can also identify potential interviewees through the Yellow Pages or professional directories of business executives. The person you interview may also refer you to some other expert. At the end of an interview, it is always a good idea to ask, "Can you recommend anyone else I might talk to about this topic?" In this way, you can expand your network of professional contacts.

DO YOUR HOMEWORK

People who grant you an interview are usually very busy. It is extremely amateurish and irritating to them if you waste their time by asking questions that you could easily have answered for yourself if you had done a bit of homework. It is important to gather as much information as you can in advance of an interview so that your shared time will be used to its greatest potential. By being informed about the subject matter, you can converse with the interviewee more intelligently, ask more focused questions, and present yourself as a more credible interviewer.

PREPARE YOUR QUESTIONS IN ADVANCE

A general outline is helpful for covering your interests in an interview. A clear set of questions or topic areas helps you cover the ground you want to explore and not ramble too far afield. Use your notes to keep you on track or to get you back on track if the conversation happens to wander. Do not be glued to your notes, however. Listen carefully to the interviewee's answers. Probe deeper for more information if you are interested. Always be ready to shift to new topics if they become more interesting than your planned agenda.

SET UP THE INTERVIEW

The easiest interview to arrange is with someone you already know, but you can easily arrange appointments with strangers as well. Most people are willing and even flattered to provide information about themselves, their business, and their success. You may occasionally encounter someone who is too busy to help you, but most business people realize the importance of information sharing and will assist you. If you get a rejection, don't pester that person, but move on to another interviewee.

An interview can be arranged through a letter requesting it, through a telephone call, or a combination of the two. If you cannot reach someone by telephone, a letter is often the most effective way to explain your purpose and to arrange a time to talk by phone.

When arranging the interview, you should explain who you are, announce the fact that you desire an interview, and explain the purpose of the interview. State your time expectations for the interview. Most people will gladly schedule 15 or 20 minutes to talk with you. If the interview is enjoyable, that time may stretch, but you should leave it up to the interviewee to expand the time limit originally agreed on. Finally, determine the exact time and place for the interview. Allow the interviewee flexibility when setting a time. Remember that the person you interview is doing you a favor, so you want the interview to be as convenient as possible for him or her—not for you. Arrive on time—or even a bit early—at the interview, and be prepared.

The hardest interview to arrange is the "cold call," in which you do not know the person you wish to meet. Figure 17.1 offers a telephone script for arranging a cold-call interview.

CALLER:	Hello, Mr. Jones?
CONTACT:	Yes, this is he.
CALLER:	This is Sarah Welder calling. I am a student at Sutter State University, and I am doing research for a business class project.
CONTACT:	Yes? How can I be of help?
CALLER:	Well, Mr. Jones, I would like to arrange a brief interview with you—about fifteen minutes of your time—in order to gather some information about the responsibilities of a sales representative for a textbook company. I am exploring sales as a career area, and I would like to meet someone and talk about what a sales career is like.
CONTACT:	Well, Sarah, I am kind of busy. How did you happen to get my name?
CALLER:	You were referred to me by Professor Martha Slader, my advisor at State.
CONTACT:	Oh, Martha! Well, if she referred you, then I suppose I can take the time. What exactly do you want to talk about?
CALLER:	I'll be glad to send you the list of questions I'd like to discuss with you. I'm interested in what is required in your job, what you think a student ought to know about preparing for a career in sales, and maybe some information on how you like your present position.
CONTACT:	Sure, I can tell you about that. Do you want to talk about it now, over the phone?
CALLER:	Well, I would really like to meet you in person, Mr. Jones. Seeing you in your office would give me a better picture of what your job is like.
CONTACT:	Sure, that's fine. I can even show you around the office.
CALLER:	That would be great! When would be a convenient time to meet?
CONTACT:	Well, let's see. How about on Wednesday morning, the ninth, at about eleven-thirty. Do you know where my office is?
CALLER:	Yes, I do. And that time is fine. Thank you, and I'll see you next Wednesday at eleven-thirty. Goodby.

FIGURE 17.1   Telephone Script for Arranging an Information-Gathering Interview

Techniques for Conducting the Interview

This section offers suggestions on conducting the information-gathering interview for the purpose of exploring a profession or a specific job. When gathering information about a career area, you will find the topics and questions suggested in Figure 17.2 helpful in preparing for the interview.

Opening conversation: Discuss people and things you have in common. Explain the purpose of the interview and the general areas you intend to cover. Introduce yourself, and allow the contact to introduce herself or himself.

Investigate job responsibilities: What do you do on this job? What is the most difficult aspect of this job? the most interesting?

Investigate job qualifications: What skills does it take to perform this job? What training is necessary? What does it take to be successful in this job? What path would you recommend for a beginner to get a job in this area? What classes, extracurricular activities, part-time jobs, or experiences would be the most valuable?

Investigate the specific company: How is this company different from and similar to other companies in the industry? What is the most enjoyable aspect of working for this company?

Investigate the industry or professional area: What do you see as the future trend in the profession? What are the growth possibilities in this field? What advice would you give a young person considering this profession? For a person with my background, how can I best use my skills in this career area?

Get to know the contact (if appropriate): What path did you take to get into this career area? How were you hired for this job? How do you like working here? What are some of the positive aspects of this career? What are some of the negative aspects of this career?

End with a "capper" question: Do you have any other advice or suggestions for a student preparing for a career in this field? Can you suggest anyone else I might talk to about this area?

FIGURE 17.2 Typical Questions for the Information-Gathering Interview

When using the interview to gather information, it is a good tactic to explain early that you are *not looking for a job*. Some jobseekers use the excuse of information gathering to meet employers face to face and then do a sales pitch on why they should be hired for a certain job. This tactic undermines the entire purpose of information-gathering interviews and makes some business people suspicious. Always be clear and honest about your intentions, and stay true to your purpose.

When beginning the interview, start with general, open-ended questions. Do not get specific too soon, or you will get sidetracked. If you do get off track, simply refer to your notes. As long as the interviewee is comfortable, the order of questions may not be very important. Check your notes, however, to make sure you are covering all the areas you want to investigate. Take notes of specific facts, but do it unobtrusively. You should record specific names, telephone numbers, addresses, dates, or facts if you are going to need them later. If a cordial climate develops, you can deepen your questions to get more personal information from the contact, but always attend to the comfort level of the interviewee. Watch for nonverbal signals like relaxed posture, smiling, and eye contact, which indicate whether the interview is on track. Be interested in what the interviewee has to say: respond to answers and ask for more clarification if something interests you. Be polite, and do not probe too deeply if you get signals that the contact is unwilling to discuss a particular subject. Let the interviewee do most of the talking—remember that you are there to gather information. Watch the time limit, and stick to it unless the interviewee appears to want to extend the time.

As you approach the end of the interview, summarizing what you have learned is an excellent technique for checking your facts and for showing the contact that you have been listening. Express your appreciation for the time and effort the contact has given you. If you want a second interview, make specific plans to meet again. A firm handshake and cordial thanks are courteous ways to terminate the interview. Once outside the interview setting, you may want to add to your notes or jot down some details that you might not remember later. A follow-up letter repeating your thanks shows professional courtesy that is universally appreciated. If an interview is extremely helpful, you might even consider sending flowers or a small gift to express your appreciation.

You need to assess the information you receive from the interview. Remember that you are getting just one person's perspective on a job or a profession. Other people may have widely divergent points of view that could be equally valuable to you. Balance your interviews by talking with several contacts from several different sources. The more information you gather, the better the decisions you can make.

There are several ways in which the information-gathering interview can be modified for a specific purpose. One adaptation is to use it as a stepping stone to finding the job you want. Richard Bolles suggests the strategy of "comparative interviewing": conducting five or six information-gathering interviews and then returning to the most attractive company and making an employment pitch—telling them why you want to work for the company and what you can do to help them succeed at their business.[1] This technique demonstrates stamina and courage, and it demands assertiveness as well as a knowledge of the industry.

Another use of the interview is to gather information on a specific job opening. If you find a help-wanted ad or a job-opening notification, you can gather more specific information in order to target your application and résumé to fit the specific requirements. This type of information-gathering interview should begin with the explanation that you are an applicant for a certain position and that you would like more information about the opening. By showing up in person to ask for the information, you may get an impromptu job interview with the decision maker. Be prepared to talk about your qualifications if that happens, but limit the interview as much as you can to gathering information so that you can complete the application and return for an in-depth interview later. By probing for additional skills re-

---

Introduction:	Remind the reader of the interview.
	Express your appreciation.
Body:	Review some surprising fact or question raised in the interview.
	Express any subsequent thoughts you had.
	Explain how the interview was of value to you.
Conclusion:	Express desire to maintain contact.
	Repeat your thanks.

FIGURE 17.3   Formula for Follow-Up Letters

quired, the specific responsibilities of the job, and particular working conditions, you may be able to make your application unique and finely tailored to the prospective employer's needs.

The Follow-Up Letter

Once you have completed an interview, a follow-up letter is usually in order to express your appreciation and to maintain professional contact with the new member of your network. This business courtesy demonstrates your level of professionalism and is a small price to pay for the value of an effective interview. Figure 17.3 outlines the points that are typically included in a follow-up letter after an information-gathering interview. The sample follow-up letter in Exhibit 17.A demonstrates the use of these points.

NOTE

1. See Richard Bolles, *What Color Is Your Parachute? A Practical Manual for Job Hunters* (Berkeley, Calif.: Ten Speed Press, 1986).

RESOURCES

Biagi, Shirley. *Interviews That Work: A Practical Guide for Journalists.* Belmont, Calif.: Wadsworth, 1986.
This book provides instruction on how to plan and conduct information-gathering interviews from a journalistic perspective. It is useful to compare the task of a reporter looking for a story to that of a jobseeker.

Bolles, Richard A. *What Color Is Your Parachute? A Practical Manual for Job Hunters.* Berkeley, Calif.: Ten Speed Press, 1986.
This book discusses the information-gathering interview technique in depth and is particularly useful in helping you identify potential interviewees when searching for a career.

Irish, Richard K. *Go Hire Yourself an Employer.* Garden City, N.Y.: Anchor Books, 1980.
This book contains a useful section on information gathering that integrates interviews into the overall career search.

Samovar, Larry A., and Susan A. Hellweg. *Interviewing: A Communicative Approach.* Scottsdale, Ariz.: Gorsuch Scarisbrick, 1982.
This book is useful for determining your purpose and developing questions for the information-gathering interview.

Walters, Barbara. *How to Talk with Practically Anybody About Practically Anything.* New York: Dell Books, 1971.
An interesting narrative by a famous newscaster and reporter about information-gathering interviews she has conducted.

```
                                        Jamie Curtis
                                        32 Pine Street
                                        Alamo, MO  74673


                                        December 3, 19XX

Ms. Eleanor Harper
Whitney Investments
4950 Excelsior Blvd.
St. Louis, MO  75849

Dear Ms. Harper:

Thank you for the time and the effort you spent in showing me the
bank and discussing my career in investment banking.

I was particularly impressed by the wide background one needs in
order to become an effective investments counselor.  The informa-
tion you shared with me will help me in my remaining year of
coursework.  I now plan to develop more interpersonal communica-
tion skills and a broader background in international economics.
As you indicated, I am sure that skill and knowledge in those two
areas will be of immense help to me in the future.

I hope we can stay in touch.  I would like to talk with you again
in about six months.  I will be in contact with you about that
later.  Again, please accept my thanks for an extremely helpful
interview.

Cordially,


Jamie Curtis

P.S.  Dr. Edison, my instructor, sends his regards to you as
well.  He liked my report on investment banking--an A!
```

EXHIBIT 17.A Follow-Up Letter

EXERCISE 17.1
Planning an Information-Gathering Interview

Directions: Use the following worksheet to plan and conduct an information-gathering interview in which you research a job area of interest to you. You may wish to do general research in a professional area or to interview someone who holds a position similar to one that you might someday like to have.

PURPOSE OF THE INTERVIEW

_____

_____

SPECIFIC AREAS TO BE COVERED IN THE INTERVIEW

1. _____

   _____

2. _____

   _____

3. _____

   _____

4. _____

   _____

PERSON TO BE INTERVIEWED

Name: _____

Position: _____

Company: _____

Areas of responsibility: _____

_____

TECHNIQUES FOR OPENING THE INTERVIEW

1. _____

2. _____

3. _____

QUESTIONS TO BE ASKED

Specific area 1:

1. _____

_____

2. _____

_____

3. _____

_____

Specific area 2:

1. _____

_____

2. _____

_____

3. _____

_____

Specific area 3:

1. _____

_____

2. _____

_____

3. _____

_____

Specific area 4:

1. _____

   _____

2. _____

   _____

3. _____

   _____

TECHNIQUES FOR CLOSING THE INTERVIEW

1. _____

2. _____

EXERCISE 17.2
Reporting on an Information-Gathering Interview

Directions: On the basis of the interview you planned and conducted in Exercise 17.1, use this worksheet to report your findings. If some categories are not applicable, omit them. If you covered other areas in the interview, add them to the outline.

PERSON INTERVIEWED

Name: _____

Position/Company: _____

Areas of responsibility: _____

_____

INTERVIEW DETAILS

Date/Time: _____

Location: _____

FINDINGS OF THE INTERVIEW

Specific area 1:

1. _____

_____

2. _____

_____

3. _____

_____

Specific area 2:

1. _____

_____

2. _____

_____

3. _____

_____

Specific area 3:

1. _____

   _____

2. _____

   _____

3. _____

   _____

Specific area 4:

1. _____

   _____

2. _____

   _____

3. _____

   _____

GENERAL REACTION TO THE INTERVIEW

_____

_____

_____

FOLLOW-UP ACTION NEEDED

_____

_____

_____

EXERCISE 17.3
Writing a Follow-Up Letter

Directions: Write a follow-up letter expressing your thanks for the interview you conducted in Exercise 17.1. Use the following worksheet to plan your letter.

Opening paragraph:

(reminder of interview) _____

_____

_____

(thanks) _____

_____

_____

Middle paragraph:

(unexpected facts or questions raised) _____

_____

_____

_____

_____

(subsequent thoughts) _____

_____

_____

_____

_____

(interview's value to you) _____

_____

_____

_____

_____

Closing paragraph:

(desire to maintain contact) _____

_____

_____

_____

(repeated thanks) _____

_____

_____

_____

_____

The Information-Gathering Interview

1. Plan and conduct an information-gathering interview with one of your classmates. The purpose of the interview should be for you to better understand your partner's career goals and aspirations. You may wish to include the following list of subject areas in planning your questions:

   General background information (age, marital status, residence, major in school, planned graduation date)

   Work experience

   Immediate goal for after graduation (or within two years)

   Long-term career goal (within five to ten years)

   Reasons for selecting these goals

   Criteria for success in chosen career

2. Interview a close relative (a parent, an aunt or uncle, or an older sibling) and gather information about his or her work experience. Use the information-gathering questions suggested in this chapter to gain a better understanding of the interviewee's attitudes and experiences in the working world.

3. Interview a working person who is employed in an industry outside of your career interests. Use the information-gathering questions suggested in this chapter to gain a better understanding of the interviewee's attitudes and experiences in the working world.

4. Prepare a list of people you would like to interview who are currently employed in your future career area. For each person, list the kinds of information that would be most helpful for you to gain.

18

Selection Interviews: The Role of the Interviewer

Business people use many types of interviews. The ability to interview efficiently and effectively is a valuable career skill for people who will have to gather information, hire employees, and manage others. Managers are rarely given instruction in how to interview, however. It is assumed that anyone can interview anybody with ease—it's just a matter of asking a few questions, right? Such an attitude leads to many problems: poor planning, poor questioning, and poor decision making.

Effective interviewing can be relatively easy and useful if certain principles and skills are applied. This chapter analyzes the *selection interview*, in which a potential employer reviews the qualifications of an applicant and makes a hiring decision. This type of interview is also called the *employment interview* or the *job interview*. This chapter outlines techniques for interviewing and focuses on the role of the interviewer in the employment selection interview. By understanding the role of the interviewer, you will be better able to use interviews effectively to recruit, hire, and manage people. Understanding the role of the interviewer will also give you an advantage as an applicant for a job. (The role of the applicant in the selection interview is discussed in Chapter 19.)

General Interviewing Techniques

All interviews consist of the exchange of information. The major technique of the interview is the use of questions and answers. Prior to an interview, both parties should prepare an agenda of information that they wish to disclose to the other person and an agenda of information that they would like to gather. Through question and answer, both parties disclose and gather the information they desire.

Introduction:	Greetings and introductions.
	Conversation to make the interviewee comfortable.
	Explanation of the purpose of the interview.
	Description of the structure of the interview.
Body:	The information the interviewer will provide.
	The questions the interviewer asks the interviewee.
	The answers the interviewee provides.
	The questions the interviewee asks the interviewer.
	The answers the interviewer provides.
Conclusion:	Any last-minute additions or questions.
	Discussion of the next step in the process.
	Thanks and farewell.

FIGURE 18.1 Common Three-Part Structure of Selection Interviews

The following general techniques are useful in the efficient exchange of information in the selection interview. These techniques will help you prepare both questions and answers that will make interviewing easier. The better you understand the process of effective interviewing, the more comfortable you will be—on either side of the table. More specific techniques for the interviewer will be covered later in this chapter.

KNOW YOUR PURPOSE

Plan the information you wish to disclose about yourself and the company you represent. By anticipating the types of questions the other person will ask, you can determine in advance how much you wish to say about a topic. Likewise, you should have a clear idea of the information you wish to gather. By having a checklist of facts you wish to learn, you can plan and use your interview time more efficiently.

DEVELOP AN INTERVIEW PLAN

A plan will guide you through your time with the other person. Some people prepare an outline of topics they want to cover and questions they wish to ask. Others rely on a general plan that consists of three steps: beginning, middle, and end. The common structure for a selection interview is summarized in Figure 18.1. Notice the areas of responsibility for the interviewer in each part of the interview.

VARY YOUR TYPES OF QUESTIONS

There are several types of questioning you can use in an interview. Knowing and using various types of questions will keep you from becoming monotonous as an interviewer and will allow you to gain a more thorough picture of the applicant's qualifications.

Use *closed questions* to gather specific facts. A closed question is one that can be answered with a simple "yes" or "no" or with a specific piece of information. Closed questions can be very direct and save time, but they also tend to limit the amount of information disclosed. Use closed questions when you want specific and simple answers.

Use *open-ended questions* when you want greater amounts of information. An open-ended question begins with a phrase such as "Tell me about . . ." or "Describe for me. . ." Such questions prompt the respondent to offer more detailed information. They also provide more in-depth information, since personal opinions and feelings often are subtly communicated in the longer answers. Open-ended questions are a useful way to get to know an applicant quickly, since the answers reflect the personality of the person.

Use *probing questions* to gather more in-depth information about specific areas. The *journalistic questions* of "who, what, where, when, and how" can bring out greater detail. *Follow-up questions*, which ask for more specific detail or for more information, will help you gain a clearer picture as well.

Use *clarifying techniques* to ensure the accuracy of your understanding. There are several ways in which to clarify. You can use a *reflecting question*, which makes the other person restate an answer; for example, "So you think it was a good thing to expand the job description?" You can *paraphrase* and watch the person's response to ensure the accuracy of your summary; for example, "What you are saying is that it was a good thing to expand the job description." *Repetition* and *summary* are also useful techniques for checking the accuracy of facts or details.

Use *hypothetical questions* to test the other person's responses. A hypothetical question asks for a specific response in an imaginary situation; for example, "What would you do if an employee said that to you?" The way the person answers may indicate how he or she would react in a real situation.

A final type of question—the *clearinghouse question*—is useful at the end of an interview. Such a question clears the air so that the participants can move on to other business; for example, "Is there anything else about that issue you want to tell me?" Common clearinghouse questions include: "Is there anything else I can tell you about my company?" "Do you have any further questions?" and "Is there anything else you want to tell me about yourself?"

At no point in the interview should you use leading and loaded questions, because they will give a faulty picture of the applicant. A *leading question* has an implied answer; for example, "Don't you agree that my solution is the best?" A *loaded question* uses emotionally charged language and name calling to imply a certain opinion in an answer; for example, "Surely you weren't stupid enough to do that, were you?" These two types of questions create an obstacle to effective information sharing, since they imply the prejudgment of a "right" answer.

Figure 18.2 summarizes the various types of questions you can use as an interviewer and provides examples of each type.

Closed Questions:

Do you have any experience?

Did you do filing at your last job?

What is your typing speed?

Open Questions:

Tell me about your last job.

How did you get along with your last manager?

Describe what you did on your last vacation.

Probing Questions:

Tell me more about what you did at school.

What did you do after he said that?

When did you get that experience?

Clarifying Techniques:

So you think you know how to do this job?

You say you worked there for three years?

Let me get this straight—you have done this before?

Hypothetical Questions:

What would you do in a situation like this?

How would you react if an employee did that?

What would you do if an employee caused a problem?

Clearinghouse Questions:

Do you have any further questions?

Anything else I should know about you?

What else can I tell you about us before we end?

Avoid Using Leading and Loaded Questions:

Surely you don't think that, do you?

Are you sure that's what you would do?

What is the right way to handle a client like that?

FIGURE 18.2 Examples of Types of Questions

CREATE A COMFORTABLE ENVIRONMENT FOR THE INTERVIEW

When both parties are relaxed, there is a greater chance for an efficient exchange of information. Interviews should be in a private and appropriate environment free from distractions or interruptions. Any interview should begin with a relaxed period of conversation to put both people at ease and to familiarize them with each other before they begin the exchange.

BEGIN WITH EASY QUESTIONS

The applicant needs to establish confidence and trust in the interviewer. It is awkward and unfair to start an interview with a very difficult question. If an applicant becomes defensive and uncomfortable, the effectiveness of the interview can be severely reduced. Easy questions are those which cover facts the applicant knows well, such as general questions about schooling or a prior position. Difficult questions test a person's skill or knowledge and serve as the basis for evaluation.

RESPOND TO ANSWERS AS YOU ASK QUESTIONS

Listen closely to the applicant, and let him or her know that you have heard and understood the answers offered. Responses can be noncommittal, such as "I see" or "How interesting," or they can reflect you own opinions and specific reactions to the answers being provided.

END THE INTERVIEW ON A POSITIVE NOTE

Explain what will happen next in the application process. Applicants always wonder when and how the decision will be made and when it will be communicated to them. Anticipate your next meeting with the person being interviewed, and create a positive relationship that will make future dealings pleasant and relaxed. Disclose as much information as you can to allay any fears or concerns the applicant might have. Small pleasantries such as statements of appreciation and anticipation of the future make the end of an interview graceful and positive.

Steps in the Selection Interview

This section explains the specific tasks of the interviewer when the purpose is to evaluate and hire applicants for an employment position. Knowing interviewing skills from the interviewer's side of the table can be valuable in several ways. First, being able to interview effectively is a useful managerial skill. Many managers never receive any training in interviewing skills, and you can save time and energy by knowing how to plan and conduct productive interviews. Likewise, you can make better hiring decisions if you are an effective interviewer. A second reason for learning interviewing skills is to prepare yourself as an applicant. When you apply for a job and know you will be interviewed, the best way to prepare for the interview is to anticipate what the interviewer will do. By understanding the role of the interviewer, you can anticipate how the interview will be structured, the types of questions that will probably be asked, and the best techniques for influencing the interviewer in a positive manner.

PREPARING FOR THE INTERVIEW

As the interviewer, you must do a certain amount of homework to prepare for an effective interview. The following list of activities surveys the preparation you should make.

1. *Know the purpose of the interview.* You must know the specific purpose of the interview in order to determine the appropriate length and depth of questioning. If the purpose is merely to screen applicants, then questions will be relatively brief and general. When the purpose is to hire someone immediately, your questions should probe the applicant's background and abilities in more depth.

2. *Know the qualifications for the job.* You must know the job duties and the qualifications that will best reflect an applicant's ability to perform these duties. Usually, an interviewer looks for prior experience, skills needed to perform the required tasks, knowledge that will be used on the job, and key personality traits that will make for a good employee. Analyze the job responsibilities and prepare a set of selection criteria that will guide you in asking questions and reviewing the applicant's qualifications.

3. *Prepare the interviewing location.* Arrange an appropriate time and place for the interview. The interview site should be free of distractions and interruptions such as telephones ringing or people dropping by to talk during the interview. If you plan a tour or a meeting with other people, arrange these details in advance so that they will take place smoothly and efficiently.

4. *Review the applicant's materials.* If an applicant has submitted a résumé or letter of application, read the materials thoroughly and critically before the interview. This review will help you design more insightful questions, probe areas of potential weakness, and gain a better picture of the applicant in a shorter time.

CONDUCTING THE INTERVIEW

Once you have prepared the interview and communicated the time and place to the applicant, you are ready to conduct the interview. The following techniques will help you guide the applicant through the exchange.

The Opening

1. *Greet the applicant and introduce yourself.* A firm handshake and consideration for the applicant's comfort are positive ways to begin an interview. Give your name and position in the organization you represent. Take note of the applicant's name, and call her or him by name during the interview; this will relax the applicant and build trust.

2. *Begin with pleasantries.* Discuss the applicant's trip to the office, the weather, people you know in common, recent noncontroversial events, or other topics that will relax the applicant and prepare him or her for the interview. Opening chit-chat may seem trivial, but it is actually very important. If you jump right into questioning without giving the applicant a chance to relax, he or she will remain defensive and uncomfortable throughout the interview. You will not receive open answers or get a real picture of the applicant's abilities. People will not trust you if you make them defensive, and their answers will be guarded and cautious.

3. *Explain the purpose of the interview.* Clarify immediately any initial misunderstandings about the purpose of the interview, the job being applied for, or how the interview will be conducted. Applicants may have applied for the wrong job, be in the wrong place, or have entirely different intentions than an interviewer assumes. By offering an opening explanation of purpose and then listening to the applicant's response, you can save time and energy if there is any confusion.

4. *Describe how the interview will be structured.* Most selection interviews include: a description of the job, questions to explore the applicant's qualifications, and answers to any questions the applicant may have about the job. By communicating this structure, you let the applicant know what to expect. This knowledge helps to reduce his or her anxiety and demonstrates that you are organized and in control of the interview.

The Body

1. *Provide a job description.* Explain the duties of the job and the areas of responsibility that the job entails. Applicants may be unfamiliar with exactly what job they are applying for, since help-wanted ads are often sketchy or vague about specific duties. Observe or ask for the applicant's responses. Is the applicant still interested in the position? There may be clarifying questions about duties and responsibilities that need to be answered before the interview can continue. Give the applicant an opportunity to decline interest in the position if the new information changes the perception of the job. It is better to end the interview early than to waste your time with an applicant who is only being polite and is no longer interested in the job.

2. *Begin with easy questions.* If the applicant is interested in the position, then you are ready to proceed with the exploration of his or her qualifications. Start with questions for which the applicant will have positive answers: school accomplishments, interests and hobbies, or successful employment experiences listed on the résumé. These questions will give the applicant a chance to settle down. The applicant will give more honest and revealing answers when she or he is relaxed.

3. *Deepen the interview with probing questions.* As the applicant offers answers, probe for specific facts that reveal his or her ability to perform the job. You may wish to test knowledge of specific details, insight about how to manage a job, or aspects of personality that are relevant to the position. Probing questions, such as journalistic or hypothetical ones, will give you a more complete picture of the applicant's skills and abilities. Refer to your checklist of questions to cover the various aspects of the job you wish to investigate with the applicant.

4. *Listen to the applicant's answers.* Evaluate the depth and sincerity of the applicant's responses to your questioning. Notice nonverbal cues that either confirm or contradict the person's claims to knowledge or experience. How confident does the applicant appear? If an answer is incomplete or weak, you may wish to probe for more specific details. Most interviewers will not usually tell an applicant that they have given a poor answer, since that tends to upset the relaxed flow of the interview. But positive responses to an applicant's answers are useful in providing feedback and will encourage the applicant to talk more.

What advancement can I expect in this job?

What new areas of responsibility will open up in this job?

What are the long-term opportunities for growth in this job?

How will I be evaluated or reviewed on the job?

What kind of working environment can I expect?

Who will be my immediate supervisor?

With whom will I work?

What will the beginning salary be?

What sorts of benefits will the compensation package include?

Do you like working here? Why?

What is a typical day like here?

Why is this position open?

FIGURE 18.3 Questions Applicants Ask Interviewers

5. *Confront the applicant's weaknesses or deficiencies.* Toward the end of the body of the interview, you should ask the most difficult questions—the ones that ask for an explanation of obvious areas of weakness, lack of experience, or other deficiencies in preparation for the job. These questions are most important for testing the true abilities of the applicant. Carefully evaluate the answers, and notice the nonverbal signals. The answers to the difficult questions are the most important basis for your ultimate decision to hire or reject.

6. *Reestablish rapport with easy questions or praise.* Once the in-depth questioning has been accomplished, regain the applicant's confidence with a few easy questions or with statements of positive regard or praise. This tactic at the end of the questioning period will relax the applicant after the tension of the hard questions and will create a more positive tone for the end of the interview.

7. *Ask if the applicant has any questions for you.* The applicant may have asked questions throughout the interview, but there may yet be some areas to discuss. Figure 18.3 lists some typical questions that applicants ask interviewers. Prepare and provide answers that are appropriate for the amount of information you wish to disclose.

The Close

1. *Review your notes and cover any last-minute details.* Have all areas of the applicant's qualifications been covered? Do you have any more questions? Does the applicant have any last questions for you? Pause for a moment to let the applicant collect his or her thoughts before you conclude the interview.

2. *Explain what happens next.* Most applicants are extremely interested in how and when the hiring decision will be made after the interview. Provide appropriate details about when the decision will be made, who will be making the decision, and how the applicant will be notified. Arranging this "contact step" lets the applicant know what to expect. If another interview will be required or if more materials are needed from an applicant, explain how to meet these requirements. It is rude to leave an applicant with the

attitude of "Don't call us, we'll call you." Help make the evaluation and waiting period after the interview less stressful for the applicant by providing as much information as you can.

3. *Thank the applicant and end the interview.* A graceful statement of appreciation for the applicant's time ends the interview on a positive note and reflects well on the manners of the interviewer. Accompany the applicant out of the interview site. A firm handshake and a smile are welcome nonverbal cues that the interview has been a productive and pleasant time shared.

Post-Interview Tasks

1. *Rate the applicant as soon as you have completed the interview.* Many interviewers use a rating or ranking form to quantify and record their impressions. Record your evaluation of a candidate immediately after an interview so that it is recent and accurate.

2. *Offer the position to the best applicant.* Communicate your offer as soon as possible to the best-qualified candidate for the position. The applicant's time is as valuable as your own, and it is considerate to be as efficient as possible in making your decision.

3. *Communicate your decision to the other applicants.* It is extremely disheartening for applicants to interview for a position and then never receive any word about the decision. A short letter or note announcing the hiring of another qualified candidate is better than no feedback at all. It is most useful, of course, for an applicant to receive a detailed explanation of why the decision was made to hire someone else. Even when you do not choose an applicant for one position, another opening may occur for which the person will be better suited. As a gracious closing gesture, you could offer to keep the applicant in mind if such an opening does occur.

RESOURCES

Donaghy, William C. *The Interview: Skills and Applications.* Glenview, Ill.: Scott, Foresman, 1984.

This book describes techniques for the selection interview as well as other types of interviews.

Einhorn, Lois, et al. *Effective Employment Interviewing: Unlocking Human Potential.* Glenview, Ill.: Scott, Foresman, 1982.

This book explains the relationship between interviewer and applicant very effectively and shows how each relies on the other to perform effectively in a selection interview.

Pell, Arthur R. *Be a Better Employment Interviewer.* New York: Personnel Publications, 1978.

This book provides useful techniques for interviewers in professional employment situations.

Stewart, Charles J., and William B. Cash. *Interviewing: Principles and Practices.* Dubuque, Iowa: Brown, 1985.

This text provides an excellent explanation of the types of interviews and interviewing techniques that business people use regularly in their jobs.

EXERCISE 18.1
What's Wrong with These Questions?

Directions: Below is a list of questions that an interviewer might ask a job applicant. Evaluate the questions by identifying the problem in each one. Rewrite the question so that the same information is elicited by the interviewer in a more appropriate way.

1. "Tell me about yourself."

   Problem: _____

   Rewrite: _____

   _____

   _____

2. "What makes you think a woman can do this job?"

   Problem: _____

   Rewrite: _____

   _____

   _____

3. "Aren't you too young to do this kind of work?"

   Problem: _____

   Rewrite: _____

   _____

   _____

4. "Are you a Catholic?"

   Problem: _____

   Rewrite: _____

   _____

   _____

5. "You don't seem to have any experience, do you?"

   Problem: _____

Rewrite: _____

_____

_____

6. "So, what should I know about you?"

Problem: _____

Rewrite: _____

_____

_____

7. "Are you sure you can do this job?"

Problem: _____

Rewrite: _____

_____

_____

8. "You surely don't think that's very important, do you?"

Problem: _____

Rewrite: _____

_____

_____

9. "You say you want to work for this company—why?"

Problem: _____

Rewrite: _____

_____

_____

10. "Do you know how to use this machine?"

Problem: _____

Rewrite: _____

_____

_____

EXERCISE 18.2
Planning a Selection Interview

Directions: In the spaces below, plan a selection interview and conduct it with a fellow student. You should play the role of the interviewer and your fellow student the role of job applicant. Ask a third student to observe the interview and to evaluate your performance as an interviewer by filling out the critique sheet given in Exercise 18.4. Be as thorough as you can in preparing the areas you will investigate. Obtain details about the specific duties and responsibilities of the job from the applicant if you are not familiar with them.

BEFORE THE INTERVIEW

What is the purpose of the interview?

_____

_____

_____

What are the job duties?

_____

_____

_____

What are the areas of responsibility in the job?

_____

_____

_____

What are the working conditions?

_____

_____

_____

What benefits can the job have for the applicant?

_____

_____

_____

DURING THE INTERVIEW

The Opening

Topics for opening conversation:

_____

_____

The purpose of the interview:

_____

_____

The structure of the interview:

_____

_____

The job description:

_____

_____

_____

_____

The Body

Opening easy questions:

_____

_____

_____

Areas to probe:

_____

_____

_____

_____

Areas of weakness to confront:

_____

_____

_____

_____

Easy questions to close:

_____

_____

Request for any applicant questions:

_____

_____

The Close

Pause to think of any additional points to cover:

_____

_____

What will happen next:

_____

_____

Friendly close:

_____

_____

AFTER THE INTERVIEW

Rate the applicant (see Exercise 18.3).

EXERCISE 18.3
Evaluating an Applicant in a Selection Interview

Directions: Use the card below to rate the performance of the "applicant" whom you interviewed in Exercise 18.2. The rating card is similar to those used by professional interviewers and recruiters. Share the results of your ratings with the applicant, and be prepared to explain your reactions in a way that will help the applicant to improve her or his interviewing performance.

Interview Rating Card

Applicant's name: _____

Date: _____

Position applied for: _____

	Low				High
Technical qualifications	1	2	3	4	5
Knowledge of the field	1	2	3	4	5
Experience level	1	2	3	4	5
Personality factors	1	2	3	4	5
Appearance	1	2	3	4	5

Outstanding strengths:

_____

_____

_____

Outstanding weaknesses:

_____

_____

_____

EXERCISE 18.4
Evaluating the Interviewer in a Selection Interview

Directions: The student who observed the selection interview you conducted in Exercise 18.2 should fill out the following critique sheet to evaluate your performance as an interviewer. Review the critique and discuss ways in which you might improve your skills as an interviewer.

Interviewer Critique Sheet

Name of Interviewer: _____

Name of Critic: _____

THE OPENING

1. Was rapport established?

   (greeting) _____

   (eye contact) _____

   (smile) _____

   (introductions) _____

   (use of applicant's name) _____

   Comments: _____

   _____

   _____

2. Was chit-chat used to relax the applicant?

   (personal inquiries) _____

   (commonalities) _____

   (environment) _____

   (social issues) _____

   Comments: _____

   _____

   _____

3. Was the purpose of the interview stated?

(information gathering) _____

(screening) _____

(hiring) _____

Comments: _____

_____

_____

4. Was the structure of the interview clear?

(sequence) _____

(time limit) _____

Comments: _____

_____

_____

THE BODY

1. Was the job description given?

(duties) _____

(responsibilities) _____

(incentives) _____

(areas for growth) _____

(applicant response) _____

Comments: _____

_____

_____

2. Were opening questions easy and relaxed?

(school accomplishments) _____

(prior work experience) _____

(interests/hobbies) _____

Comments: _____

_____

_____

3. Were probing questions used?

(skills) _____

(knowledge) _____

(prior work experience) _____

(relevant personality traits) _____

(interest in organization) _____

(future career plans) _____

Comments: _____

_____

_____

4. Were difficult questions used to confront weaknesses?

(lack of experience) _____

(deficiencies in training) _____

(problems in prior work experience) _____

_____

Comments: _____

_____

_____

5. Did the interviewer listen and respond to answers?

Comments: _____

_____

_____

_____

6. Was rapport reestablished at the end of the interview body?

Comments: _____

_____

_____

7. Did the interviewer invite questions?

Comments: _____

_____

_____

THE CLOSE

1. Were clearinghouse questions used?

Comments: _____

_____

_____

2. Was the contact step made clear?

(who makes the decision) _____

(when the decision will be made) _____

(how applicant will be notified) _____

Comments: _____

_____

_____

3. Was the close friendly and courteous?

Comments: _____

_____

_____

Selection Interviews: The Role of the Interviewer

1. As you prepare for your role as interviewer in Exercise 18.2, write a description of the "perfect candidate" for the position. List as many specific qualities as you can in the following areas:

   Technical qualifications
   Knowledge of the field
   Experience level
   Personality factors
   Appearance
   Outstanding strengths

   Share this description with the applicant whom you are going to interview in Exercise 18.2 so that he or she will be familiar with your expectations and criteria for evaluating candidates.

2. Prepare your own evaluation sheet to replace Exercise 18.3. Would you use different categories to rank applicants?

3. Arrange to videotape the selection interview you hold with an applicant in Exercise 18.2. Critique your own performance as the interviewer on the basis of the guidelines suggested in this chapter.

19

Selection Interviews: The Role of the Applicant

Most people face employment interviews with a mixture of excitement and dread. Selection interviews can be pleasant experiences because they provide gateways to rewarding jobs, to new ways of growing in a career, and to new experiences. Selection interviews are also threatening, however, because of the inherent judgment involved. Will you interview well? Are your qualifications attractive? Are you wanted for this new job? Employment interviewing need not be threatening. By knowing what to expect in an interview and by developing some basic interviewing skills, you can make interviews work for you rather than against you. Ideally, an interview is an opportunity to learn, to explore, and to discover new career possibilities. This chapter investigates the techniques for making interviews valuable career experiences. These suggestions will help reduce nervousness and improve your performance in selection interviews.

Making Interviews Work for You

Most people feel threatened by interviews because of their assumptions about the situation. If you are desperately searching for a job or if you feel that your skills and abilities appear inferior to those of other applicants, then you have automatically placed yourself in a powerless and defensive position. This chapter looks at an effective interviewing philosophy that will help you exert more control over the situation. This improved position will make you feel more confident and comfortable. It will serve as the basis for giving a better presentation of yourself and will make interviewing a career learning tool rather than an unpleasant, judgmental trial. The five steps to making interviews work for you are as follows.

KNOW WHAT YOU HAVE TO OFFER AN EMPLOYER

The more clearly you understand your skills, abilities, and experiences, the more confident you will appear in an interview. Chapter 13, on job-search skills, emphasized the importance of knowing your own abilities. Everyone has unique capacities—skills, experiences, or personality traits—to offer a potential employer. Objectively analyze the unique contributions you can make to a business. Approach the interview with the attitude that you have something to offer an employer rather than focusing on what he or she has to offer you. This is the familiar "you"-orientation principle of all business communication.

REALIZE THAT YOU ARE INTERVIEWING EMPLOYERS

In an interview you are evaluating prospective employers just as much as they are assessing you. Try to assume the attitude that you are a "hot property" who is looking for a position in which to perform well. With this attitude, you have as much control over the interview as the interviewer does. There is information you need to know about the potential employer before you will consider working for the organization. By having confidence that many opportunities are available to you, you can be more objective and independent about the interview—traits that are usually more attractive to an employer than lack of confidence, desperation, and uncertainty.

DON'T BE AFRAID TO TAKE CONTROL OF THE INTERVIEW

In most cases the interviewer will direct the interview, but you should be prepared to take control if the interviewer does not do a good job. Some interviewers have poor interviewing skills, and if you wait for them to ask the right questions so that you can explain your best skills and abilities, they may never get around to it. Remember that the purpose of the interview is twofold: for the employer to get to know you *and* for you to get to know the employer. If the interviewer asks only vague, general questions or never touches on your strongest abilities, be sure you supply that information somewhere in the process by volunteering the information gracefully. Likewise, if the interviewer never contributes the information you want to know about the company, ask your own questions gracefully. You should be in as much control as the interviewer. Allow the interviewer to exert control initially, but if the interview seems not to be going well, step in and gracefully redirect the interview questions so that the session focuses on your assets and the information you want to know.

ESTABLISH CLEAR GOALS

The clearer you are about what you want from a job or from an interview, the easier it is to plan strategies that will help you accomplish these objectives. If you approach an interview with the attitude that you are just "shopping around," the interviewer will probably pick up on it and will consider you as a less likely prospect than someone who is more serious. To make the strongest impact in an interview, demonstrate that you know what you want and why you want it. A sense of dedication and professionalism is the best message you can send an interviewer, so try to develop those attitudes about yourself and your reasons for applying for a job.

RELAX—AND BE PREPARED TO LEARN FROM THE INTERVIEW

No single interview will make or break your career. You will probably face dozens of them in your lifetime, so do not be overly concerned about any single interview performance. Of course, you want to prepare thoroughly and present yourself as well as possible, but a relaxed confidence makes for a better interview than nervous anxiety. Try to take the pressure off yourself by reducing some of the unknown elements:

Practice interviewing with friends or with "dry runs."

Use information-gathering interviews extensively.

Prepare answers in advance to the typical interview questions.

Get feedback about your interview performances.

Realize that you are a "hot property." If you are not selected for the position, remember that there will be many other opportunities, because you have something valuable to offer.

Successful Interviewing Techniques

The interview is the last of the series of career-search activities we have investigated. You have determined your career goals, analyzed your skills, investigated your career area, uncovered job leads, identified an employment target, and gotten in touch with the potential employer. The résumé you submit gives the employer a brief overview of your experience and technical skills. Your letter of application explains your reasons for wanting the job, highlights your outstanding skills and abilities, and gives some sense of your personality. You are at last ready to present your best case—an actual face-to-face encounter in which you give in-depth information about your qualifications for the job. The following suggestions will help you address this challenge successfully.

The general history of the company.

The products or services the company provides.

Prior years' sales figures.

Projected sales for coming years.

New developments in product line or expansion.

Locations of offices and centers of activity.

Key individuals in the firm.

Management philosophy and statement of the company's mission.

FIGURE 19.1   What to Look For in an Annual Report

BEFORE THE INTERVIEW—DO YOUR HOMEWORK

You must complete several tasks before the interview takes place. The more time and care you give to these preliminaries, the better your interview performance will be.

1. *Do research on the company.* The more you know about the company, the more you know about what it may want from you. You are also better prepared to ask meaningful questions. Sources of information about a company include people you know who work there, information-gathering interviews with experts or employees, and secondary sources in the library. A standard industrial profile, such as *Moody's Industrial Guide*, will give you facts about large companies. Smaller companies are often profiled in city or state indexes, which your local reference librarian can locate for you. Another useful source of information is the company's annual report, which is often on file in business libraries or at a college's placement center. Figure 19.1 illustrates the kind of information you can gather from a company's annual report to help you prepare for the interview.

Other kinds of information that might be useful include the company's competitors, the relative standing of the target company in comparison to competitors, general industry trends, and recent outstanding news about the company. These facts can often be learned from local publications or from interviews with knowledgeable industry sources. Having this kind of information makes you appear informed, interested in the company, and professional. It takes time to unearth these facts, so you should start early in your academic career to gather as much industry-related information as you can.

2. *Anticipate the qualifications.* Know the criteria by which you will be evaluated as an applicant. What skills, abilities, and traits is the company looking for in an employee? You probably did some of this investigation when you analyzed the help-wanted ad, but prepare even more carefully to meet the expectations the interviewer will have. You may have to do some information gathering to uncover hidden qualifications or criteria the company may have.

3. *Prepare a list of probable questions.* On the basis of your anticipation of the qualifications, prepare a practice list of questions that the interviewer will probably ask. Plan answers to these questions that emphasize your unique skills and abilities. Do not memorize your responses, since you want

your answers in the interview to be spontaneous and naturally expressed, but do have a clear idea of what information you want the interviewer to know about you. As questions arise in the interview, provide statements of your skills and abilities that demonstrate the particular contribution you can make to the company. If the interviewer does not ask the right questions, you can volunteer the information in a graceful way. Exercise 19.1 at the end of this chapter provides practice in anticipating questions and planning answers. Use it to plan good answers that reflect well on you.

4. *Prepare to explain your weaknesses.* Every candidate for a position has certain weaknesses or deficiencies. One of the main tasks of the interviewer is to uncover and probe these areas of weakness—lack of experience, lack of skill or training, poor performance on a prior job, poor relationships with prior co-workers, and problematic personality traits. You must prepare plausible and convincing answers to questions in these areas. Be honest in the way you answer, but also be positive. Almost any negative aspect can be presented in a positive light. For example, if you have a low grade-point average because you worked full-time while going to school, you could emphasize the real work experience you gained. If you have a high grade-point average but lack work experience, you might explain that you preferred to get a solid understanding of principles rather than focus on a specific job too early in your career. Tactful explanations for weaknesses can be honest and still not detrimental to your qualifications. In short, know your weaknesses and be prepared to explain them.

5. *Prepare a list of the information you want.* Your homework may not reveal some information you need before making a decision to join a company. Plan a checklist of areas you want to probe in the interview. Some of the points may surface in the course of the interview, but there is usually time at the end to take care of any unfinished business, and the interviewer will ask if you have any further questions. Figure 18.5 listed typical questions asked by applicants. Review these questions or devise your own before an interview, but also gather as much information as you can through your homework. You will look amateurish if you ask questions about information that is readily available to you.

DURING THE INTERVIEW— EMPHASIZE THE POSITIVE

Once the interview is underway, keep in mind the objectives you have set: to create a positive impression, to get to know the interviewer and the company, to provide information so the company can get to know you. Try to be objective about yourself as an applicant and keep a "third eye" on your performance—monitor how you are doing, what has been covered so far, and what remains to be covered. This mental organization helps keep you in control during the interview.

1. *Create a strong and positive first impression.* Arrive a little early for the interview so that you have time to organize your thoughts and relax a bit before you begin. The interviewer may be ahead of schedule and will appreciate your saving him or her time by being ready early. Dress appropriately for

the situation. Know the dress code for the company, and if there is any doubt, dress more conservatively than necessary. Smile at the interviewer, offer a firm handshake, and use eye contact to convey your self-confidence.

2. *Respond to the interviewer's opening.* Most interviewers will try to engage you in relaxed small talk in the opening phase of the interview. Respond as naturally and as gracefully as you can. Enjoy getting to know the interviewer. Be yourself, behaving as you would at any professional social gathering. This attitude will communicate your confidence and your ability to talk comfortably with other professional people.

3. *Let the interviewer take charge.* Some interviewers like to chat quite a while before beginning the questioning, but keep your time limit in mind. If you have to exert some control in the interview, begin by volunteering some information about yourself. That approach may prompt the interviewer to get down to business. The interviewer should explain how the interview will be structured and how much time you will have. If he or she does not, you may ask for that information.

4. *Provide strong, positive answers to questions.* The interviewer will probably begin with easy questions and then progress to more difficult and challenging ones. Give answers that emphasize your skills and positive traits. Avoid vague or short answers; give specific examples, illustrations, and facts to support your answers. Show that you understand what it takes to be a good employee. See the interview from the interviewer's side, and demonstrate that you understand his or her needs. Try to avoid revealing anything negative about yourself. Do not be humble or self-defeating—state only positive interpretations of events.

Figure 19.2 lists typical questions that interviewers ask. Prepare answers for these questions about yourself when you plan an interview. Consider the strength of your answers, or discuss them with a friend to see if they can be improved.

There are an infinite number of questions that an interviewer might ask, but a thorough knowledge of what the job requires, what skills you have, and your reasons for wanting to work for a certain employer should prepare you for almost any question. The most difficult questions are those that pinpoint your weaknesses as an applicant. Have reasonable explanations prepared for them.

Tell me about yourself.

What are your career goals?

Where do you want to be in five (or ten) years?

What did you like best about school?

Why do you want to work for this company?

What experience do you have?

Why did you leave your last job?

How did you get along with people (or the boss) on your last job?

What are your greatest strengths (or weaknesses)?

Can you perform the skills we need?

Do you have the information you need for the job?

Do you have the personality traits necessary to perform well?

FIGURE 19.2 Questions Interviewers Ask Applicants

The most awkward questions are those which are vague—the most common being "Tell me about yourself." When confronted with such questions, merely pretend that the interviewer asked a different question. "Tell me about yourself" is merely an invitation to provide information about your skills, your experiences, your training, or your reasons for wanting to work. Do not give vague answers to vague questions. Instead, emphasize specific and positive information about yourself and your abilities.

5. *Be prepared for tricky or unfair questions.* Despite legal restrictions on discrimination, some employers will imply that you may not be qualified because of certain traits: sex, age, physical condition, handicap, race, sexual preference, ethnic background, religion, or other factors. Questions that refer to these traits often reflect a bias on the part of the employer and are considered illegal if the question does not relate directly to the job requirements. You need to consider in advance how you want to answer these questions. Otherwise, a surprise question may catch you off guard and provoke a less than desirable response. The best response is to ask how the question is relevant to the qualifications for the position. This response will lead to a discussion that helps clarify the issue. Less effective responses are: stating indignantly that the question is irrelevant; cleverly avoiding the issue by making light of it; ignoring the question and changing the subject; or confronting the interviewer as an insensitive lout. Each choice creates certain predictable responses in the interviewer, and you should determine in advance how you want to handle these situations.

CLOSING THE INTERVIEW—END GRACEFULLY

An interviewer usually signals the end of the interview by asking if you have any further questions. At that point, you should check your list of items and ask for any information you still need. The close of the interview should consist of the interviewer's telling you when the decision will be made and how the decision will be communicated to you. If the interviewer does not give you this information, ask for it so that you will know what to expect. You do not want to be hustled out the door with a "Don't call us, we'll call you." Ask approximately when the employer will make the decision and when you can expect to be notified. A good strategy to show your interest is to ask whether you may call if you have not heard by a certain date. Interviewers are usually willing to give you their number so that you can call them directly.

Two other effective strategies that you can use as an applicant in closing the interview are the summary and the statement of interest. As the interview winds down, summarize your major strengths and the contributions you could make as an employee. The summary demonstrates your self-assertiveness and confidence. If you are particularly interested in a position, a strong statement of interest is a good way to leave the interviewer with a positive final impression of you. State that you want to work for the employer, summarize your major strengths, and ask the interviewer to consider your application carefully.

Introduction:	Reference to the recent interview.
	Appreciation for the chance to meet.
	Praise of the interviewer or company.
Body:	Reminder of your strengths as an applicant.
	Any additional information you want to stress.
Conclusion:	Statement of your continued interest in the position.
	Courteous close.

FIGURE 19.3 Formula for Follow-Up Letters

AFTER THE INTERVIEW—DON'T GIVE UP

Once the interview has been completed, assess your performance. Consider ways in which it could be improved. Use these reflections as a lesson for improving your answers, doing more thorough homework, or creating a stronger impression in future interviews. If the interview went well and you remain interested in the position, a follow-up letter is a useful strategy for keeping your name and interest in the interviewer's mind. Figure 19.3 lists the items that are typically included in the follow-up letter.

If you receive a rejection for a position, do not give up. The follow-up letter, even after a rejection, demonstrates that you are a serious professional committed to a career. It is good to stay on positive terms with other professionals in your chosen field—they become part of your network, and you may encounter them in the future. Checking back with the employer also demonstrates your interest in a specific company. Even if you do not receive the first open position, subsequent openings may come to your attention if you check in occasionally.

RESOURCES

Donaho, Melvin W., and John L. Meyer. *How to Get the Job You Want: A Guide to Résumés, Interviews, and Job-Hunting Strategy.* Englewood Cliffs, N.J.: Prentice-Hall, 1976.

This is a good guide to various aspects of the job-search process.

Einhorn, Lois, et al. *Effective Employment Interviewing: Unlocking Human Potential.* Glenview: Ill.: Scott, Foresman, 1982.

This book offers excellent suggestions and drills to prepare for selection interviews.

Medley, H. Anthony. *Sweaty Palms: The Neglected Art of Being Interviewed.* Belmont, Calif.: Lifetime Learning Publications, 1978.

This is an excellent and entertaining approach to preparing for interviews. The author helps dispel much of the fear of interviewing for people with little experience.

Robertson, Jason. *How to Win in a Job Interview.* Englewood Cliffs, N.J.: Prentice-Hall, 1978.

This book provides suggestions for developing an aggressive, winning attitude toward job interviewing.

EXERCISE 19.1
What's Wrong with These Answers?

Directions: The following answers have actually been given by applicants in selection interviews. Identify the principle of interviewing that is violated by each answer, and compose a better answer that the applicant might have given.

1. "Yes, that's right. I don't have any experience."

   Principle violated: _____

   _____

   Better answer: _____

   _____

2. "Well, I took Lotus 1-2-3, but it never made much sense."

   Principle violated: _____

   _____

   Better answer: _____

   _____

3. "No, I don't know how to do that process—but I am a quick learner."

   Principle violated: _____

   _____

   Better answer: _____

   _____

4. "What matters to me? Gee, that's a hard question. Boy, it's hard to say."

   Principle violated: _____

   _____

   Better answer: _____

   _____

5. "I don't know much about your company. I've been so busy that I haven't had a chance to read your annual report."

   Principle violated: _____

   _____

   Better answer: _____

   _____

6. "Weaknesses? I don't have any—unless you consider workaholism a weakness."

   Principle violated: _____

   _____

   Better answer: _____

   _____

7. "I spend most of my free time skydiving. It's a great sport!"

   Principle violated: _____

   _____

   Better answer: _____

   _____

8. "I want to work for you because you offer the highest salaries in the industry."

   Principle violated: _____

   _____

   Better answer: _____

   _____

9. "I left my last job because my boss and I just couldn't seem to get along with each other."

   Principle violated: _____

   _____

   Better answer: _____

   _____

EXERCISE 19.2
Finding the Hidden Questions

Directions: Interviewers often ask vague or open-ended questions to get information indirectly. The answer to a vague question often reveals more than an applicant knows. Each of the following questions reflects an ulterior motive—there is an underlying reason for asking the question in addition to the obvious reason. Determine what piece of information an interviewer is looking for when he or she uses each of the following questions. Write a good answer that addresses the hidden question being asked.

1. "Tell me about yourself."

   The hidden question: _____

   _____

   Good answer: _____

   _____

2. "Why do you want this job?"

   The hidden question: _____

   _____

   Good answer: _____

   _____

3. "Why did you leave your last job?"

   The hidden question: _____

   _____

   Good answer: _____

   _____

4. "What do you do outside of work?"

   The hidden question: _____

   _____

   Good answer: _____

   _____

5. "What is your greatest weakness?"

The hidden question: _____

_____

Good answer: _____

_____

6. "What is your greatest strength?"

The hidden question: _____

_____

Good answer: _____

_____

7. "What did you think of your last boss?"

The hidden question: _____

_____

Good answer: _____

_____

8. "What salary are you interested in?"

The hidden question: _____

_____

Good answer: _____

_____

EXERCISE 19.3
Applicant Planning for a Selection Interview

Directions: In conjunction with a fellow student, plan and conduct a selection interview in which you apply for a position. Refer to Exercise 18.3, in which the interviewer planned the interview. Exchange information so that the interviewer is aware of the job description and qualifications. The applicant can use the following planning sheet to prepare answers and to list questions that may be asked in the interview.

BACKGROUND INFORMATION

Position applied for: _____

Required skills: _____

_____

_____

_____

Required experience: _____

_____

_____

_____

Required knowledge: _____

_____

_____

_____

Required personal traits: _____

_____

_____

_____

QUESTIONS THE INTERVIEWER WILL PROBABLY ASK

1. Question: _____

   _____

   Answer: _____

   _____

   _____

2. Question: _____

   _____

   Answer: _____

   _____

   _____

3. Question: _____

   _____

   Answer: _____

   _____

   _____

4. Question: _____

   _____

   Answer: _____

   _____

   _____

5. Question: _____

   _____

   Answer: _____

   _____

   _____

6. Question: _____

_____

Answer: _____

_____

_____

7. Question: _____

_____

Answer: _____

_____

_____

8. Question: _____

_____

Answer: _____

_____

_____

9. Question: _____

_____

Answer: _____

_____

_____

10. Question: _____

_____

Answer: _____

_____

_____

QUESTIONS TO ASK THE INTERVIEWER

1. _____

_____

2. _____

_____

3. _____

_____

4. _____

_____

5. _____

_____

6. _____

_____

7. _____

_____

8. _____

_____

9. _____

_____

10. _____

_____

SUMMARY STATEMENT

_____

_____

_____

_____

EXERCISE 19.4
Critiquing an Applicant in a Selection Interview

Directions: Observe two students who are conducting a selection interview. Pay close attention to the applicant. Complete the following critique sheet and provide feedback to the applicant about the strengths of his or her presentation and ways in which he or she could improve the performance. When completing the critique, note the specific behaviors that are the basis of your evaluation.

Critique Sheet for Selection Interview

Applicant: _____ Critic: _____

THE OPENING

1. Was rapport established?

   (response to greeting) _____

   (response to introduction) _____

   (eye contact) _____

   (smile) _____

   Comments: _____

   _____

   _____

2. Was the opening comfortable?

   (response to chit-chat) _____

   (relaxed posture) _____

   (voice quality) _____

   Comments: _____

   _____

   _____

3. Were the purpose and structure of the interview clear?

(response to interviewer's explanation) _____

Comments: _____

_____

_____

THE BODY

1. Was the job description clear?

(response to the job description) _____

(questions asked about the job) _____

Comments: _____

_____

_____

2. Were opening answers positive and confident?

(school accomplishments) _____

(prior work experience) _____

(interests/hobbies) _____

Comments: _____

_____

_____

3. Was the response to probing clear and relaxed?

(skills) _____

(knowledge) _____

(prior work experience) _____

(relevant personality traits) _____

(interest in the organization) _____

(future career plans) _____

Comments: _____

_____

_____

_____

4. Were the answers to difficult questions positive and complete?

(lack of experience) _____

(deficiencies in training) _____

(problems in prior work experience) _____

Comments: _____

_____

_____

_____

5. Did the applicant cover all his or her relevant qualifications?

(skills) _____

(knowledge) _____

(personality traits) _____

Comments: _____

_____

_____

_____

6. Was rapport reestablished at the end of the interview body?

Comments: _____

_____

_____

_____

THE CLOSE

1. Were clearinghouse questions used?

    Comments: _____

    _____

    _____

    _____

2. Was the contact step made clear?

    Comments: _____

    _____

    _____

    _____

3. Did the applicant offer a summary of his or her qualifications?

    Comments: _____

    _____

    _____

    _____

4. Was a strong statement of interest made?

    Comments: _____

    _____

    _____

    _____

5. Was the close friendly and courteous?

    Comments: _____

    _____

    _____

    _____

Selection Interviews: The Role of the Applicant

1. Interview two people who have undergone several selection interviews. Ask them what went well, what went badly, what they would have done differently, and how they handled their nervousness. Compile a list of suggestions on preparing for interviews that you can share with your classmates.

2. As you prepare for Exercise 19.2, describe what your competition may be like. Visualize the "perfect applicant" for the same job you are applying for. List the specific qualities this person would have in the following areas:

   Technical qualifications
   Knowledge of the field
   Experience level
   Personality factors
   Appearance
   Outstanding strengths

   How do your qualifications compare to those of this "perfect candidate"? How will you handle the differences when they are brought up in the interview?

3. Arrange to videotape your selection interview as an applicant in Exercise 19.2. Critique your performance on the basis of the guidelines provided in this chapter.

BUSINESS SPEAKING

20

The Principles of Business Speaking

Public speaking is perceived as one of the most important business communication skills. The ability to speak effectively to others, whether in a planned presentation or in spontaneous remarks in a meeting, reflects intelligence and general competence. Much business is conducted in meetings, and business people are often called upon to address speeches to large groups. For these reasons, effective public speaking is a necessity if you want to succeed in your career.

Effective business speaking requires skills in a variety of situations: informative talks, training programs, speeches to persuade, sales presentations, and motivational speeches. In Chapters 21–25 each of these five speaking situations will be discussed in detail so that you can develop skills in each area. This chapter introduces you to the basic principles that underlie all types of speeches. Later chapters will deal with the unique elements of specific speaking contexts. By combining the principles in this introductory chapter with the specific guidelines provided in later chapters, you will be able to plan, practice, and present effective and interesting public speeches in most business situations.

Six basic steps are necessary to plan an interesting and effective speech:

Determine your purpose and topic.

Research your topic and select materials.

Establish your credibility.

Organize and outline your speech.

Prepare the delivery of the speech.

Anticipate and deal with stage fright.

This chapter investigates each of these areas and provides suggestions to help you master all six steps. Once you have mastered these skills, you can apply them to other types of speaking purposes and situations.

Determine Your Purpose and Topic

The first step in giving any speech is to analyze exactly what you are trying to accomplish. What is your topic? Who is your audience? Why are you talking to them? It sounds obvious to say that these considerations should be dealt with first, but it is amazing how often a speaker will skip over this essential analysis of the situation and just start talking without giving much thought to what the central message of the speech is, who is listening, or why the message is important to the audience.

Knowing your audience is important because it helps you determine what you should say and how best to express it. In most business situations you give a speech because the audience members need the information to do their own work or to make decisions about the topic. Consider carefully what your audience needs. How much information do they already have about the topic? How much information do they need in order to accomplish the purpose for which they are listening? Answering these questions helps you determine the scope and time limits of your speech. You need to determine how detailed or superficial to be in each of the areas of information you might cover. You have probably heard at least one speaker who rambled on and on and on, long after he or she had given the necessary information. That is an example of poor analysis of audience need. You need to know how much information to include and what information is irrelevant or unnecessary.

The second aspect of the audience that you should consider is their interests. The best way to be an interesting speaker is to talk about what the audience is interested in—their experiences, their concerns, and themselves. A careful speaker will analyze the topic from the audience's point of view. Why is the audience listening? How can the speaker benefit the audience? What are the most interesting aspects of the topic area from the audience's perspective? The answers to these questions are the guidelines to making your speech interesting and lively. Again, you have probably heard a speaker whose information seemed to be totally irrelevant to your concerns. It was as though he or she was talking to a brick wall instead of to an audience of busy people. By analyzing audience members' interests, you can select materials that will capture their attention and hold their interest throughout the presentation.

The final aspect of audience analysis is to determine your shared purpose. Why has the audience come to hear you talk? What are their expectations? The answers to these questions help you determine what to talk about and how much to say. You also need to consider your own purposes as a speaker. In some situations the audience may not know what you are going to say. You need to analyze carefully their needs and interests to make sure your material is relevant and interesting. If, after having analyzed the audience and the situation, you feel that certain information is important for an audience to hear, then you have done all you can do to ensure relevance. You are ready to gather your materials and prepare the presentation.

Research Your Topic and Select Materials

The second step in speech preparation is to collect your information. In some business situations, you may have all the information you need right at your fingertips—you may be the expert and you will not need to do any research. When that is the case, you can move directly into organizing your materials once you have analyzed the audience and your purpose.

In many situations, however, you will need to do some research to supplement what you already know about the topic. When it is necessary to research a topic, consider the available sources of information before you start. The best place to begin your research is with a pen and paper and your own brain. Make a list of what you already know and the things you need to find. Then make a list of the places where you can most easily and quickly find the information you need. Organize your information needs into the general categories you want to cover in your speech. This list becomes your preliminary or *tentative outline*. It will evolve into the final outline as you add information and delete unnecessary details.

You may want to discuss your list with people whose opinions you trust. They may be able to refer you to sources of information that you have overlooked. Another useful set of people to consult are local experts on your topic. If you can find experts with whom you can discuss your information needs, they may be able to provide some shortcuts to help you locate what you need. Professors, business people, or researchers may help you find useful materials quickly and easily. They can also give you feedback on your planned coverage of the topic.

Once you have determined your information needs, resources such as books, magazines, professional periodicals, clipping file services, and reference materials in local libraries will fill in needed details. Specialized industry information may be obtained through special libraries. Information-gathering interviews with experts on your topic can help you locate hard-to-find data. Another important source of information is personal experience. Analyze your own experiences and those of the audience for examples and applications of the points you want to make in your speech. Personal examples are often relevant and interesting and can enliven the topic for the audience.

You are likely to uncover much more information than you can possibly include in the time allotted for the speech. You must then begin the process of weeding out the less interesting and less relevant materials. Select the information that best accomplishes the purpose of the speech and is the most interesting. The more you refine your information, the greater the likelihood that your speech will be successful.

Establish Your Credibility

When you have listened to speakers, have you noticed that you readily believe and trust some but are skeptical of or dubious about others? This perception of believability is called *speaker credibility*. It is imperative for a speaker to establish credibility so that the audience will be favorably disposed toward the speaker and what he or she has to say. Research has shown that high speaker credibility increases the speaker's chances of being persuasive and of retaining the audience's attention.[1]

Credibility consists of many factors. Researchers in speech communication have isolated five major dimensions of speaker credibility: authority, good sense, good character, good will, and dynamism.[2] Figure 20.1 provides definitions of these dimensions of credibility and suggests ways in which you can develop credibility as a speaker.

Authority: having knowledge, power, or influence

Demonstrating thorough research or knowledge of the topic.
Having personal experience in the topic.
Having degrees, awards, honors, achievements, reputation.
Having social standing, status, and position.
Being associated with or introduced by other authority figures.

Good sense: being fair and open-minded

Using reasonable and objective language.
Using ethical speaking strategies.
Demonstrating attitudes of equality and respect for the audience.

Good character: trustworthiness and appropriateness

Being honest and sincere toward the audience.
Using accurate facts and relevant data.
Avoiding rude, vulgar, or insulting language.

Good will: having the audience's best interests at heart

Establishing common experiences and values with the audience.
Being relevant to audience needs.
Being friendly, helpful, and concerned about the audience.
Showing personal concern about and commitment to the topic.

Dynamism: force and liveliness of delivery

Showing vocal and physical enthusiasm and energy.
Showing interest in the topic and the occasion.
Appearing calm and relaxed when presenting the speech.
Using direct eye contact and audience awareness.
Being flexible about interruptions and last-minute changes.

**FIGURE 20.1 Dimensions and Examples of
Speaker Credibility**

Organize and Outline Your Speech

Once you have determined your purpose, selected materials, and considered ways of establishing your credibility, you are ready to prepare the actual speech. The tentative outline you used in researching your topic may have organized your planning to some degree, but now you need to consider the shape of the final version of the speech.

Most speeches use a three-part organizational structure: introduction, body, and conclusion. Each of the parts has a unique function, but you should adapt each part to suit the specific purpose of the speech.

In general, the *introduction* should grab the attention of the audience members and prepare them for what follows. The very first line of the speech is important for grabbing attention and creating interest. Therefore, select an opening line that is unique and engaging. Announce the topic and the purpose of the speech, and explain the relevance of the topic for the audience. Speakers often include some devices for increasing their credibility to create a positive first impression. It is effective to orient the audience by ending the introduction with a preview of the main points of the body.

The *body* contains the bulk of the information you want to tell the audience. It consists of the main points of information and the supporting materials for the arguments of the speech. You should organize the body into several main points. The longer the speech, the more main points you will have. Remember the attention span and information needs of your audience, however, and do not overwhelm them with too much information. Each main point should be supported with subpoints. Common types of supporting subpoints are facts, statistics, quotations, examples, illustrations, and visual aids.

The *conclusion* varies tremendously, depending on the purpose of the speech itself. In general, the conclusion fulfills the overall objective of the speech and provides a sense of completion and closure. Common concluding devices in informative speeches are summaries, reiteration of the main point, and closing quotations. Persuasive speeches often end with strong appeals for action by the audience. Whatever the purpose of the speech, however, the last line of the speech is an important place to provide a carefully chosen device, since the last line of the speech is what the audience will remember best. Therefore, select a strong and memorable last line for the speech.

Outlines are extremely useful tools for helping you organize and deliver a speech. As you prepare, maintain a thorough outline of every element you want to include in the speech. Organize your outline along the lines presented in Figure 20.2.

Outlines vary tremendously because you must adapt them to the situation and the purpose of the speech. Whatever the case, take care to organize clearly and use a framework that allows you to see at a glance how the speech is structured. A good outline will assist you in staying organized as you speak, in adjusting the speech to time constraints, in adding or subtracting material, and in helping you find your place if you become lost during the speech. Prepare your outline using complete sentences, partial sentences, key phrases, or key words. Experiment with various forms of outlines until you find one that is particularly useful to you.

Speaker's Name
Title of Speech
Purpose of Speech
  I. Introduction
    A. Device to grab the audience's attention
    B. Topic of speech
    C. Relevance of topic
      1. Subpoint 1: reason
      2. Subpoint 2: reason
    D. Establish your credibility
      1. Subpoint 1: personal experience
      2. Subpoint 2: research done
    E. Preview of the main points to follow
  II. Body
    A. Main point 1
      1. Subpoint 1
        a. supporting point
        b. supporting point
      2. Subpoint 2
        a. supporting point
        b. supporting point
    B. Main point 2
      1. Subpoint 1
        a. supporting point
        b. supporting point
      2. Subpoint 2
        a. supporting point
        b. supporting point
    C. Main point 3
      1. Subpoint 1
        a. supporting point
        b. supporting point
        c. supporting point
      2. Subpoint 2
        a. supporting point
        b. supporting point
        c. supporting point
  III. Conclusion
    A. Summary of the main points
    B. Emphasis of the most important point
    C. Strong last line to close

FIGURE 20.2 Sample Skeletal Outline for a Speech

Prepare the Delivery of the Speech

The most challenging aspect of speechmaking for many people is the actual delivery of the speech—standing in front of the crowd and talking. The best way to overcome this difficulty is to prepare thoroughly and to practice the delivery. If you know your material thoroughly and have rehearsed it several times, you will be able to speak with a minimum of discomfort and awkwardness. Most speakers say that they are extremely nervous when they speak in public. Accomplished speakers, however, say that they have learned to control their nervousness by preparing thoroughly. The following suggestions about delivery will help you deal with any discomfort you may have and show you how to prepare to speak.

The first step in preparing your delivery is to determine the mode of speaking you will use: manuscript, memorized, or note card. Each delivery mode has advantages and disadvantages. Some formal situations require that a speaker write a manuscript and read directly from it. The *manuscript* speech ensures good word choice, but it is potentially boring for the audience. There is not much personal contact between speaker and audience. The *memorized* mode helps the speaker hold eye contact and interest with the audience, but the danger of memory slips is great. The best alternative in most situations is to speak from *note cards*—either full sheets of paper that contain the outline or small cards with key points. The use of note cards allows you to be thoroughly prepared but still spontaneous with your word choice and interest factors. You should practice delivery with different types of notes and outlines—key words, key phrases, and full sentences—to find the style you prefer.

The second step in preparing your delivery is to rehearse your wording of ideas so that you can speak fluently and clearly. Take care to talk loudly and distinctly. Focus your voice on the people who will be farthest away from you in the room or hall. If you use a microphone, practice using it in advance so that you will not have embarrassing squawks and screeches. It is best to practice your speech aloud with live listeners if possible. Watch for their feedback as they listen and discuss the speech afterward. Make use of that feedback to strengthen the final performance.

When you face the actual audience, concentrate on good eye contact. More than any other nonverbal signal, eye contact increases interest and attention in an audience. Take care not to exhibit distracting physical movements such as swaying, pacing, or tapping of hands or feet. Gestures should be natural and relaxed. If you normally do not gesture in conversation, do not try to include artificial gesturing in your speech. Finally, take a deep breath every now and then. This technique will help you and the audience relax and enjoy the speech more fully. The time you take for deep breaths lets the audience think about what you just said, and it allows you to prepare to present your next thought by glancing at your outline.

Anticipate Stage Fright

Every speaker experiences stage fright to some degree. By concentrating on the preparation and practice of your speech, you are taking the best possible measures to ensure an effective and interesting speech. The better you know your material, the more relaxed you will be in front of a group of people.

Prepare thoroughly: know your material and be well organized.

Select topics that interest you and your audience.

Relax with your audience: breathe deeply and smile.

Concentrate on your audience, not on yourself.

Get to know the audience before you begin.

Get the audience involved immediately with a story, a joke, or a question that forces them to respond to you.

Don't try to be "perfect": just present your information clearly, and the audience will appreciate what you have to say.

FIGURE 20.3 Techniques for Dealing with Stage Fright

Stage fright is also a matter of attitude. If you focus on yourself—how you look, how you sound, how you feel—then you will become self-conscious and your stage fright will get worse. However, if you focus on the audience members—their interests, their needs, their understanding—then you will be able to forget your nervousness. Try to make public speaking a pleasant experience, not a dreaded event to be avoided at all costs. Certainly, you will not be very dynamic or impressive when you are a beginning orator, but with practice you can become a valuable and effective communicator.

Figure 20.3 lists several suggestions that speakers have found useful for dealing with stage fright. Incorporate these suggestions as much as you can into the preparation of your speech.

Good speechmaking is a simple matter of practice: the more speaking you do, the more effective you will become. Comfortable and efficient public speaking is a valuable tool for a business person. By watching other effective speakers and incorporating the techniques discussed in this chapter, you can become successful. You may actually come to enjoy speaking in public. Learning dynamic and effective public speaking is quite a challenge, but the rewards it can bring to your business career are worth the effort.

Figure 20.4 (on facing page) summarizes the points made in this chapter. Use it as a basic checklist as you prepare the various kinds of speeches discussed in the following chapters.

NOTES

1. See James C. McCroskey, "Scales for the Measurement of Ethos," *Communication Monographs* 33 (1966): 65–73.
2. A discussion of these five traits appears in Rudolph E. Busby and Randall E. Majors, *Basic Speech Communication* (New York: Harper & Row, 1987), pp. 199–203.

Determine Your Purpose and Topic

Who is your audience?

What is your topic?

Why are you talking to this audience?

How much information does the audience need?

What are the audience's interests?

What does the audience expect from the speaker?

What do you want to accomplish?

Research Your Topic and Select Materials

What do you already know about the topic?

What information do you need to gather?

Where can you find the information you need?

Who are the local experts you can interview?

What library materials will be useful?

What personal experience can you include?

Establish Your Credibility

Who are you?

Why are you talking to this audience about this topic?

Why do you care about them?

What credentials do you have for talking to them?

Organize and Outline Your Speech

What are your main points?

What information factors should you include: facts, statistics, quotations, examples, illustrations, assertions?

What interest factors should you include: personal experiences, demonstrations, audience participation, stories, anecdotes?

What visual aids can you include?

Which concluding devices can you use?

Which introductory devices should you use?

Have you included transitional statements among all parts?

Prepare the Delivery of the Speech

Determine the delivery mode: manuscript, memorized, note cards.

Practice the wording of your ideas.

Practice aloud with a live audience.

Practice physical movement, voice, and eye contact.

Breathe deeply and relax when speaking.

FIGURE 20.4 Checklist for Business Speakers

EXERCISE 20.1
Assessing Your Speech Skills

Directions: In light of the speechmaking skills discussed in this chapter, assess your present speech skills in each of the following categories. Rate yourself in each of the skill areas on the scale, from 1 for the lowest score to 10 for the highest.

1. *Determining your topic and purpose*

   If you were asked to give an impromptu one-minute speech on any topic, how easily could you select an interesting subject?

   Low   1   2   3   4   5   6   7   8   9   10   High

   How well can you determine an audience's needs and interests concerning a topic when you have to give a speech?

   Low   1   2   3   4   5   6   7   8   9   10   High

2. *Researching your topic and selecting materials*

   How familiar are you with local library resources?

   Low   1   2   3   4   5   6   7   8   9   10   High

   How conversant are you with local experts whose advice you can seek for developing a speech?

   Low   1   2   3   4   5   6   7   8   9   10   High

   How knowledgeable are you about resources in your chosen career area?

   Low   1   2   3   4   5   6   7   8   9   10   High

3. *Establishing your credibility*

   How credible a speaker would you be with your classmates?

   Low   1   2   3   4   5   6   7   8   9   10   High

   How credible a speaker would you be within your career area?

   Low   1   2   3   4   5   6   7   8   9   10   High

4. *Organizing and outlining your speech*

   How comfortable are you with outlining a five-minute speech?

   Low   1   2   3   4   5   6   7   8   9   10   High

   How easily do you use note cards when speaking?

   Low   1   2   3   4   5   6   7   8   9   10   High

5. *Preparing the delivery of the speech*

   How effective is your eye contact with an audience?

   Low   1   2   3   4   5   6   7   8   9   10   High

   How relaxed are your hands when you are giving a speech?

   Low   1   2   3   4   5   6   7   8   9   10   High

   How easily do you project enthusiasm with your voice?

   Low   1   2   3   4   5   6   7   8   9   10   High

6. *Dealing with stage fright*

   What is your general confidence level about giving speeches?

   Low   1   2   3   4   5   6   7   8   9   10   High

   How comfortable are you when speaking in public?

   Low   1   2   3   4   5   6   7   8   9   10   High

   How well do you channel your nervousness and control your voice and body when speaking in public?

   Low   1   2   3   4   5   6   7   8   9   10   High

EXERCISE 20.2
Analyzing the Situation for a Speech

Directions: Use the following worksheet to analyze a speaking situation. Describe a speech that a business person would give on the job. Complete the worksheet to assist the speaker in making choices about developing the speech.

The situation

Describe a typical situation in which a business person would give a public speech.

_____

_____

_____

_____

_____

_____

_____

Determine the purpose and topic

Who is the audience?

_____

_____

_____

_____

How much information do the audience members need?

_____

_____

_____

_____

What is the purpose of the speech?

_____

_____

Research the topic and select materials
What does the speaker already know?

_____

_____

_____

_____

What information does the speaker need to find?

_____

_____

_____

_____

What resources are available to the speaker?

_____

_____

_____

_____

Establish credibility
What can the speaker do to establish his or her credibility?

_____

_____

_____

_____

EXERCISE 20.3
Building Your Credibility as a Speaker

Directions: Many beginning public speakers feel that they do not have much credibility. In fact, however, they have many potential resources for establishing their credibility with an audience. Imagine that you have to give a five-minute informative speech to a group of your peers on a topic of your choice. On the following worksheet, list the techniques you could use to establish or enhance your credibility as a speaker.

Topic of the speech: _____

1. How could you create *authority* in the following areas?

   Research: _____

   _____

   Knowledge: _____

   _____

   Personal experience: _____

   _____

   Achievements: _____

   _____

   Associations with other authority figures: _____

   _____

2. How could you show *good sense* in the following areas?

   Reasonable and objective language: _____

   _____

   Using ethical speaking strategies: _____

   _____

   Attitude of equality with and respect for the audience: _____

   _____

3. How could you show *good character* in the following areas?

   Honesty and sincerity: _____

   _____

Accurate facts and data: _____

_____

Avoiding inappropriate language: _____

_____

4. How could you show *good will* in the following areas?

Common experiences and values with the audience: _____

_____

Relevance to audience needs: _____

_____

Friendly, helpful, concerned attitude: _____

_____

Personal concern about and commitment to the topic: _____

_____

5. How could you show *dynamism* in the following areas?

Vocal and physical enthusiasm: _____

_____

Interest in the topic and occasion: _____

_____

Calm and relaxed presentation: _____

_____

Direct eye contact: _____

_____

Flexibility about necessary interruptions or changes: _____

_____

EXERCISE 20.4
Critiquing a Speech

Directions: Attend a public speech of any kind—a lecture, a debate, a sales presentation, or some other public address. Look for the elements in the following guidesheet. Critique the speaker on these points by recording your comments in the speeches provided.

Introduction of the Speech

How clear were the topic and the purpose of the speech? Why?

_____

_____

_____

What introductory devices did the speaker use?

_____

_____

_____

How effective were these devices in building rapport and interest?

_____

_____

_____

Body of the Speech

Were the main points of the body clearly organized? How?

_____

_____

_____

What types of subpoints did the speaker use to support the main points?

_____

_____

_____

What visual aids did the speaker use?

_____

_____

_____

Conclusion of the Speech

What concluding devices did the speaker use?

_____

_____

_____

How effective were these devices in ending the speech?

_____

_____

_____

Delivery of the Speech

Which delivery mode did the speaker use? Was it effective?

_____

_____

_____

How effective were the speaker's voice and use of eye contact?

_____

_____

_____

How effective was the speaker's use of gestures and movement?

_____

_____

_____

ACTION ASSIGNMENT

20

The Principles of Business Speaking

1. Form into groups of five people. Discuss with your group the reasons you feel stage fright. Does anyone in the group have techniques for coping with stage fright? Discuss the methods that group members use. Brainstorm other possible techniques for controlling stage fright when you are speaking in public.

2. Locate a current issue of *Vital Speeches*, a collection of recent speeches of national importance. Select one speech, read it closely, and analyze it in terms of the following elements:

   Situation (the speaker, the audience, the occasion)
   Speaker's purpose
   Organizational pattern of the speech
   Introductory devices
   Main points of the body
   Types of support the speaker used
   Concluding devices

3. Plan a two-minute speech on the topic "My Strengths and Weaknesses as a Speaker." Incorporate introductory and concluding devices in your speech as well as the main points of the body (your strengths and weaknesses). Rehearse the speech until you feel well prepared. Arrange to deliver the speech and videotape your performance. Once you have delivered the speech, review the videotape and determine ways in which your delivery could be improved. Repeat the delivery of the speech and record it again. Review the videotape again and critique your delivery. Was the delivery better the second time? Deliver the speech a third time and record it. Review the videotape. Was there even greater improvement the third time?

21
Informative Speeches

By far the most common speaking situation in business is the informative speech. Often a group needs some information that a speaker can give. The purpose might be to explain a new situation, to report the findings of a project, to recount the history of an issue, or to give reasons for a decision.

A good place to begin discussing speechmaking skills is with informative speaking, because it provides the basic foundation for all other kinds of speaking. Once you master informative speaking, then you will find the other types of speaking easier. By becoming an accomplished informative speaker, you can easily adapt your skills to the other types of speaking.[1]

Preliminary Considerations

As the preceding chapter suggested, you should begin the construction of your speech by determining your purpose and topic. In informative speaking, it is important to determine the scope of your topic. How much information does the audience need? How much do they already know? How do they plan to use this information? The answers to these questions will help you in selecting the amount and kinds of material to include in your speech.

Once you have narrowed or broadened the topic until it is appropriate to the audience's needs and interests, you must gather the information you will present. Search your own experience first to find useful personal stories and insights. You will usually have to supplement this information with material from expert sources. Research in local libraries or through local experts will help to make your information more credible and authoritative.

As you collect materials, give close attention to ways in which you can increase your credibility as a speaker. Look for elements you can include in the speech to heighten your authority, relevance, and dynamism. Pay particular attention to the needs of the audience. Select materials that will be helpful and applicable to audience members. This effort will be repaid in the heightened interest and receptivity of the audience.

Organize and Outline the Body of Your Speech

For an informative speech, it is easiest to plan the body of the speech first. Analyze the material you have to present and divide it into main points. Which division makes the most sense? How can you organize the material into a few main ideas that provide an overall structure for the speech? Many speakers try to limit themselves to just three or four main points. With only a few main points, the audience can more easily remember the material, and your organizational structure will be clearer. All other materials should be subordinated to these main points.

Each main point of information should be supported with subpoints. There are two basic types of support: information factors and interest factors. *Information factors* are the actual pieces of information you present in your speech. The more information factors you present, given the time limit, the stronger the speech usually is. Test your informative support for relevance, accuracy, and timeliness to make sure it is suitable for inclusion in your speech. The second form of support, *interest factors*, makes your speech grab the attention and hold the interest of the audience. These factors are the uniquely "rhetorical" aspects of a speech—the elements that make a speech different from reading information in a book. The interest factors create a sense of personality and rapport between the speaker and the audience. They make people want to listen. Figure 21.1 lists types of support, both information factors and interest factors, that you can use in building an informative speech.

Information Factors

Facts: statements of what is true.

Statistics: numerical data.

Quotations from expert sources: highly credible opinions.

Examples: cases and instances of your ideas.

Illustrations: complex examples that show many details.

Explanations: lengthy discussion of facts to show relationships.

Interest Factors

Personal opinions: your own feelings and thoughts.

Personal experiences: your own insights and activities.

Audience applications: relevant experiences of the audience.

Demonstrations: actual physical and visual examples.

Audience participation: getting the audience involved through a demonstration, a discussion, or questions.

Humorous stories and anecdotes: clever or entertaining examples.

Visual aids: visual representations of data.

FIGURE 21.1   Types of Support: Information and Interest Factors

Analyze your speech for a balance of information factors and interest factors. A speech with nothing but information can be rather dry. A speech composed of purely interest factors can be entertaining, but may not contain all the necessary information. Also, select the most credible support. For example, personal opinions may be interesting, but they are not as credible as the opinions of experts.

Visual presentations of information are particularly useful because they help you compress much information into a smaller time frame. You can cover much more data visually than you can in words alone. Visuals are also helpful in increasing the retention of information. Audiences remember up to three times more information when it is presented visually.[2] Charts, graphs, lists, diagrams, pictures, objects, and models are the most common forms of visual aids. These devices can be presented by means of posters, overhead projectors, slide projectors, blackboards, and handouts. Visual aids are a very powerful interest factor and should be included in speeches whenever appropriate. Figure 21.2 illustrates several examples of the major types of visual aids.[3]

You will find these suggestions helpful when preparing and using visual aids. Make sure that your visuals are necessary and appropriate for your speech. Cluttering your talk with too many visuals may distract the audience from your message. Use visual aids to enhance and clarify, not just to attract attention. Keep your visual aids simple so that they are easy to make and easy to understand. Limit the number of words on your visuals to key elements, and do not try to get too much information on one visual. Use color and pictures whenever possible—lists of words are less interesting than visual images. Print or draw neatly, and use large lettering that can be seen by everyone in the audience. You want your aids to have a professional appearance. Finally, practice the use of your visuals so that they fit easily and comfortably into the delivery of your speech. Anticipate what might go wrong with your aids and practice their use to avoid any last-minute glitches.[4]

Prepare the Conclusion

Once the body of the speech has been organized, you need to prepare the concluding devices. These techniques end the speech gracefully and ensure that your purpose is fulfilled. The most common concluding devices are the summary of all the main points or the reiteration of the single most important point of the speech. These reviews remind the audience of the key elements of information in the speech and emphasize their importance. Some speakers use the conclusion as a time to answer any questions or clarify any misunderstandings that audience members might have. Sources for more information are often included in the conclusion if the speaker wishes to share resources. In some speeches, the answer to the question "Where do we go from here?" is addressed in the conclusion. If information is presented as a springboard to some action, the speaker may use the conclusion to get the audience started thinking about the next steps to take with the information presented in the speech.

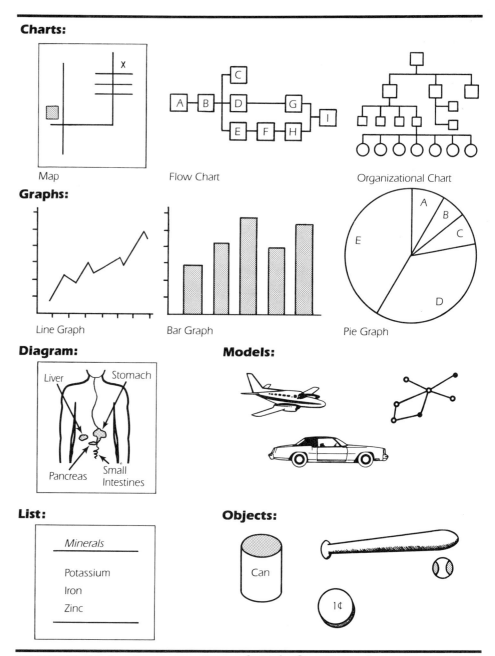

Charts:

Map

Flow Chart

Organizational Chart

Graphs:

Line Graph

Bar Graph

Pie Graph

Diagram:

Liver

Stomach

Pancreas

Small Intestines

Models:

List:

Minerals

Potassium

Iron

Zinc

Objects:

Can

1¢

FIGURE 21.2 Common Visual Aids for Speeches

The final lines of the speech are very important for creating a sense of closure and a graceful ending to the presentation. You should select an impressive or powerful last line for your speech. A quotation from an authority or a bold assertion about the topic creates an impressive and memorable ending that is the capstone to the entire speech. As you assemble materials for your informative speech, watch for powerful quotations or lines you can use to end your speech on a strong note.

Prepare the Introduction

Once you have completed the body and the conclusion, you are ready to prepare the introduction. Some speakers like to write the introduction first, since it comes first in the order of speaking. Many speakers have found, however, that introductions are easier to write once the rest of the speech is completed. When you know what you are going to say in the body and conclusion, it is easier to introduce this material in the opening.

Whichever method you use for constructing the speech, you should cover these five main points in your introduction:

> Grab the attention of the audience.
> Announce the topic and purpose of the speech.
> Explain the relevance of the topic for the audience.
> Establish your credibility as a speaker.
> Preview the main points of the body, which follows.

The opening line of a speech is the most important for creating a positive impression with an audience. Therefore, take special care to select a device that grabs attention and creates interest. Common opening devices are startling statistics, references to audience benefits, rhetorical questions, interesting anecdotes, and challenges to the audience. The opening line should be relevant to the topic and should focus audience attention on the information that will follow, not on the speaker as a performer.

The purpose of informative speaking is to be clear and well organized so that the audience will understand and remember the information. A careful explanation of the topic at the beginning of the speech helps ensure this clarity. If you have limited the topic in some way, you should explain these restrictions. The audience may also need some explanation of unusual terminology or jargon that you use.

Explaining the relevance of the topic for the audience increases interest and attention throughout the presentation. You should explain how the information will benefit the audience, how they can use it, why you are presenting it, and what needs the information will fulfill. You cannot assume that the audience will automatically understand the importance or relevance of a body of information. They often have other things on their minds, which may distract them from your presentation. A strong statement of relevance and importance focuses their attention on the topic.

Techniques for establishing your credibility as a speaker were discussed in the preceding chapter. Insert several credibility-enhancing devices in the introduction of the speech to create a positive impression with the audience. Likewise, occasionally insert these devices throughout the body of the speech to maintain your credibility.

The final element of the introduction is a preview of the main points that will be covered in the body. This advance notice of the structure of your speech helps the audience understand the logical organization of the speech and will help them remember the main points longer. A preview demonstrates that you are highly organized and that you have prepared the material carefully and efficiently. Both of these qualities increase your credibility and enhance audience comprehension of the information.

Develop Transitions in the Speech

Transitions are signposts that tell audience members where you are in the speech and where you are going. All parts of the speech should be linked together by simple statements of transition, which demonstrate the organizational pattern you are using. The introductory preview acts as a transition to the body of the speech. When you move from one main point to another, use a statement announcing the move: "Now that we have looked at point 1, let's look at point 2." Likewise, you should announce demonstrations, examples, digressions, or comparisons and contrasts when they occur: "An example of point 2 occurs when . . . ." Finally, make a clear transition when you begin the conclusion of the speech: "Now that we have discussed each of the three main points, let's summarize the key elements."

Poor speakers often overlook these simple transitional sentences, but they can be one of your most effective devices in helping the audience follow your points. The members of the audience do not have the outline of the speech in front of them, so you must verbalize the structure of the outline in order to keep them on track. Figure 21.3 lists several other transitions you might use in organizing your speech.

Informative speaking challenges your ability to organize information and present it in an interesting way. By following the suggestions in this chapter, you will be able to select a topic, assemble your information, and organize it in an engaging and effective fashion. A sample outline for an informative speech on listening is included in Exhibit 21.A. Note how it incorporates the suggestions presented in this chapter.

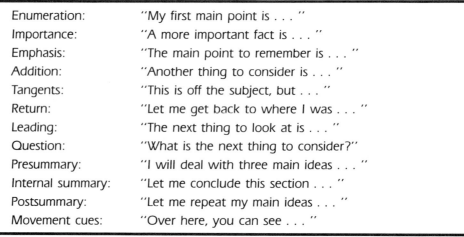

Enumeration:	"My first main point is . . . "
Importance:	"A more important fact is . . . "
Emphasis:	"The main point to remember is . . . "
Addition:	"Another thing to consider is . . . "
Tangents:	"This is off the subject, but . . . "
Return:	"Let me get back to where I was . . . "
Leading:	"The next thing to look at is . . . "
Question:	"What is the next thing to consider?"
Presummary:	"I will deal with three main ideas . . . "
Internal summary:	"Let me conclude this section . . . "
Postsummary:	"Let me repeat my main ideas . . . "
Movement cues:	"Over here, you can see . . . "

FIGURE 21.3 Transitions for Speeches

EXHIBIT 21.A Informative Speech Outline

Topic: Effective Listening

Speaker: Mary E. Whiteley

I. Introduction

  A. Ask: How many of you have ever heard people say:

    1. "What was that you said?"
    2. "I didn't hear anything."
    3. "He never told us that."

  B. Hearing is not the same as listening.

    1. Hearing is automatic and requires no effort.
    2. Listening requires physical and mental effort.

  C. While I am talking some of you will be:

    1. Mentally drifting.
    2. Critiquing my presentation or mannerisms.
    3. Tuned out completely.

  D. Listening is an important skill to prevent these from happening.

    1. As students, listening helps you:
      a. Retain lecture material and get better grades.
      b. Grasp main ideas and follow instructions.
      c. Understand material and get more out of courses.
    2. As future workers/employees, listening helps you:
      a. Judge work situations more effectively.
      b. Make better decisions.
      c. Develop better relationships with superiors, peers, and subordinates.
    3. In your personal life:
      a. Nothing is as important as good listening in a relationship: Hite survey showed that the most frequent complaint women have in relationships is that their men do not listen to them effectively.
      b. Get more cooperation from people:
        1. Example: listening builds trust with parents.
        2. Example: listening builds respect with friends.

  E. Presummary: Today I will cover three areas:

    1. Reasons for poor listening.
    2. Two types of effective listening: attentive and empathic.
    3. Techniques for developing effective listening.

II. Body

A. Reasons for Poor Listening:

    1. Lack of training: listening not taught as academic subject.
    2. Mind drifting:
        a. People can listen at 600–800 words per minute.
        b. Speakers usually talk at 125–150 words per minute.
        c. Extra time is spent daydreaming and drifting away.
    3. Busy criticizing speaker's performance or mannerisms.
    4. Judging and rejecting content before speaker is done.
    5. Allowing emotions to get in the way:
        a. Reactions to key words that seem negative.
        b. Getting angry at the speaker for the ideas.
    6. Busy planning your own response.
    7. Failure to concentrate:
        a. Giving in to distractions: noise, people, situation.
        b. Not listening to complete message of speaker and trying to understand it fully before responding.

B. Two Types of Effective Listening

    1. Attentive Listening
        a. Use when retention of information is important:
            1. Classroom lecture.
            2. Important information presented orally.
        b. See and hear simultaneously:
            1. Listen to words and ideas.
            2. Watch for meaning cues: gestures, nonverbal.
    2. Empathic Listening
        a. Used mostly in interpersonal relationships.
        b. Attempt to understand the other person's emotions:
            1. Listen closely for emotional wording.
            2. Withhold judgment—it prevents problems.
        c. You do not have to agree with the speaker, but by understanding the emotion, you create a more effective relationship and better understanding.

C. Techniques for Effective Listening

    1. Attentive Listening Techniques (Show Overhead)
        a. Pick out key words and relate them to main ideas.
        b. Listen for main concepts and ideas—do not get lost in details.
        c. Be open and flexible to new ideas being presented—withhold judgment until the speaker is done.
        d. Try to structure the speaker's ideas:
            1. Take notes.
            2. Outline the speaker's thoughts.
        e. Use excess time to summarize ideas mentally.
        f. Concentrate closely.
    2. Audience Participation
        a. Ask: What other techniques have you found to be effective for this type of listening?
        b. List answers on overhead.

3. Empathic Listening Techniques (Show Overhead)
   a. Try to understand the emotional level.
   b. Listen for emotional words.
   c. Listen "between the lines" for what is not said.
   d. Watch for nonverbal emotional cues.
   e. Use your own nonverbal cues:
      1. Lean forward.
      2. Maintain eye contact.
      3. Encourage the speaker to continue.
   f. Try not to let your own emotions interfere.
   g. Set aside time to listen fully.
4. Example of Empathic Listening
   a. Tell story of my friend who was considering whether to quit school or change majors.
   b. Point out empathic listening techniques I used.

III. Conclusion

A. There are many other techniques:

1. You may have developed your own.
2. I have covered only the major ones.

B. Much information is available:

1. Magazine articles, such as "Learn How to Listen" in *Fortune*, August 17, 1987.
2. Books, such as *Are You Listening?* by Nichols and Stevens.
3. Classes in interpersonal communication.

C. I hope that you have gotten some useful information and will use it to become more effective listeners.

D. Remember:

1. Effective listening is not the same as just hearing—good listening takes effort and concentration.
2. Two types of effective listening:
   a. Attentive listening.
   b. Empathic listening.

E. You may be surprised at the things you will learn when you listen.

BIBLIOGRAPHY

Anthony Allessandra, "How Do You Rate as a Listener?" *Data Management,* February 1987.
Walter Keichell, "Learn How to Listen," *Fortune,* August 17, 1987, pp. 107–108.
Ralph Nichols and Leonard Stevens, *Are You Listening?* (New York: McGraw-Hill, 1957).
Dan Strother, "On Listening," *Phi Delta Kappan,* October 1987, pp. 127–129.

NOTES

1. For more complete coverage of informative speaking, see Rudolph E. Busby and Randall E. Majors, *Basic Speech Communication: Principles and Practices* (New York: Harper & Row, 1987).

2. The power of visual aids is discussed in Judy C. Pearson and Paul E. Nelson, *Understanding and Sharing*, 3rd ed. (Dubuque, Iowa: Brown, 1985).

3. For more information on types and uses of visual aids, see Douglas Ehninger, Bruce Gronbeck, Ray McKerrow, and Alan Monroe, *Principles and Types of Speech Communication*, 10th ed. (Glenview, Ill.: Scott, Foresman, 1986).

EXERCISE 21.1
Planning an Interesting Introduction for an Informative Speech

Directions: Select one of the following topics for a five-minute informative speech to your peers. Prepare an interesting introduction for the speech by brainstorming devices you might use. In each of the following categories, develop 3 introductory devices that would be interesting and relevant to the topic. Once you have developed all 15 devices, select the best ones from each category to include in your introduction.

Topics: Why You Should Buy a Personal Computer
What You Can Do About Environmental Pollution
Protecting Your Health on the Job
Traits of the Effective Manager

Topic selected: _____

Introduction

Attention-grabbing devices:

1. _____
_____
_____

2. _____
_____
_____

3. _____
_____
_____

Announcing the topic:

1. _____
_____
_____

2. _____
_____
_____

3. _____

   _____

   _____

The relevance of the topic for the audience:

   1. _____

      _____

      _____

   2. _____

      _____

      _____

   3. _____

      _____

      _____

Establishing your credibility:

   1. _____

      _____

      _____

   2. _____

      _____

      _____

   3. _____

      _____

      _____

Preview of the main points of the body:

1. _____

_____

_____

2. _____

_____

_____

3. _____

_____

_____

EXERCISE 21.2
Planning Visual Aids

Directions: Using the topic you selected in Exercise 21.1, imagine the kinds of visual aids that would assist you in creating interest in and understanding of your topic. For each of the following categories, develop at least two visual aids that you might use for your speech. Draw a rough sketch showing what each aid would look like. Indicate the means by which you would present the aid: poster, overhead projector, slide projector, blackboard, or handout.

Charts (maps, flow charts, organizational charts):

_____

_____

Graphs (line graphs, bar graphs, pie graphs):

_____

_____

Lists:

_____

_____

Pictures, objects, or models:

_____

_____

EXERCISE 21.3
Speech Organization Drill

Directions: Below is a list of the elements for an informative speech on the topic of "The Importance of Libraries." The elements of the speech are in jumbled order. Reorganize the elements so that a logical speech could be given from them. Enter the elements in the spaces provided in the outline form that follows, and identify the function that each item plays in the speech. Label the main points, the subpoints, and the type of introductory or concluding device.

Introductory Elements

I have worked in several libraries and I know their usefulness.

In this speech I will analyze three values of libraries: their holdings, their reference services, and their lending services.

Do you want to be knowledgeable in your profession?

Libraries can benefit you by providing much needed information.

The library is a valuable resource for people in business.

Elements of the Body

Reference librarians can help locate materials.

You can borrow from libraries around the country through inter-library loan services.

The most obvious asset of libraries are their holdings.

Reference books provide unique information that helps you find other sources quickly.

Books are the most obvious holding of libraries.

If you are doing a long-term project, you can often place books on long-term lending in a carrel.

One of the most valuable services of a library is the reference department.

Many libraries have reference materials on learning how to use the library.

An often-overlooked resource in the library is lending services.

Clipping files and pamphlets are also useful resources.

Many libraries have short-term reserve lending services.

Most libraries have extensive collections of government publications.

Concluding Elements

Know the services of your library and use them to succeed in your profession.

The holdings are the most obvious feature, but other services are useful too.

A wise man once said, "I bless God in the libraries of the learned."

The three main services of libraries are their holdings, their reference services, and their lending services.

ORGANIZATION OF THE SPEECH

I. Introduction

    A. _____

    B. _____

    C. _____

    D. _____

    E. _____

II. Body

    A. _____

        1. _____

        2. _____

        3. _____

        4. _____

    B. _____

        1. _____

        2. _____

        3. _____

    C. _____

        1. _____

        2. _____

        3. _____

        4. _____

III. Conclusion

    A. _____

    B. _____

    C. _____

    D. _____

EXERCISE 21.4
Planning an Informative Speech

Directions: Select a topic for a five-minute informative speech. Use the following planning sheet to determine your purpose and to develop your preliminary outline.

Speaker's name: _____

Topic of the speech: _____

Audience and Situation Analysis

Audience for the speech: _____

_____

Reasons the audience may need the information: _____

_____

Relevant audience interests and needs: _____

_____

Why you are interested in the topic: _____

_____

The purpose of the speech: _____

_____

Researching the Topic

What the speaker already knows: _____

_____

Areas to be researched: _____

_____

Resources for information: _____

_____

Local experts available for interviews: _____

_____

Preliminary Outline

I. Introduction

    A. _____

       _____

    B. _____

       _____

    C. _____

       _____

    D. _____

       _____

    E. Preview of the main points: _____

       _____

II. Body

    A. Main point: _____

       _____

       1. Subpoint: _____

          _____

          a. Information factors: _____

             _____

             _____

          b. Interest factors: _____

             _____

             _____

       2. Subpoint: _____

          _____

          a. Information factors: _____

             _____

             _____

b. Interest factors: _____

_____

_____

B. Main Point: _____

_____

1. Subpoint: _____

_____

a. Information factors: _____

_____

_____

b. Interest factors: _____

_____

_____

2. Subpoint: _____

_____

a. Information factors: _____

_____

_____

b. Interest factors: _____

_____

_____

C. Main point: _____

_____

1. Subpoint: _____

_____

a. Information factors: _____

_____

_____

b. Interest factors: _____

_____

_____

2. Subpoint: _____

_____

a. Information factors: _____

_____

_____

b. Interest factors: _____

_____

_____

III. Conclusion

A. _____

_____

B. _____

_____

C. _____

_____

D. Strong last line: _____

_____

IV. Bibliography (if used)

ACTION ASSIGNMENT

21

Informative Speeches

1. Review the outline of the speech on listening in Exhibit 21.A. Locate in the outline where one example of the following forms of support is used. If there is no example of the form of support, create one that the writer of the outline might incorporate.

Information Factors	*Interest Factors*
Facts	Personal opinion
Statistics	Personal experience
Quotations	Audience application
Examples	Demonstration
Illustration	Audience participation
Example	Humorous story or anecdote
	Visual aid

2. Review the outline for the speech on listening in Exhibit 21.A and the list of types of transitions in Figure 21.3. Create transitions and write them into the outline in the following locations:

   Between the main points of the introduction (A, B, C, D, E)
   Between the introduction and the body
   Between the main points of the body (A, B, C)
   Between the first level of subpoints in the body (A: 1, 2, 3, 4, 5, 6, 7; B: 1, 2; C: 1, 2, 3, 4)
   Between the body and the conclusion
   Between the main points of the conclusion (A, B, C, D, E)

3. Attend a meeting of a business or professional organization (such as Kiwanis, Rotary, or Business and Professional Women), a student chapter meeting of a professional association, or a guest lecture at an academic meeting. Critique the speaker in terms of the following categories:

   Introduction:
       How clear were the topic and the purpose of the speech?
       What introductory devices did the speaker use?
       How effective were the devices in building rapport and interest?
   Body:
       Were the main points of the body clearly organized?
       What types of subpoints did the speaker use to support them?
       What visual aids did the speaker use?
   Conclusion:
       What concluding devices did the speaker use?
       How effective were the devices in ending the speech?
   Delivery:
       Which delivery mode did the speaker use?
       How effective was the speaker's use of eye contact and voice?
       How effective was the speaker's use of gestures and movement?

22
Training Presentations

Employee training is a huge industry in the United States. Estimates suggest that companies spend from $30 billion to $40 billion a year on internal training for their employees.[1] General Motors alone spends over $1 billion annually on employee development.[2] What do companies get for this money? Training is aimed primarily at helping employees do their job-related tasks more efficiently. Improve interpersonal and communication skills are also major training goals. The result of training is better performance, higher profitability, and increased job satisfaction.[3] Workers also report that training is invaluable in helping them advance in their careers and move up the company ladder.

Training is done in many ways in American industry. Large organizations have centralized training departments that develop, test, and conduct training courses. Many companies hire outside consultant trainers to provide expertise in course development and delivery. Far more commonly, however, informal training is done with minimal preparation and for small groups within an individual office. Given the size and scope of training, most administrators and managers can expect to do some training in their jobs.

Unfortunately, managers are often asked to do training because they are adept at their jobs—not because they are good trainers. This chapter investigates the techniques of effective training and gives you experience in assessing training needs, developing training materials, and anticipating the delivery of training presentations.

Types of Training Presentations

Some training is designed merely to *transmit information* from one person to a group of people. In this type of training, the audience is passive. For example, a company may want to inform its employees of new safety procedures or revised documentation policies. Training of this sort is essentially like an informative speech. A question-and-answer period may be added to the end of the speech to deal with any uncertainties listeners might have.

Other training is designed to *share information* by allowing the audience to become active participants. Such participative training allows more experienced employees to pass along valuable information to newer workers. Group discussions are a good means for letting members of an organization share their knowledge and get to know one another.

Another common purpose of training is to impart *behavioral skills* to a group of workers. Information can be supplemented with hands-on experience that gives employees the chance to practice and learn new skills in a risk-free environment. When dealing with machinery operation, interpersonal skills, or other behaviors, trainers often use guided practice sessions as the best means for educating trainees.

No matter which type of training is used, the fundamentals of informative speaking, which were discussed in the last chapter, are the basis for all training presentations. Concepts must be explained, procedures clarified, information distributed, and questions answered. Training often goes beyond the bounds of mere informative speaking, however, when it incorporates additional group discussion, behavioral experiences, and numerous handouts. This chapter describes additional training techniques and provides suggestions for using them effectively in training situations.

Techniques for Effective Training

Planning a training presentation is almost identical to planning a speech. The difference lies in the desired outcome. Training is designed to impart useful knowledge and skills to workers. Thus, training must always be guided by the outcome. Will the training improve workers' abilities? To accomplish its purpose, training is best designed when you consider the following steps:

Determine the needs of the trainees.
Establish the objectives and benefits of the training.
Select suitable training devices.
Organize the presentation logically.
Rehearse the presentation for maximum impact.
Evaluate the training for effectiveness and value.

Each of these guidelines is dealt with more fully in the sections that follow.

DETERMINE THE NEEDS OF THE TRAINEES

Good training is a response to employees' needs for information to accomplish their jobs better. In determining the need for training, you should consider the questions posed in Figure 22.1. The answers to these questions will help you determine whether training is needed, what type would be most effective, how much information to include, and when to hold the presentation. Use these questions as a guide for determining training needs.

Regarding the content of the training:

What are workers' perceptions of their need for training?

What is management's perception of the need for training?

What do new employees need to know in order to do their jobs?

What do experienced employees wish they had known earlier?

Regarding the timing of the training:

What would be the most efficient way to organize the material to be presented?

When should the training units be presented?

How long should the training units be?

Regarding the delivery of the training:

Who should deliver the training?

Where should the training take place?

What materials will be necessary for the training?

Which training devices are most suitable for the training?

FIGURE 22.1   Questions to Determine Training Needs

DETERMINE THE OBJECTIVES AND BENEFITS OF THE TRAINING

As noted earlier, training can have multiple objectives. It is imperative that the trainer determine the desired outcomes for the training presentation. Without a clear picture of what the training should accomplish, presentations run the risk of being irrelevant, uninteresting, and useless.

Trainers should also be aware that objectives may vary among the different groups involved. Management's goals may be different from those of workers, and the needs of new employees may be very different from those of experienced workers. Considerable attention should be paid to these differences so that the training presentation fills as many needs as possible. Competing or different groups may negotiate what is included in the training. Whatever the outcome of this planning, the trainer needs a clear set of stated outcomes in order to be able to plan an effective presentation.

Training objectives generally cover two elements: information and skills. Most training contains both of these ingredients. The trainer should analyze the desired outcomes for the training and create a set of written objectives. The objectives should outline the exact knowledge and skills that will be included in the training. They should also be written in clear, specific, and measurable terms so that the results of the training can be measured against the objectives once the training is completed. Figure 22.2 lists sample training objectives. Note how each is clearly expressed, specific in detail, and measurable.

(A bank wishes to train new employees on their responsibilities regarding the new Automated Teller Machines.)

At the end of this training session, participants will be able to:

Explain in specific detail the operation of the Automated Teller Machine (ATM).

Demonstrate complete proficiency in operating the ATM.

Give thorough directions to customers on the use of the ATM.

Answer commonly asked customer questions about the ATM.

Perform routine maintenance functions on the ATM.

Know the proper procedures for emergency maintenance on the ATM.

FIGURE 22.2   Sample Training Objectives

Another useful planning device is a written set of benefits that the participants will gain from the training. While the objectives explain what will happen during the training, the statement of benefits explains what the employees will gain from active participation. Analyzing the training for benefits to participants helps the trainer stay relevant and useful—important qualities for audience rapport and interest. The statement of benefits may be used as a promotional device to get people to take the training, or it may be included as opening material in the training itself to create a more receptive attitude in participants. Figure 22.3 lists sample benefits for the bank training described in Figure 22.2.

SELECT THE SUITABLE TRAINING DEVICE

The trainer has four major resources for providing information and skills: lecture, group discussion, experiential exercises, and reading materials. The needs of the participants and the objectives of the training determine which devices are likely to be most suitable for the presentation. As you prepare a training presentation, carefully consider the strengths and limitations of each of the following training devices so that you may select the appropriate one for your goals.

Training lectures are similar to informative speeches. They are used mainly when the objective of the training is to impart large amounts of information. Lectures are often presented in a more casual style than a formal

Upon completion of the ATM training, new employees will:

Provide better customer service.

Be able to prevent mechanical malfunction, thereby relieving their workload at the teller window.

Increase efficiency of their customer load, thereby increasing their chances for involvement in more demanding financial transactions.

Become qualified for advancement to areas of greater responsibility within the bank.

FIGURE 22.3   Sample Statement of Training Benefits

speech so that participants will feel free to interrupt with questions. The informal style also encourages the participants to relax and enjoy the training. Information is often repeated several times by means of internal summaries, printed handouts, or supplemental devices that reinforce the material. Training lectures also make heavy use of visual aids and demonstrations in order to hold attention and aid retention of the material.

Lectures can be very effective when the same material must be given to large numbers of employees, when the material is fairly simple and will need little detailed explanation, and when there is no skill component to the training. A major drawback of the lecture is that the effective attention span of most employees will not permit lectures to exceed an hour or two. If large amounts of material must be transmitted to employees, then the training should be broken down into several lectures or supplemented with reading material. Another way to overcome the relative weakness of lecturing is to combine it with group discussion and experiential exercises in order to provide a well-rounded training presentation.

Group discussion is a popular method for encouraging participants to share information with one another. The discussion leader can insert some new material, but the main purpose of discussion is to let participants explain their opinions, experiences, and knowledge to one another.

Leading a group discussion is significantly different from giving a speech. The trainer must use questions to guide the exchange of information and control the flow of the discussion so that the objectives of the training are met. These skills require practice and patience; but once they are mastered, discussion can be an extremely effective tool for helping participants understand and integrate information. Figure 22.4 lists several suggestions for leading a group discussion. Use them as a guide for planning any group interaction.

Determine the objectives for the discussion.

List the main points that you want the discussion to cover.

Develop a tentative outline by which the discussion may be guided.

Prepare key questions that will start the discussion along the path you want it to follow.

Use "overhead questions" (for example, "Does anyone know . . . ") to get general reactions to ideas.

Use "direct questions" (for example, "Bob, what do you think . . . ") to get specific reactions to ideas.

Encourage participants to express themselves. Ask for reactions from quiet participants and avoid letting outspoken members control or dominate the discussion.

Act as a referee among participants if you must. Your role is to facilitate the discussion, not to control it. Let the members do most of the talking.

Be flexible in letting the discussion take its own course, but be prepared to pull it back on course if it wanders too far afield.

Provide a summary of what has been discussed and decided at the end of the discussion.

FIGURE 22.4   Suggestions for Leading a Group Discussion

PARTICIPANT A:	You are a customer of ABC Bank. You enjoy coming to the bank and talking to the tellers to make sure your money is safe. You do not know how to use the ATM, and you are somewhat resistant to learning how to use it. You will agree to learn to use the ATM only if the teller gives you good reasons and adequate instructions.
PARTICIPANT B:	You are a teller at ABC Bank. You are requested to try to convince customers to use the ATM as often as possible. The reasons include more efficient use of tellers, greater convenience for customers (since the ATM is open 24 hours), and foolproof security of the ATM system.
INSTRUCTIONS:	A customer comes to the teller's window and wants to make a deposit. The teller should convince the customer to learn and to use the ATM system. A mobile ATM unit is at the teller's window for purposes of instruction.

FIGURE 22.5 Sample Role-Play Instructions

Experiential exercises are powerful devices for learning and integrating training materials, especially behavioral skills. If a worker needs hands-on training in order to learn a skill, then experiential exercises give him or her a chance to practice in a safe environment and perfect the skill before being required to use it on the job. While there are many types of exercises a trainer might use, three of the most common are experiential handouts, role plays, and simulations.

Experiential handouts are simple, and usually short, exercises that require participants to react to ideas on paper. Examples of this type of exercise are paper-and-pencil tests, attitude surveys, and self-assessments about the material to be presented. Many of the exercises at the ends of chapters in this book could be used as experiential handouts in a training course. The purpose of an experiential handout is to focus attention and interest on the training material and to get the participants to think about the information. These exercises are often used at the beginning of training presentations to get participants warmed up.

Role plays are spontaneous dramatic representations of a situation in which a skill is needed. Trainers use role plays to point out the lack of a skill or to give the participant a chance to practice a skill. Sample instructions for a role-play exercise are presented in Figure 22.5. Note how the two participants are given specific goals and suggestions for playing their role.

Simulations are training devices, much like games, of more complex situations that require employee skills. Instead of a single situation, like the role play, a simulation requires the integration of skills in several situations and in ongoing relationships among people. An example of a simulation is the war game played by an army, in which large groups of people engage in complex maneuvers to develop and test their abilities. Similarly, businesses use simulations by creating an artificial work environment that demands complex and multiple reactions from workers. By experiencing the simulation, training participants can practice skills and measure their abilities to perform them. They also see other workers using the skills and can learn from these models.

Reading materials often supplement training presentations when large amounts of information must be presented. Participants may be asked to read materials before or during the presentation. The reading may also serve as homework or review material for participants once the presentation is completed. These materials are often collected in a training manual or binder for convenience.

ORGANIZE AND PRACTICE THE PRESENTATION

Once you have selected the appropriate training devices to accomplish your goals, you are ready to organize the entire presentation. Most training uses a combination of several devices. Consider a logical balance and sequence for the combination you wish to use. You can accomplish only so much within a certain time frame, so consider your priorities in selecting material and devices for the presentation. Anticipate realistic time limits for each of the activities, and prepare an agenda to help you manage your time. You may need to practice some of the devices to determine how long they will take to deliver.

You should also consider the number of participants and the resources you have available for materials. The time needed for preparation and the cost of materials are important factors in determining training presentations. Likewise, space and facilities requirements must be determined and budgeted. Consider these elements in the planning stage, and be prepared to be flexible in adjusting to environmental constraints.

Once you have completed the planning for the presentation, it is advisable to give the materials a practice run-through. A critical "dress rehearsal" can identify flaws in time planning, illogical organization, or ineffective devices. Professional trainers often use pilot training sessions to perfect materials and ensure top-quality presentations.

EVALUATE THE TRAINING

Once you have delivered a training presentation, you should evaluate both the content and the methods of the training. Evaluation is often integrated into the conclusion of training by means of an evaluation form or questionnaire. Has the training had any impact on the job performance of workers? What are their opinions of the training? Are there certain areas of the training presentation that could be improved? Should there be any follow-up activity to reinforce the training? Asking these questions helps you identify both strengths and weaknesses in training presentations. Any weaknesses should be corrected in order to ensure success the next time the training is given.

Strong training presentations are exciting and valuable parts of any manager's responsibility. They are also valuable assets to a company. If you find you enjoy training, it can become an opportunity for career growth. By following the principles of effective informational speaking presented in the preceding chapter and the guidelines for training presentations in this chapter, you are well on the road to presenting dynamic, interesting, and valuable training of your own.

NOTES

1. B. J. Middlebrook and F. M. Rachel, "Who Receives Training and What Kind of Training Do They Get?" *Training* 20 (October 1983): 41–45.

2. D. Gayeski, "Educating the Training Professional," *Training and Development Journal* 35 (1981): 60–66.

3. K. E. Hultman and G. Cunningham, "Preparing Employees for Upward Mobility," *Training and Development Journal* 32 (1978): 10–14.

EXERCISE 22.1
Determining Objectives and Benefits for Training

Directions: Consider your current or past work situation. Was there a need for training? In the worksheet below, describe the situation and the need for training as you saw it. Imagine that it was your responsibility to plan this training. Develop the objectives and benefits for the training you would propose. If you do not have a current or past example, create a fictional situation in which you might be required to provide employee training.

The Situation:

_____

_____

_____

_____

_____

_____

_____

The Need for Training:

_____

_____

_____

_____

_____

_____

_____

_____

_____

Objectives:

1. _____

_____

2. _____

_____

3. _____

_____

4. _____

_____

5. _____

_____

Benefits:

1. _____

_____

2. _____

_____

3. _____

_____

4. _____

_____

5. _____

_____

EXERCISE 22.2
Planning an Experiential Exercise

Directions: Using the situation you described in Exercise 22.1, plan an experiential exercise that would accomplish one or more of the objectives you listed. Select an experiential handout, a role play, or a simulation that would develop the skills or knowledge you wish to impart to the participants. In the following worksheet, explain the objective(s) for the exercise, describe the materials and time needed, and provide a brief description of the steps in the exercise. Conclude your planning with a statement of your expected outcome.

Objective(s) for the Exercise:

_____

_____

_____

_____

Materials and Time Needed:

_____

_____

_____

Instructions for Conducting the Exercise:

_____

_____

_____

_____

Anticipated Problems (if Any):

_____

_____

_____

Expected Outcomes of the Exercise:

_____

_____

_____

EXERCISE 22.3
Planning a Training Presentation

Directions: Imagine that you are a manger in an office of 30 workers. Your immediate supervisor has discovered that the people in your office are making far more mistakes than the company average in the work they do. The reason seems to be poor listening skills in understanding and following directions. Your boss has asked you to design a two-hour training presentation on listening skills in order to reduce this high rate of errors. Outline a tentative plan for the training presentation.

Objectives:

1. _____

2. _____

3. _____

4. _____

5. _____

Benefits:

1. _____

2. _____

3. _____

4. _____

5. _____

Outlined Agenda for the Training Presentation:
(For each part, include objective, materials and time needed, steps in or main points of the training device)

_____

_____

_____

_____

_____

_____

_____

_____

_____

Agenda (continued):

_____

_____

_____

_____

_____

_____

_____

_____

_____

_____

_____

_____

_____

_____

_____

_____

_____

_____

_____

_____

_____

_____

_____

ACTION ASSIGNMENT

22

Training Presentations

1. In your community, find a provider of one of the following areas of training:

   Word processing
   Spread-sheet analysis
   Typing (keyboarding)
   Speed reading
   Study skills
   Test-taking skills
   Recreational sport (e.g., skydiving, horseback riding, kayaking)

   Interview the training provider and gather information to critique the training in the following categories:

   Traits of the provider (qualifications, reputation, skill level)
   Objectives of the training
   Benefits of the training
   Schedule of activities
   Types of training activities
   Cost of the training

2. Recall some training you have received in a business situation. It may have been as brief as a five-minute introduction on how to use a cash register. (Business training is often very informal.) If you have had no business training, recall a skills training activity in a youth organization (Boy Scouts, Brownies, 4H Club). Was the training as effective as it could have been? Using the guidelines given in this chapter, critique the training you received and suggest ways in which it might have been improved.

3. Plan a ten-minute training program on one of the following topics:

   How to Balance Your Checkbook
   Napkin Folding
   Designing Your Own Personal Stationery
   How to Take Better Photographs
   How to Design Your Own Physical Training Program
   Designing a Weight Reduction Plan
   How to Study Effectively for Tests

   Form groups of four people, and deliver your training programs to one another. Ask for feedback from the group on ways in which you were effective and ways in which you could improve your presentation.

23

Speeches to Influence

In the world of business, the ability to influence others is a powerful skill. Business people constantly work in situations that require the ability to persuade others to agree, to accept, or to act. Knowing the principles and techniques of persuasion makes you appear successful, and you can exert greater control in work situations because of your ability to influence others.

This chapter analyzes the basic principles of persuasion, which you can use in public-speaking situations to influence others: stating a clear purpose, analyzing audience values, constructing good arguments, and coping with counterarguments. These principles are then applied in four speaking situations common in business: convincing others that a problem exists, reaching agreement about the cause of a problem, influencing others to consider alternative solutions to a problem, and persuading others that one solution is better than the rest. If you can organize your thoughts and present persuasive arguments in these four situations, you will be a powerful member of your chosen field. (The sales presentation is another common persuasive situation, dealt with separately in Chapter 24.)

Clarify Your Persuasive Purpose

The first step to being influential with others is to know exactly what you want done and who should do it. Far too often, persuasion is watered down by the attitude that "somebody ought to do something." Who is the somebody? And what is the something? If you have a clear idea of what you think ought to be done and who ought to do it, then you are well on the way to being influential. Better yet, if you have ideas about how things should be done, you can shine. Most employers want managers who can find solutions, not just identify problems. If you can analyze problems and solutions in a clear and logical way, then you will greatly increase your value as an employee.

Before presenting a speech to influence, you need to analyze carefully your purpose in speaking. Effective persuasion demands a critical awareness of the many sides of a problem situation. Who thinks there is a problem? What are the negative effects of the problem? Who is affected by the problem? What are possible causes of the problem? The answers to these questions help you focus your investigation and arrive at more effective solutions.

Once you have analyzed the cause of the problem from all perspectives, you may be able to form an opinion about what should be done. In presenting this opinion to a group of people, you need a precise purpose. The more precisely you state who ought to do what and how it ought to be done, the more effectively your arguments can be focused to get the results you desire. A speaker cannot be effective if the audience walks away from the speech saying, "Those were good arguments, but what am I supposed to do about the problem?" In planning your speech, determine exactly what you want done, then test each of your arguments to see if they contribute to your ultimate purpose.

Analyze Your Audience's Values

In order to develop good arguments to convince an audience to agree with your purpose, you must understand the values of the people you address. If a person does not value saving money, for example, an argument that your solution is economical will be wasted on that person. Likewise, if another person values saving money above everything else, then you need to include the economy argument or you will never convince that individual. You must identify the dominant values of your audience and use them as the foundation of your arguments. This process is called "anchoring."[1] You anchor your ideas to the values that the audience already holds.

People value many different things, and they value them to varying degrees of intensity. The more you understand about the values of your audience members, the better equipped you are to make choices about the arguments and kinds of evidence to use. Figure 23.1 lists common values of Americans, based on the research of one social scientist.[2] As you read this list, reflect on your own values. Which of these items are of value to you? How would you rank them in terms of their importance to you?

Values vary in different situations. What you value in the purchase of a house may be different from what you value in the selection of a life partner. However, the more clearly you understand how values affect perceptions of problems and solutions, the better equipped you are to influence other people's decisions. You must also be able to separate your values from those of others. A common flaw in persuasion is the assumption that other people will value the same things as you and that they will agree with your value choices. You must carefully analyze your own values and compare them with the audience members' values. If they are not the same on key issues, then you must decide how to address the inconsistency. In most cases, you can find common values that will serve as the basis for your arguments.

Pioneer morality: "The good guys versus the bad guys."

Rugged individualism: "Give me elbow room."

Achievement and success: "We're number one!"

Change and progress: "Things are getting better and better."

Ethical equality: "All people are created equal."

Effort and optimism: "Puritan work ethic: If you don't work, you don't eat."

Efficiency, practicality, and pragmatism: "If it works, don't fix it."

Rejection of authority: "Don't trust anyone over 30."

Science and secular rationality: "Better living through science."

Social acceptance: Being a "regular guy" and "keeping up with the Joneses."

Material comfort: "Because you deserve the very best."

Quantity: "Bigger is better."

External conformity: "Be in with the 'in crowd.'"

Humor: "You better smile when you say that, mister."

Generosity: "Give me your tired, your poor . . . ."

Patriotism: "Land of the free, home of the brave."

FIGURE 23.1 Common American Values

Develop Good Arguments

Once you have determined your purpose and considered the values of the audience, you are ready to begin selecting arguments that will support your position. An *argument* is a proposed statement of fact that is supported with evidence. For example, a person might argue: "We are polluting Lake Michigan with our factory waste, and we should stop it." The claim that the company is polluting the lake must be supported with facts that prove the case: testimony of experts, statistical data, laboratory tests, or other forms of support. Figure 23.2 lists common forms of evidence you can use in building

Expert testimony: "Dr. Smith measured the pollution and found . . . ."

Statistics: "The pollution is a 27.5 percent level of tar."

Personal experience: "I went out and inspected and saw . . . ."

Explanation: "By pollution I mean . . . ."

Analogy/comparison: "The drain is like a cesspool."

Illustration: "These pictures show what I mean . . . ."

Demonstration: "I have a sample here of the outflow."

Contrast: "This is not up to EPA standards."

Application: "Would you want this discharged into your yard?"

Incremental agreement: "Can we at least agree that this is not a very pleasant situation?"

FIGURE 23.2 Common Forms of Evidence

sound arguments. As you read the list, notice the examples that are provided for the pollution argument.

Most persuasive speeches consist of several main arguments. Each argument—or *reason,* as it is sometimes called—must be supported with evidence proving the point the speaker is trying to make. As you plan your speech, select the arguments that are most likely to be accepted by the audience. Find the forms of support that are most convincing to that particular group. These choices of argument and evidence are always matters of judgment, since you can never be sure how an audience will decide what to think or do. The stronger your evidence, however, the greater your chances of persuading effectively.

Some evidence is stronger than other evidence. When an audience is confronted with conflicting evidence, which set of facts will they believe? Three tests of evidence will help you determine the strength of your facts: credibility, relevance, and accuracy.[3] *Credibility* refers to the authority of the source of the facts. Experts are generally more authoritative than lay people. Thus, expert testimony is more credible. *Relevance* refers to the applicability of the facts to the case at hand. Is the evidence immediately relevant or only tangentially so? The more relevant the data, the stronger the support will be. *Accuracy* refers to the lack of errors or bias in the selection and presentation of the evidence. Accurate evidence is complete, up to date, and not distorted in the way it is presented. By applying these tests to the evidence you want to use, you can make your arguments stronger and more acceptable to an audience.[4]

Finally, one aspect of evidence to avoid is the use of fallacious argumentation. Some forms of evidence sound as though they could be true, but in fact violate logical rules. Figure 23.3 illustrates common fallacious forms of arguments that you should avoid when building persuasive arguments.[5]

Ad hominem arguments: Attacking the opponent personally rather than refuting his or her argument.

Bandwagon conformity: Appealing to irrational follow-the-leader instincts rather than weighing the evidence.

Exaggeration: Overstating or stretching the truth to make it more attractive or acceptable.

Falsehood: Lying or misrepresenting facts.

Faulty causal reasoning: Implying that one thing causes another when there is no evidence to prove that relationship.

Glittering generality: Making a sweeping statement when there is no evidence that it is always true.

Scapegoating: Laying blame for a problem on a defenseless person or group to direct attention away from the real cause.

"Straw man" argument: Creating an intentionally weak argument and then easily disproving it for dramatic effect.

FIGURE 23.3 Common Fallacious Arguments

Anticipate Counterarguments

In most persuasive situations there are at least two sides to the case. You can expect that the other side will have arguments and evidence that contradict yours. You should plan a way of dealing with those arguments. For example, if you know that opponents intend to bring out expert testimony to support an argument, you should have equally impressive or even more credible experts to argue your position. If you cannot refute evidence in a certain area, then you can balance your case with stronger evidence in some other area.

Many persuasive speeches anticipate the arguments of the other side of the case and attempt to defeat them early. This "beating the opponent to the punch" is called the *inoculation effect.*[6] By warning the audience about what the other side will probably say, you can focus their attention on your argument's strengths and force your opponents to deal with your arguments rather than their own. By appearing to consider both sides of the case, you also seem to be fairer and more concerned about the audience making a good choice—thereby increasing your credibility as a speaker.

When planning your persuasive speech, anticipate the arguments the other side of the case will present. If there is no opponent presenting a contrary position, then consider what the critics in your audience will probably be thinking. Develop good evidence that will outweigh, or at least counterbalance, the opposing evidence. This anticipation will make your own case more nearly complete and will enable you to deal with opposing positions more effectively.

Organize Your Speech

There are several organizational patterns that you can use in a persuasive situation. The best choice depends on the nature of the situation and your specific purpose. Four common speaking situations are discussed in this section. Each has a persuasive pattern that can assist you in organizing your speech.

The *problem-awareness pattern* is useful when your main purpose is to bring attention to a condition. In this pattern you do not propose a solution but only point out that a problem exists that needs to be solved. This pattern is most useful when you think the group needs time to consider solutions or when you do not have an opinion about the best solution. Figure 23.4 lists the steps in the problem-awareness pattern of a speech to influence.

I. Introduction
   A. Grab the audience's attention.
   B. Show relevance of the topic to the audience.
   C. Establish your credibility.
   D. State your purpose—to show that a problem exists.

II. Body
   A. Describe the nature of the problem.
      1. Provide examples of the problem.
      2. Offer evidence that the problem exists.
   B. Show the relevance of the problem to the audience.
      1. Assert that the problem affects the audience.
      2. Provide specific evidence of negative effects.
   C. Show the consequences if nothing is done.
      1. Provide evidence of short-term effects.
      2. Provide evidence of long-term effects.
      3. Give specific applications of effect on audience.

III. Conclusion
   A. Summarize the problem situation.
   B. Outline a specific plan for approaching the problem, if you have one.

FIGURE 23.4   The Problem-Awareness Pattern of a Speech to Influence

The *cause-and-effect pattern* is effective when your purpose is to demonstrate the cause of a specific problem. In some instances, the cause of a problem may be a matter of controversy. Your persuasive purpose may be to get agreement about the actual cause. Again, you do not propose a solution. You only wish to clarify the cause so that possible solutions can be examined later. The cause-and-effect pattern is outlined in Figure 23.5.

I. Introduction
   A. Introductory devices (see Figure 23.4).
   B. Establish that a problem exists (see Figure 23.4).

II. Body
   A. Propose the possible causes of the problem.
      1. List factors that support each causal relationship.
      2. Determine who is responsible for each cause.
      3. Clarify any overlapping or confusing causes.
   B. Eliminate the unlikely causes.
      1. Dismiss the impossible causes.
      2. Provide evidence to dismiss unlikely causes.
   C. Focus attention on the probable cause.
      1. List factors that support the likelihood of cause.
      2. Clarify who is responsible for the cause.

III. Conclusion
   A. Summarize your case for the probable cause.
   B. Call for action to find solutions to the problem.

FIGURE 23.5   The Cause-and-Effect Pattern of a Speech to Influence

I. Introduction
  A. Introductory devices.
  B. Review the problem (see Figure 23.4).
  C. Review the cause (see Figure 23.5).
  D. State your purpose—to review possible solutions.

II. Body
  A. Consider solutions already tried.
    1. Provide details of the solutions.
    2. Describe how and why they failed.
  B. Consider unworkable solutions.
    1. Provide details of the solutions.
    2. Provide evidence for their ineffectiveness.
  C. Consider likely solutions.
    1. Provide details of the solutions.
    2. Provide evidence for the likelihood of each.
  D. Compare the most likely solutions.
    1. Compare relative advantages of each solution.
    2. Compare relative disadvantages of each plan.
    3. Compare relative long-term effects of adoption.

III. Conclusion
  A. Review possible solutions.
  B. Emphasize the most likely alternatives.
  C. Review relative advantages and disadvantages.
  D. Call for adoption of the most suitable solution.

FIGURE 23.6   The Possible-Solutions Pattern of a Speech to Influence

In some situations, the problem and the cause of the problem may be obvious. The *possible-solutions pattern* focuses the audience's attention on the means available to solve the problem and prepares them to make a decision. You may wish to argue the pros and cons of the possible solutions and leave the decision to the audience. This pattern does not argue for the acceptance of a specific solution but allows the audience to choose the best solutions available. Figure 23.6 outlines this pattern.

The most commonly used persuasive scheme is the *best-solution pattern.* This organization is designed to prove that one solution is the best of all possible solutions. It combines elements of the problem-awareness, cause-and-effect, and possible-solution patterns and leads to the conclusion that one solution should be adopted. It organizes supporting evidence in a logical fashion, and it ends with a strong appeal for acceptance of the proposed solution. The best-solution pattern is outlined in Figure 23.7.

I. Introduction

A. Introductory devices.

B. Establish that a problem exists (see Figure 23.4).

II. Body

A. Review the cause of the problem (see Figure 23.5).

B. Review the possible solutions (see Figure 23.6).

C. Identify the best solution.

1. Provide evidence for its effectiveness.
2. Provide evidence that it will address the causes of the problem.
3. Consider any negative side effects.

D. Deal with counterarguments.

1. Identify the opponents of the solution.
2. Provide evidence to refute their arguments.

III. Conclusion

A. Review the best solution.

B. Provide specific plan for implementation of the solution.

C. Establish criteria for determining whether the solution actually works.

D. Visualize the positive results of the solution.

E. Call for action to adopt and implement the solution.

FIGURE 23.7   Best-Solution Pattern of a Speech to Influence

Persuasive speaking is an important part of any business setting. The keys to effective influence are clear purpose, audience analysis, good arguments, and an appropriate organizational scheme. With the techniques described in this chapter, you can organize your thoughts and prepare dynamic and effective persuasive presentations.

A sample outline for a speech to influence using the best-solution pattern is provided in Exhibit 23.A. Note how it uses the structure outlined in Figure 23.7 and incorporates the suggestions offered in this chapter.

EXHIBIT 23.A   Outline for Speech to Influence

Topic: Support Mothers Against Drunk Driving (MADD)

Speaker: Mary A. Whiteley

I. Introduction

A. Did you know that in a ten-year period drunk drivers killed a quarter of a million people?

1. Average of 70 per day.
2. Three people will die while we are in this class today.

B. Drunk driving is a national catastrophe.

1. In 1984, National Transportation Safety Board reported:
   a. On any weekend night, 10 percent of drivers are drunk.
   b. Thirty percent of drunk drivers are repeat offenders.

C. This means that you and I are endangered every time we drive.

D. I know firsthand the tragedy.

 1. Story of sister who was injured in auto accident caused by drunk driver.
 2. Story of woman at work whose child was hit by drunk driver.

E. Today I want to talk about:

 1. History of MADD.
 2. What MADD does.
 3. What MADD has accomplished.
 4. How you can help MADD accomplish its goals.

II. Body

A. History of MADD.

 1. MADD formed in 1980 by Cindy Lightner, whose daughter was killed by a drunk driver—who had four prior arrests for drunk driving.
 2. Since 1980, MADD has grown to 430 regional chapters in 47 states—usually founded by people who have lost loved ones.
 3. National chapter lobbies Congress for legislation to control the problem of drunk driving.
 4. MADD is totally nonprofit—relies on donations, grants, fundraisers, and volunteers.

B. What MADD Does.

 1. Regional chapters:
 a. Provide individual attention to victims and families to help them during crisis.
 b. Provide information on victims' rights and criminal process.
 c. Make referrals for grief counseling.
 d. Encourage families to talk to district attorney and testify in court.
 e. Attend court proceedings and report judgments to media and interest groups.
 2. National chapter:
 a. Attempts to increase public awareness through media.
 b. Works for changes in legislation:
 1. Harsher penalties.
 2. More enforcement.
 3. Prevent repeat offenders from driving.
 c. Sets goals for state legislation.
 d. Assists regional chapters.

C. What MADD has accomplished.

 1. Ignited public support for stricter laws.
 a. Tougher laws adopted in 25 states.
 b. Local example of law enforcement.

2. Supports laws to increase legal drinking age to 21 in all states.
3. Results:
   a. Since 1981, deaths caused by drunk driving have fallen by 24 percent in United Sates.
   b. Estimated 5,000 lives saved in past five years.

III. Conclusion: How You Can Help

A. Donate money to MADD for the fight (show overhead of MADD's address).

B. If you cannot donate money, then volunteer time.

   1. Types of things volunteers do (show overhead):
      a. Receive training.
      b. Assemble mailings.
      c. Telephone people to support legislation.
      d. Social-support groups and counseling services.
   2. Benefits of being a volunteer:
      a. Meet pleasant people.
      b. Develop skills in grass-roots organization.
      c. Satisfaction of saving lives.

C. Become politically aware and support local and state legislation endorsed by MADD.

D. Remember—a person may have died in the time I have taken to give this speech.

E. If you cannot do any of these things to support MADD— please don't drink and drive!

BIBLIOGRAPHY

"Ahead: Minimum Drinking Age of 21," *U.S. News and World Report*, June 25, 1984, p. 8.
"Drunk Driving," *Ladies Home Journal*, February 5, 1985, p. 110.
John Leo, "One Less for the Road?" *Time*, May 20, 1985, pp. 76–78.
"One Woman Can Make a Difference," *Vogue*, April 1986, p. 170.
Margie Sellinger, "Already the Conscience of a Nation, Candy Lightner Prods Congress into Action Against Drunk Drivers," *People's Weekly*, July 9, 1984, pp. 102–105.

NOTES

1. See Roderick Hart, Gustav W. Friedrich, and Barry Brummett, *Public Communication* (New York: Harper & Row, 1983).

2. See James C. McCroskey, *An Introduction to Rhetorical Communication*, 3rd ed. (Englewood Cliffs, N.J.: Prentice-Hall, 1983).

3. Hart, Friedrich, and Brummett, *Public Communication.*

4. For a complete discussion of the effective use of evidence, see James C. McCroskey, "A Summary of Experimental Research on the Effects of Evidence in Persuasion," James W. Gibson (ed.), *A Reader in Speech Communication* (New York: McGraw-Hill, 1971), pp. 297–306.

5. These and other logical fallacies are discussed fully in Howard Kahane, *Logic and Contemporary Rhetoric*, 2d ed. (Belmont, Calif.: Wadsworth, 1976).

6. Hart, Friedrich, and Brummett, *Public Communication.*

EXERCISE 23.1
Analyzing an Audience

Directions: Assume that you are a manager in an office. You have determined that the present system of ordering supplies is extremely inefficient and needs restructuring. You must convince the other three managers in your company to accept your plan if the president is to agree to adopt a new system. You plan to give a speech at the next managers' meeting and propose your plan.

Below are profiles of the three other managers whom you will have to convince. For each manager, list three values that you think would be effective anchors for arguments in getting them to approve your idea. Then explain how you could incorporate each of their values into an argument in support of your plan.

John is a very enthusiastic and energetic worker. He seems to run at full speed constantly. He works well and efficiently, but he is sometimes a bit disorganized. He likes new ideas and is always open to suggestions for ways to improve the office. He takes criticism and feedback easily and was not threatened when you proposed improvements in the past. You and John get along well together, and you have lunch with him occasionally.

Value #1:

_____

_____

_____

Value #2:

_____

_____

_____

Value #3:

_____

_____

_____

Martha has been a manager in the office longer than anyone else. She originally designed the supply-ordering system that is currently in need of overhaul. She realizes that it is not as efficient as it could be, but she does not want to lose face by having someone else criticize the system. She is concerned about saving the company money because she respects the president and wants the company to succeed.

Value #1:

_____

_____

_____

Value #2:

_____

_____

_____

Value #3:

_____

_____

_____

Ernest is a shy and very quiet manager who performs extremely exacting work but does not enjoy dealing with other people. He is quite number-oriented. He is highly organized and likes to keep precise records on all expenditures. He agrees that something should be done to improve the current ordering system, but since he has little contact with other people in the office, he does not have any opinion about what should be done. He is willing to leave the decision up to someone else as long as the new system is efficient and precise and does not force him to have to deal with sales people.

Value #1:

_____

_____

_____

Value #2:

_____

_____

Value #3:

_____

_____

EXERCISE 23.2
Evaluating the Strength or Weakness of Evidence

Directions: Below is a list of evidence in support of the argument that buying a personal computer (PC) is a good investment for a business student. Apply the tests of evidence—credibility, relevance, and accuracy—to each of the pieces of evidence. Which pieces of evidence are the most persuasive? Which are the least powerful? Also, be on the lookout for any fallacious arguments (see Figure 23.2). In the blanks in the right-hand column, comment on the strength or weakness of each piece of evidence.

Proposed fact: Buying a personal computer is a good investment for a business student.

EVIDENCE	COMMENT ON STRENGTH OR WEAKNESS
1. Almost all business students have PCs.	_____
2. Fifty percent of business students have cars.	_____
3. Your economics professor says this is true.	_____

4. Anybody who disagrees with you is a dope.

_____

_____

_____

_____

5. The president of Apple Computer thinks this is a good idea.

_____

_____

_____

_____

_____

6. All the business students you know have PCs.

_____

_____

_____

_____

_____

7. Be one of the in-crowd—buy a computer.

_____

_____

_____

_____

8. By 1990, every business student will own a PC anyway.

_____

_____

_____

_____

EXERCISE 23.3
Developing Support for Arguments

Directions: Assume that you want to give a speech to your peers about reasons for participating in the Red Cross blood drive. From your research, you determine that there are three main arguments: the Red Cross badly needs your blood donation, it is not painful or dangerous to give blood, and it can save you money if you ever need blood from the Red Cross. For each of these three arguments, develop four supporting pieces of evidence from the list of the following types of support. Make sure that all forms of support are represented somewhere in your speech. Invent whatever facts you need to in order to create the evidence.

Forms of Support: personal experience   explanation
                          expert testimony   analogy
                          statistics   comparison
                          illustration   contrast
                          demonstration   application
                          incremental agreement

Argument #1: The Red Cross badly needs your blood donation.

Evidence 1: _____

_____

_____

Evidence 2: _____

_____

_____

Evidence 3: _____

_____

_____

Evidence 4: _____

_____

_____

Argument #2: It is not painful or dangerous to give blood.

Evidence 1: _____

_____

_____

Evidence 2: _____

_____

_____

Evidence 3: _____

_____

_____

Evidence 4: _____

_____

_____

Argument #3: You will save money if you ever need blood from the Red Cross.

Evidence 1: _____

_____

_____

Evidence 2: _____

_____

_____

Evidence 3: _____

_____

_____

Evidence 4: _____

_____

_____

EXERCISE 23.4
Planning a Speech to Influence

Directions: Below is a list of four possible topics for a speech to influence. Select one of the topics and plan a tentative outline. Refer to the outlines of persuasive patterns in this chapter for ideas in developing your outline.

Topics: Air Pollution is a Problem in Our Office
   Poor Study Habits Cause Failing Grades
   Ways of Combating Sexism in the Office
   The Office Needs to be Redecorated to Improve Our Image

Topic: _____

I. Introduction

A. _____

_____

_____

_____

B. _____

_____

_____

_____

C. _____

_____

_____

_____

D. _____

_____

_____

_____

E. _____

_____

_____

_____

II. Body

    A. _____

       _____

       1. _____

         _____

         _____

         _____

       2. _____

         _____

         _____

         _____

       3. _____

         _____

         _____

         _____

    B. _____

       _____

       1. _____

         _____

         _____

         _____

       2. _____

         _____

         _____

         _____

       3. _____

         _____

         _____

         _____

C. _____

    _____

    1. _____

      _____

      _____

    2. _____

      _____

      _____

      _____

    3. _____

      _____

      _____

      _____

III. Conclusion

    A. _____

      _____

      _____

    B. _____

      _____

      _____

    C. _____

      _____

      _____

    D. _____

      _____

      _____

ACTION ASSIGNMENT

23

Speeches to Influence

1. Select one of the following topics to convince an audience:

   To change an attitude (e.g., tuition should be raised)
   To take a risky behavior (e.g., to give blood in the next Red Cross blood drive)
   To change a behavior (e.g., not to litter)
   To experience a new environment (e.g., to join a student organization)

   Review the following list of values and create an argument in support of your topic based on each value. See Figure 23.1 for examples.

Pioneer morality	Science
Rugged individualism	Social acceptance
Achievement/success	Material comfort
Change/progress	Quantity
Ethical equality	External conformity
Effort/optimism	Humor
Efficiency/practicality	Generosity
Rejection of authority	Patriotism

2. For the same topic as in the Action Assignment above, develop one example of each of the following fallacious arguments:

   Ad hominem argument
   Bandwagon conformity
   Exaggeration
   Falsehood
   Faulty causal reasoning
   Glittering generality
   Scapegoating
   "Straw man" argument

3. Identify the organizational pattern you would use for the topics listed below for a speech to influence. Outline the main points of the speech you would give to illustrate your use of the pattern.

   Patterns: problem-awareness pattern
   cause-and-effect pattern
   possible-solutions pattern
   best-solution pattern

   Topics: What Should Be Done About Absenteeism?
   Is There Waste in Spending?
   How to End the Parking Problem
   What Can We Do About Quality Control?
   Dealing With Sexism in the Office
   The Cost of Alcoholism

24
Sales Presentations

Aggressive selling is the hallmark of American business. Since the days of the "Yankee traders," Americans have profited by their abilities to analyze needs, provide benefits, and close a deal. Unfortunately, sales speaking has acquired a bad reputation. Many people assume that sales speaking is pushy, overly aggressive, and even obnoxious. While that may be true in a few cases, sales is a necessary part of any business.

Sales speaking is not just the responsibility of sales people. More than 7 million Americans are employed as "sales workers," but every professional— politician, doctor, teacher, mechanic, or factory worker—is actually involved in selling ideas, services, or products to potential consumers.[1] Any member of an organization may be called upon to represent its products or services. Therefore, in an age of increasing competitiveness among businesses, all members of businesses need to be able to speak effectively about the products or services that their companies offer. Effective sales speaking is a skill that can advance your career dramatically if you are a sales professional, and it is useful even if you do not have a sales position. Knowing the elements of effective selling prepares you to be a powerful persuader, whatever responsibility you may have within a company.

This chapter discusses five major aspects of sales speaking:

Analyze your buyer's needs and values.
Know your product's features.
Determine your product's benefits.
Know your competitors.
Prepare for customer objections.

With these elements, you can construct a sales speech that is dynamic enough to get your audience to "sign on the dotted line."

Sales presentations depend greatly on the nature of the situation. There is no one perfect sales speech. Each presentation must be adapted to the needs of the customer, the nature of the product or service, and the competitive environment surrounding the transaction between buyer and seller. The effective sales speaker will be aware of the complexity of the sales situation and will adapt accordingly. However, the basic methods for analyzing the situation and adapting the sales presentation can be learned and are discussed in the sections that follow.

Analyze the Buyer's Needs and Values

The purchase of a product or service often takes place in several stages. The potential buyer may not be aware of a need, may not know that a product or service exists, may be gathering information to make a decision, may be shopping for comparative value, or may be ready to purchase. At each of these stages, a sale can take place. The sales presentation will vary, depending on the stage of readiness of the purchaser. Thus, the first step in the sales presentation is to determine how close the customer is to making a purchase.

In the early stages, the most effective type of sales presentation is informative. You need to give the customer objective information in order to raise his or her interest and to satisfy the need for data on which to base a decision. In the later stages of the decision-making process, persuasive elements such as comparative statistics and appeals to values are more effective. The most effective presentation provides the consumer with whatever he or she needs at the moment. A customer may move through the stages quickly, so the seller must be able to analyze the changing situation and adapt to each new level of readiness as it develops.

Customers buy things for vastly different reasons. The same product may be bought because it is inexpensive, because it is functional, because it is pretty, or because it is made in the United States. The most effective sales presentation does not waste valuable time presenting arguments that will be ineffective. The sales presenter needs to assess the values of the potential buyer and adapt the presentation to match those values.

You can assess the values of a consumer in several ways. In some situations, you must do your analysis completely in advance. An example of this type of presentation is the "canned" presentation designed to fit a typical audience. You must determine as accurately as possible the most probable needs and values of the audience you will address. The more specifically you understand what the audience members want and the values they hold, the better you can target your remarks to satisfying those needs and interests.

In other situations, you may have the opportunity to talk with the prospective buyer before actually beginning the sales presentation. The most powerful tool in a face-to-face situation is listening to the buyer's own opinions. Ask the buyer what he or she wants and needs—and then listen to the answer! Embedded in people's opinions are statements of what is valuable to them. They often leave unstated what is not valuable to them. You can test these perceptions by asking direct questions about values; for example, "Do you want good gas mileage, or are you more concerned about performance in a car?" The answers to these questions may help you focus your arguments more effectively.

Figure 24.1 lists common values that are often relevant in sales situations. Use these values as the basis for building arguments.[2]

Personal values: status, comfort, group acceptance, friendship, personal satisfaction, beauty, morality.

Practical values: economy, convenience, longevity, efficiency, cost comparison, service, workmanship, availability.

Situational values: reputation of seller, other satisfied buyers, endorsements/testimonials, authoritative evidence.

Personality of seller: enthusiasm, optimism, good will, sincerity.

FIGURE 24.1 Common American Values for Sales

Know Your Product's Features

Any item has hundreds of elements that make it appealing: cost, shape, size, color, packaging, construction materials, convenience, versatility, and many more. In addition, many intangible elements make a product attractive: conditions of purchase, such as credit or discount; the availability of the product; the nature of the purchasing environment (retail store, mail order, and so on); and add-on services, such as delivery or service guarantees. These elements are called *features*.

As a seller, it is imperative that you know every feature of your product intimately in order to adapt your sales presentation effectively. If you know only a few of the features, the types of arguments you can create will be severely limited. The more features you know, the better you can emphasize features that match the particular needs and values of your customer.

As you plan a sales presentation, carefully analyze the features of the product or service you represent. Create an exhaustive list of every feature—both tangible and intangible—that might be a selling point. More complex products may require that you group the features into categories. The more time you spend familiarizing yourself with product features, the more raw material you have for building effective sales arguments.

Determine Your Product's Benefits

An important distinction to make as you prepare your sales talk is the difference between features and benefits. *Features*, as we have seen, are the tangible and intangible elements of the item being sold. *Benefits* are the perceived value of those features to the consumer. For example, price is always a feature of a product. What are the benefits of a low price? A cost-conscious customer might perceive the benefits of a low price to be savings, thrift, or the self-perception of being a "smart shopper." But there might be benefits to a high price as well: prestige, implied worth of the product, or the self-perception that "I deserve the finest quality." Thus, any feature can be interpreted in many ways, depending on the values of the individual customer.

Feature	Benefit (Value)
Cost of 69 cents	Saves you money (economy)
Research-designed shape	Works effectively (hygiene)
USDA approved	Good reputation (authority)
Red handle	Pretty color (color preference)
Non-slip grip	Won't slip out of hand (safety)
Made in New Jersey	Support American economy (patriotism)
High-quality materials	Will last a long time (longevity)
Money-back guarantee	Ensured satisfaction (security)

FIGURE 24.2 Sample Features-Benefit Analysis for a Toothbrush

The task of the seller is to match the features of the product with the values of the potential buyer. If the feature satisfies some value or need of the buyer, then that satisfaction is a benefit. For example, if a buyer values safety, you should identify all the features that are in any way related to safety benefits and emphasize these features in your presentation. This analysis isolates the key persuasive elements of a sales presentation. In the language of professional sales people, "Benefits sell, features don't." The only way you can be truly effective is to develop a sense of which benefits are preferred by a particular customer. Features may be appealing, but they will not sell a product—benefits will.

Inexperienced sales people often overlook this important distinction and assume that a mere recitation of the attractive features of a product or service will sell it. A far more persuasive approach is to present features and then to explain how the feature will benefit the customer. You cannot assume that the buyer will automatically see the relationship between feature and benefit. You must point out the relevant features and directly emphasize the benefits.

Figure 24.2 illustrates a features-benefits analysis of a toothbrush. Notice how each feature listed is matched with a benefit that a customer might perceive. In parentheses after each benefit is the value on which that benefit is based.

Know Your Competitors

In a highly competitive marketplace such as the United States, few products or services are without competitors. Most consumers know they have a choice. Thus, sellers must be thoroughly familiar with competitors and must be prepared to deal with comparisons between their products or services and others.

Just as you analyzed your own product for features and benefits, you need to do the same for your competitors' products. The more you know about how your product compares with those of your competitors, the more easily you can present yours as superior. One of the major benefits you can give a customer is the knowledge that your product is superior to competing products. In order to do that, you need specific examples and evidence of that superiority.

Apply the same analysis of features and benefits to all major competitors. Of course, if one competitor's product is superior in some aspects to yours, you may wish to omit that feature from your presentation. If the weakness is a major feature that is sure to be questioned by an astute customer, you should prepare a reasonable explanation for the weakness. You can usually do this by balancing the weakness with some compensating strong feature.

R. T. C. LETTERKENNY

Prepare for Customer Objections

In addition to their awareness of competing products, some customers are certain to present purchase resistance. This reluctance to buy is often couched in the form of an objection—a claim that a product does not fulfill some need or value that the consumer has. For example, a buyer might object that a product is too expensive, too limited in use, too complicated, or not very convenient.

You should anticipate the typical objections you will receive whenever you represent a product or service. Prepare good explanations that compensate for the perceived weakness. In some cases, you may be able to present authoritative information that counteracts the objection. In other instances, you may trade off a weakness against a greater strength. A third technique for dealing with objections is to ask customers what they want you to do about the weakness. Some customers have specific ideas for meeting their own objections. For example, if a product is too expensive for an outright purchase, you might ask if the buyer would like to pay on installments or to finance the purchase through your company's credit department. Almost any objection can be met with a skillful counterargument. The better prepared you are for objections, the easier it is to deal with them when they arise.

Plan the Sales Presentation

A great deal of work must be done in advance of the actual sales presentation. As you have seen in this chapter, you must analyze your audience, identify your product's features and benefits, and select the lines of argument that will be most effective with your audience. In addition, you must know your competition and prepare for objections that your audience may raise. Once you have done this preliminary analysis, you are ready to plan the actual presentation of your sales message.

The outline of the presentation can be quite flexible. It is vital, however, that the body of the speech deal with the four major elements: features, benefits, analysis of the competitors, and the handling of objections. These steps may be combined or given in any order that you feel most effectively presents your case. Some speakers describe one feature at a time, explain its benefits, compare it to competitors, and overcome any objections; they then move on to the next feature and do the same thing. Other speakers describe all the features first, then explain the benefits, then deal with the competitors, and finally overcome any objections. Either of these approaches may be effective, but other organizational patterns can work well, too. The key is to select features and benefits that match the potential buyer's values and needs. As long as you address the customer's needs, you can maintain his or her attention. The order of presentation is less critical than a focus on the buyer's values.

The introduction of the sales speech performs many of the same functions as that of the informative speech. It should grab attention, create interest, establish your credibility, and announce the topic of your presentation. A major difference, however, is the persuasive element you add to the opening by emphasizing the listener's needs and values. Throughout the introduction, refer to things your audience values and needs. The opening line should grab attention and interest because it refers to a need the audience has. Establish your credibility as a speaker in order to satisfy the audience's need for information about your expertise. Emphasize some major benefit provided by your product or service in order to entice the audience to pay close attention to what follows. Finally, make sure that the audience understands exactly what you are trying to sell. Provide a general explanation of the product or service and of your purpose in talking to them. Emphasize that you have information that will be of great benefit to them. Encourage them to listen to the body of your speech, in which you present more specific details.

The conclusion of the sales speech differs dramatically from that of an informative speech, since you want the audience to act on the information you have presented, not just to be aware of the choices. Thus, the concluding devices for a sales speech are designed to motivate action. In order to do this, you need a clear picture of the specific action you want from the audience. Do you want them to buy today? to consider buying soon? to buy from a certain dealer? to buy a certain brand? These types of questions must be made explicit in the conclusion, or the audience will not know how to do what you want. As you plan the conclusion, consider all the steps involved in the buying decision and purchase. Make sure that you have covered each of these steps and that the audience is totally ready to act in the manner you desire.

Useful devices that you might include in the conclusion include a reiteration of the audience's need for the product, a review of the main features and benefits of the product, a reemphasis of the product's outstanding features or benefits, a specific plan of action for the audience to take, and any clarifications not given in the body of the speech. Some sales speakers include a short question-and-answer session at the end of a presentation to address any concerns or last-minute objections that audience members may have. The speech should end with a strong appeal to real action. With the information and arguments you have provided, the audience members should be ready to act. A strong last line motivates them to act and brings the speech to a forceful, enthusiastic close.

Figure 24.3 outlines the elements of a sales presentation. This outline will be useful in planning your sales presentations, and it can be adapted to create many effective variations.

I. Introduction
    A. Grab audience attention and interest.
    B. Establish your credibility as a speaker.
    C. Create in the audience a sense of need for the product.
    D. Emphasize one major benefit of the product.
    E. Introduce the general idea of the product.

II. Body
    A. Present the features of the product.
        1. Describe the features.
        2. Describe how the product works.
        3. Describe how the product can be used.
        4. Emphasize the unique features of the product.
    B. Explain the benefits of the product's features.
        1. Show how the audience will benefit.
        2. Show how audience's needs will be met.
        3. Show how future needs or problems will be avoided.
    C. Deal with the competition.
        1. Compare your product to competitors' products.
        2. Show how your product is superior.
        3. Rationalize or avoid your product's shortcomings.
    D. Counter the obvious objections.
        1. Anticipate the audience's negative reactions to the product.
        2. Explain cost and price.
        3. Rationalize and overcome other objections.

III. Conclusion
    A. Reiterate the audience's need for the product.
    B. Review the main features of the product.
    C. Emphasize the main benefits.
    D. Present a specific plan for acquiring the product.
    E. Clarify any issues of price or availability.
    F. Make a strong appeal to act now.
    G. Close with a strong last line.

IV. Question and Answer Session (if used)

FIGURE 24.3 Plan for a Sales Presentation

NOTES

1. Patrick E. Murphy and Ben M. Enis, *Marketing* (Glenview, Ill.: Scott, Foresman, 1986), p. 453.
2. Drawn from Richard Cummings, *Contemporary Selling* (New York: Harcourt Brace Jovanovich, 1987).

EXERCISE 24.1
Analyzing Customer Needs and Values

Directions: How would you go about selling a down-filled sleeping bag? The following worksheet demonstrates the use of values analysis to create arguments for selling. Assume that your potential customer has the values listed below. Write a sentence describing a feature of your sleeping bag that satisfies each of these values.

1. Security: _____

_____

_____

_____

2. Beauty: _____

_____

_____

_____

3. Friendship: _____

_____

_____

_____

4. Patriotism: _____

_____

_____

_____

5. Courage: _____

_____

_____

_____

6. Honesty: _____

_____

_____

_____

7. Conformity: _____

_____

_____

_____

8. Reason over emotion: _____

_____

_____

_____

9. Upward mobility: _____

_____

_____

_____

10. Workmanship: _____

_____

_____

_____

EXERCISE 24.2
Analyzing a Product's Features and Benefits

Directions: List as many features as you can for a new dictionary. For each feature listed, demonstrate the benefit of that feature to a potential buyer of the dictionary.

Example: Feature: cloth binding. Benefit: long-lasting wear.

FEATURE   **BENEFIT**

1. _____   _____
   _____   _____

2. _____   _____
   _____   _____

3. _____   _____
   _____   _____

4. _____   _____
   _____   _____

5. _____   _____
   _____   _____

6. _____   _____
   _____   _____

7. _____   _____
   _____   _____

8. _____   _____
   _____   _____

9. _____   _____
   _____   _____

10. _____   _____
    _____   _____

EXERCISE 24.3
Overcoming Customer Objections

Directions: If you were trying to sell a dictionary, what objections might you encounter? In the following worksheet, list six possible objections to buying the dictionary you described in Exercise 24.2 and think of a counter-argument you could use to deal with each objection.

Example: Objection: Customer doesn't like cloth-bound books. Counterargument: Dictionary also comes in a paperbound edition.

OBJECTION	COUNTERARGUMENT
1.	
2.	
3.	
4.	
5.	
6.	

EXERCISE 24.4
Planning a Sales Presentation

Directions: Plan a five-minute sales presentation that you will give to a group of your peers to sell them an actual product. You can either have the product with you (for example, a garage-sale item) or encourage the audience to purchase the product in a local store. Complete the following checklist before you plan the actual presentation.

Who is the audience? _____

_____

_____

_____

What are major values of the audience to which you can appeal? _____

_____

_____

_____

What are the features of the product? _____

_____

_____

_____

What are the benefits of the product for this particular audience? _____

_____

_____

_____

Who is your competition? _____

_____

_____

_____

What objections will you probably get from this audience? _____

_____

_____

_____

OUTLINE OF SALES PRESENTATION

I. Introduction

A. _____

_____

_____

B. _____

_____

_____

C. _____

_____

_____

D. _____

_____

_____

E. _____

_____

_____

II. Body

A. _____

_____

1. _____

_____

2. _____

_____

_____

3. _____

_____

_____

_____

B. _____

_____

1. _____

_____

_____

_____

2. _____

_____

_____

_____

3. _____

_____

_____

_____

C. _____

_____

1. _____

_____

_____

_____

2. _____

_____

_____

_____

3. _____

_____

_____

_____

III. Conclusion

A. _____

_____

_____

B. _____

_____

_____

C. _____

_____

_____

D. _____

_____

_____

E. _____

_____

_____

ACTION ASSIGNMENT

24

Sales Presentations

1. Select an advertisement that appears on national television. Analyze the effectiveness of the ad in terms of the following categories:

   Values appealed to
   Features presented
   Benefits presented
   Support for arguments
   How the competition is dealt with
   How objections are handled

2. Identify a product that you are considering but have not yet decided to purchase. List three reasons you have for wanting to purchase and at least three reasons for delaying. If you were a sales person and were aware of these reasons in a customer's mind, what types of arguments would you build into a sales presentation in order to encourage the customer to buy? Hint: You will want to reinforce the compelling reasons and attempt to overcome the reasons for the delay (objections).

3. Locate a recent issue of *Consumer Reports* magazine that compares leading brands of a product. Select one brand and prepare an outline for a sales presentation that focuses on the comparative advantages of your product. Also consider how you would overcome objections to your product based on unfavorable comparison to other brands.

25

Speeches to Motivate

Motivation is a major responsibility of anyone in a leadership position in business. Not only must a manager supervise the work of others, but he or she must also create an environment that is conducive to meeting their work goals. Despite the benefits of effective motivation in increasing worker productivity and job satisfaction, the task of motivation remains a puzzle to many administrators. How do you inspire your co-workers to achieve their best, and how do you do so in a pleasant and respectful way?

Business people are often called upon to speak at ceremonies or dinners that have a motivational purpose, and you can become an effective motivator if you incorporate the principles of motivation as you plan your speeches. This chapter investigates the basic needs that motivate people and suggests public speaking techniques that you can use to motivate your fellow employees.

How to Motivate People

What motivates a person in a work situation? People are motivated by the things they value, and, as we have seen in earlier chapters, values differ tremendously among people. Thus, workers are motivated by many different things. In a work environment, motivation is determined by the values people have about the nature of the tasks they have to do, the people with whom they share the task, and the organizational climate—such factors as rules, policies, physical conditions, reward systems, and management philosophy. Each of these elements can influence—either positively or negatively—worker attitudes and performance. Management has a large role in creating and maintaining employee motivation. One of the attributes of an effective manager is the ability to motivate subordinates and co-workers to reach high levels of performance.

Your ability to motivate an employee depends on your skill in assessing the values that person holds. People can be motivated by many different things, and the skilled motivator must be able to perceive what will serve as

Security and freedom from anxiety: Physical safety and mental serenity create a pleasant environment.

Satisfaction of physical needs: Hunger, thirst, and physical comfort are provided for.

Sense of general well-being: A positive and optimistic attitude makes work an enjoyable activity.

Success, mastery, and achievement: People are given a chance to accomplish goals and enjoy a sense of mastery.

Recognition and admiration: People are rewarded in some fashion for good performance.

Respect and approval: People are valued as unique and worthwhile individuals.

Being loved and wanted: An attitude of group "belonging" makes workers feel accepted and valued.

Adventure, excitement, and challenge: New experiences and the opportunities for personal growth prevent stagnation and boredom.

FIGURE 25.1   Motivating Factors in the Workplace

the greatest incentive for another person. Figure 25.1 lists values that workers commonly have.[1] These values are the basis for motivating. If an administrator satisfies these values in the work environment, then the employee will be more motivated to perform at a high level. The worker will also be more satisfied with the job and will feel better about the other people in the work environment.

Many management-science theorists have studied the ways in which effective managers motivate workers and have found many approaches that create high motivation. The best motivating technique for a specific situation depends on the people involved and the nature of the task environment. Every situation requires adaptation to the needs of the people involved. Figure 25.2 outlines several general techniques that have been shown to be effective in creating motivation. Note how each technique is related directly to the list of needs in Figure 25.1.

Establish clear objectives: If people know exactly what is required of them, they are more likely to achieve those goals.

Create positive expectations: The higher the opinion a manager expresses of workers' abilities, the harder they will strive to match those perceptions.

Use positive incentives: People respond more to reward systems than to punishment.

Maintain objective feedback and evaluation: People need corrective feedback to know how they measure up to the established objectives.

Establish dynamic role models: People will trust and follow an enthusiastic and competent leader.

Show concern for worker well-being: Workers must believe that a manager cares for their safety and comfort.

Use open communication to create a climate of trust: People work harder when they know their opinions are valued and their suggestions are listened to.

FIGURE 25.2   General Techniques for Motivating Workers

Effective managers must select specific methods for manifesting the general goals listed in Figure 25.2. There are usually many ways to embody these principles. For example, positive incentives may be created through monetary rewards, recognition, praise, advancement, or other positive means. Generally, the more opportunities a manager takes to satisfy workers' needs in a specific situation, the more those workers will be motivated.

Creating Motivation Through Public Speaking

While motivating is often done in a one-to-one context, managers also use public speaking situations to boost worker morale and motivation. A public speech is a good chance for an administrator to reaffirm the organization's commitment to workers' needs, to provide recognition to excellent performers, and to apply techniques that foster higher motivational levels in employees.

The following sections analyze four specific public speaking situations in which a manager may increase motivation. For each type of speech, specific methods are suggested that combine motivational needs and techniques.

SPEECHES OF INTRODUCTION

In many ceremonial situations you may be called upon to introduce another speaker or a person to a group. This occasion provides you with the opportunity to establish the credibility of the person and to motivate the audience to listen to the person's remarks. The speech of introduction is especially important when the audience does not know the person who will be speaking. As the introducer, you can significantly increase the audience's willingness to listen and to accept what the speaker has to say. You can also incorporate several general motivating techniques of your own if the topic of the speech is related to employee concerns.

Begin the speech of introduction with a direct explanation of your purpose—the occasion and the speaker whom you are introducing. You may wish to stress the importance of the occasion and explain why the speaker was asked to talk. If the occasion is related to motivational issues such as recognition or incentives, use motivating techniques that emphasize these positive aspects.

The main part of the introductory speech should cover the background of the speaker: his or her reputation, awards, rank, positions held, or other credibility factors that will create a favorable impression with the audience. If the speaker has qualifications that are related to worker needs or concerns, these should be highlighted. You can also include your knowledge of some of the speaker's personal characteristics to give a more candid view of the speaker. If the speaker desires, you can announce the topic of the speech and explain its relevance for the audience.

Explain your purpose and the occasion.

Emphasize motivational aspects of the occasion.

Provide the background of the speaker: credibility factors and personal characteristics.

Announce the general topic and its relevance for the audience.

Create a positive emotional tone for the speech.

Be brief and accurate in your remarks.

FIGURE 25.3 Formula for Speeches of Introduction

In general, your purpose should be to create a positive emotional tone for the speaker who follows you. Your remarks should be brief and relaxed. Check with the speaker in advance to get important facts about what to include in your introduction. Do not make the speaker correct your inaccuracies. Also avoid overpraising the speaker. Find the right balance of praise, objective fact, and candor that builds the audience's trust in and respect for the speaker.

Figure 25.3 reviews the techniques used in a speech of introduction. Use it as a checklist when you give this type of speech.

SPEECHES OF AWARD OR TRIBUTE

An awards ceremony is the perfect occasion to reinforce employee morale by praising the positive role model of an excellent performer. Likewise, speeches on the occasion of an employee's retirement can be good opportunities to emphasize motivational factors.

The award speech may have two general purposes: praise for the recipient of the award and praise for the organization that is providing the award. The first purpose—praise for the recipient—is accomplished by explaining the criteria for the award and spelling out how the recipient met those standards. You may wish to recount specific acts of service or performance that led to the recipient's selection. You can emphasize the unique contributions of the recipient to the organization and point to his or her impact on the community.

The second purpose—praise for the organization—is the place to bring in motivational elements. You should explain the nature and purpose of the award—why it was instituted and the values that it is intended to reward. You can also provide praise for the occasion of the award itself and for others involved in the awards process—additional candidates, judges, voters, or other people. When sincere praise is shared among many people, everyone feels more like a part of a worthwhile organization. These are important motivating factors to inspire listeners.

When you are paying tribute to an employee, you might not present a specific award, but you can use many of the same elements of the award speech. The valued employee can be praised for excellent achievement, but the organization should also be recognized for the caring attitude exhibited in providing the tribute.

Figure 25.4 lists the elements of the speech of award or tribute. Use it as a checklist when you are planning this type of speech.

Explain the nature and history of the award.

Praise the occasion and the group presenting the award.

Congratulate the recipient of the award: skills, abilities, traits.

Describe specific aspects of the recipient's performance.

Explain the importance of the recipient to the group and to the larger community.

Inspire the audience to follow the recipient's example.

Provide thanks for everyone involved in the awards process.

Be sincere with praise.

FIGURE 25.4 Formula for Speeches of Award or Tribute

SPEECHES IN ACCEPTANCE OF AN AWARD

If you are so fortunate as to receive an award from a group, you are often expected to make remarks in acceptance of the award. As a manager, you can take advantage of this opportunity to motivate the audience to follow the example you have set. In essence, the group is rewarding you for exemplifying its highest values. You can reciprocate by praising the group for the ways in which they have motivated you to perform so well.

Most acceptance speeches begin with lavish thanks—to the providers of the award, to people who have assisted you in your achievement, and to other people involved in the awards process. Often, the achievement behind the award is meaningful, and you may wish to discuss the values involved—especially if those values will be motivating to the audience. You should keep your remarks positive. Do not underrate your achievement in an attempt to be humble.

Figure 25.5 summarizes these suggestions for the speech of acceptance.

Give thanks to the group providing the award.

Thank everyone involved in the awards process.

Praise contributors to your success.

Explain the meaningfulness of the award to you.

Emphasize the values in your achievement.

Be positive in your remarks.

**FIGURE 25.5 Formula for Speeches in Acceptance
of an Award**

SPEECHES TO INSPIRE

A common motivational occasion for a business person is to be the featured speaker after a meal. This occasion demands that the speaker be somewhat entertaining as well as inspirational. Thus, the event is a relaxed and comfortable one, with a semi-serious purpose.

The inspirational speech should reflect this dual purpose. It should begin with a relaxed and comfortable tone and end on a more serious note. The relaxed opening is often accomplished by telling amusing anecdotes of common situations that illustrate a problem or a need the audience faces. The serious ending is often accomplished by deriving a moral from the anecdotes. The speaker draws a conclusion from the situations that face the audience and impresses them with the need to behave in a certain way if they are to accomplish their goals.

The body of the inspirational speech may be organized in any of several ways. The *quotation speech* begins with a significant quote that reflects the theme of the speech. The body of the speech then consists of an explanation of the various parts of the quotation and their relevance to the audience. The speaker demonstrates how the quotation serves as a guide and encourages the audience to follow that model. The speech concludes with a challenge or an appeal to fulfill the lessons embedded in the quotation and to make them come to life. This approach is most motivating when the quotation is relevant to employees' needs and concerns.

Another common technique for inspirational speaking is the *acronym speech*. The speaker takes the first letter of the main points of the body and creates an acronym that organizes the speech. For example a speaker might talk about the DRAW of effective advertising: *D*ynamic copy, *R*ealistic expectations, *A*dvance planning, and *W*riter creativity. The acronym can be cleverly used as a pun or as a visual reminder of the speech's main points. Amusing anecdotes can be organized under the main points of the body to provide examples of how to accomplish the group's goals.

A third common pattern for inspirational speeches is the *allegory speech*. An allegory is a complex story with several characters and situations that symbolically represents the audience. The speaker uses the elements of the allegory—and it can often be a humorous resemblance—to make telling points about the audience's situation. An example of an allegory speech would be an explanation of how the situation facing the audience resembles the story of the tortoise and the hare in Aesop's well-known fable. By warning of overconfidence, the speaker challenges the audience to use careful planning and time management to meet the group's objectives. The allegory speech ends with a challenge to audience members to fulfill their potential and to apply themselves to their work.

Figure 25.6 reviews the elements of these three types of inspirational speeches.

The patterns used for inspirational speeches are more explicit than other types of talks. As a result, they are generally easier to construct and listen to. While they are simple, however, they can be quite powerful in inspiring your audience and motivating them to pursue the company's goals and values.

The Quotation Speech:

Read the quotation.

Separate the quotation into parts (if applicable) and explain the meaningfulness of each part.

Demonstrate the relevance of the quotation to the audience.

Conclude with an appeal that the audience learn the lesson of the quotation.

The Acronym Speech:

Introduce the general topic of the speech.

Unveil the acronym.

Explain the parts of the acronym.

Demonstrate the relevance of each part to the audience.

Conclude with a summary of the acronym and an appeal that the audience learn the lesson implied in the parts.

The Allegory Speech:

Introduce the general topic of the speech.

Tell the allegory as a story.

Explain the elements of the allegory and show their relevance to the audience's situation.

Conclude with an appeal that the audience learn the lesson of the allegory.

FIGURE 25.6   Formulas for Speeches to Inspire

NOTE

1. Jon Eisenson, Jeffrey Auer, and John J. Irwin, *The Psychology of Communication* (New York: Meredith, 1963).

EXERCISE 25.1
Creating Methods of Motivation

Directions: Figure 25.2 of this chapter lists techniques for motivating people in the workplace. The main elements of that list are included below. Imagine that you are a manager in a work situation that you will probably encounter in the future. Work with a partner and develop three methods for implementing each technique.

TECHNIQUES FOR MOTIVATING PEOPLE

Establish clear objectives

1. _____

   _____

2. _____

   _____

3. _____

   _____

Create positive expectations

1. _____

   _____

2. _____

   _____

3. _____

   _____

Use positive incentives

1. _____

   _____

2. _____

   _____

3. _____

_____

Provide objective feedback and evaluation

1. _____

_____

2. _____

_____

3. _____

_____

Establish dynamic role models

1. _____

_____

2. _____

_____

3. _____

_____

Use open communication to create trust

1. _____

_____

2. _____

_____

3. _____

_____

EXERCISE 25.2
Planning a Speech to Motivate

Directions: Imagine that you are an administrator in a work situation that you will probably actually hold in the future. You are requested to plan and present a motivational speech to your staff. You can select any topic you wish to address. Use the worksheet below to plan your speech.

The situation: _____

_____

_____

The topic of the speech: _____

_____

The audience: _____

_____

Major motivational techniques you can include in your speech: _____

_____

_____

The speech plan you will use: _____

_____

_____

Tentative outline:

_____

_____

_____

_____

_____

_____

_____

_____

_____

Speeches to Motivate

1. Locate an audio tape (or a videotape, if possible) of a professional motivational speaker. Famous examples are Leo Buscaglia, Peter Drucker, and Tony Robbins. Analyze the speech in terms of the following categories:

   Purpose
   Introductory devices
   Organizational pattern of the speech
   Motivational factors appealed to
   Main points of the speech
   Type of support used
   Concluding devices

2. Imagine that you could invite any famous living or historical person to your class to give a 30-minute speech. Whom would you select? Your task is to give a two-minute speech of introduction that will motivate the audience to listen to this speaker. (For nationally famous people who are living, you may wish to consult *Who's Who in America* for biographical data. For historical persons, consult the *Dictionary of American Biography*.)

3. Prepare a two-minute speech in which you make an award to a classmate. (The instructor may wish to distribute names at random so that everyone receives an award.) The awards can be either humorous or serious, as illustrated in the following examples:

   Some positive personality trait: Most Industrious, Most Humorous, Best Smile, Most Helpful to You
   Some professional skill or aspiration: Sales person of the Month, Secretary of the Year, Writer of the Decade, Most Likely to Succeed
   Some personal activity or ability: Volunteer of the Year, Most Valuable Player, Most Effective Club Officer, Most Creative Chef

   See Figure 25.4 for suggestions on what to include in your speech.

4. You are the recipient of an award in Action Assignment 3 above. Give a one-minute impromptu speech accepting your award. See Figure 25.5 for suggestions on what to include in your speech.

INDEX